THE ACTIVE LIFE

SUNY series in the Philosophy of the Social Sciences

Lenore Langsdorf, Editor

THE ACTIVE LIFE

MILLER'S METAPHYSICS OF DEMOCRACY

Michael J. McGandy

State University of New York Press

Published by
State University of New York Press, Albany

For information, address State University of New York Press,
194 Washington Avenue, Suite 305, Albany, NY 12210-2384

Production by Judith Block
Marketing by Michael Campochiaro

Library of Congress Cataloging-in-Publication Data

McGandy, Michael J.
   The active life : Miller's metaphysics of democracy / Michael J. McGandy.
     p. cm. — (SUNY series in the philosophy of the social sciences)
   Includes bibliographical references and index.
   ISBN 0-7914-6537-3 (alk. paper) — ISBN 0-7914-6538-1 (pbk : alk. paper)
   1. Miller, John William. 2. Act (Philosophy) 3. Democracy—Philosophy. I. Title.
II. Series.

B945.M4764M34 2005
191—dc22
                           2004062623

10 9 8 7 6 5 4 3 2 1

Contents

Preface

This book begins with two suppositions: The idea of the active life is worth retrieving and the philosophy of John William Miller commands serious attention. Neither the idea nor the philosophy is given much consideration in current discussions. Yet the possibility of a viable and compelling metaphysics of democracy is liable to attract attention and strike many as worth some intellectual effort. My claim here is that the strength and viability of a metaphysics that comports with and informs democratic life comes by way of joining the ancient idea of the active life with the contemporary thought of Miller. If we are to undertake a serious reflection on our democratic way of life, we will be well served by turning our attention to Miller's recuperation of the active life as a leading philosophical idea.

The last thinker to give serious consideration to the active life was Hannah Arendt. Across all of her philosophical writings, but most especially in *The Human Condition*, Arendt articulated the state of contemporary affairs (political, social, and psychological) in terms of how persons understood and held themselves in relationship to action and contemplation. Thus, for her, there was nothing old about the ancient distinction between the active life (*bios politikos* or *vita activa*) and the contemplative life (*bios theoretikos* or *vita contemplativa*). Arendt thought there was nothing more diagnostic of the meaning of life than what we (individually and collectively) thought about these two modes of existence.

I take my cue from Arendt and place this distinction at the heart of the project of crafting a metaphysics of democracy. My claim is that this distinction is also central to Miller's thinking about philosophy and democracy. I assert this despite the fact that Miller did not write much directly about the active and contemplative lives. There are, to be sure, passing mentions here and there. Moreover, like Arendt, Miller thought that the Greek experience in the polis served as a touchstone for all public philosophy. Yet Miller's interest in the active life did not begin to approach the degree of articulation that one finds in Arendt. The idea was alive in Miller's thinking but always implicitly and partly concealed in an alternate

vocabulary. Here I undertake to make the implicit clear and highlight the power
of Miller's political thought by borrowing a little light from Arendt. This is especially so early on when, in the introduction, I rely on her clear statements and
penetrating insights in order to state succinctly the historical and intellectual background of Miller's innovation in the relationship of action and contemplation.[1]

The apparent divide as well as the fundamental bond between the active
and contemplative lives provide a basis for this investigation into a metaphysics
of democracy. Some terms of reconciliation between action and thought have to
be offered if one is to bring together *metaphysics* (the height of contemplation)
and *democracy* (the most vigorous form of politics). There is no escaping a consideration of this distinction if one is to understand Miller's philosophy and its
political importance. Moreover there is no gainsaying the significance of looking
at politics in light of this distinction.

Prior to embarking on this course, the reader deserves an introduction to Miller,
a philosopher who remains relatively unknown. A précis of Miller's intellectual
biography situates his early career at the end of what is known as the Golden Age
of American philosophy and his mature period amid the reign of the contrary
philosophical stances of positivism and existentialism. Given the fact that he
came into his own intellectually at such a time of transition, it is not surprising
that Miller's philosophy was a hybrid. His philosophical influences included
pragmatism, idealism, existentialism, and phenomenology. (The positivism of
the Vienna Circle was never accepted by Miller but was a constant point of contrast as well as an object of criticism.) This hybrid philosophy, which goes under
the name *actualism*, was given coherence by Miller's overriding interest in action
and history. Each philosophical influence was filtered through these interpretative skeins. His paramount concern was finding a way of thinking that best com-
ported with responsible and history-making agency. Thus the attention that
Miller gave to the various schools of thought that touched his thinking was anything but doctrinaire, and his writing was far from dry scholarship.

The details of Miller's biography are presented in various places.[2] A brief
sketch of his intellectual biography shows Miller's philosophical life to be defined
by his association with two institutions—Harvard University and Williams College.
Miller (1895-1978) was born and educated in Rochester before arriving as an un-
dergraduate at Harvard University in 1912. These were the waning years of the influence of William James and Josiah Royce, but Miller was fortunate enough to
take at least one class with Royce during this period. After completing his B.A. in
philosophy in 1916, Miller declared himself a conscientious objector to World War
I and then volunteered for service in the ambulance corps in which he saw active
duty in France. In 1919 he returned to Harvard to begin graduate studies in

philosophy. Among his teachers were William Ernest Hocking, Edwin Bissell Holt, Clarence Irving Lewis, and Ralph Barton Perry. During this period Miller worked closely with Hocking and it was under Hocking's direction that Miller wrote his dissertation. The work, titled "The Definition of the Thing," earned him his doctorate in 1922. Following a short time teaching at Connecticut College, in 1924 Miller took up an appointment at Williams College. He would remain at Williams (excepting sabbaticals and visiting teaching appointments) until his retirement in 1960. At Williams Miller taught courses across the whole philosophical curriculum, served as department chair from 1931 through 1955, and was named, in 1945, Mark Hopkins Professor of Intellectual and Moral Philosophy (a title inherited from his colleague and predecessor as chair, James Bisset Pratt).

Both Harvard and Williams were, for Miller, defining institutions. At Harvard University Miller was steeped in a philosophical culture and became intimately familiar with a set of philosophical problems—many of which were the personal property of James and Royce. One of the tasks of graduate students at Harvard in the 1920s was resolving the Battle of the Absolute that had been waged by these genial adversaries. (Indeed one important way of conceiving of Miller's actualism is as a synthesis of pragmatism and idealism.) While he would change many of the terms and would venture into new philosophical territory, the intellectual charge of making sense of the dispute that animated the Harvard Philosophy Department remained with Miller the whole of his philosophical career.

In the case of Williams College, Miller was not captivated by a philosophical figure or school. He was transformed and redefined by teaching. Research and scholarly interests were made subordinate to the primary task of liberal education and Miller's own sense of scholarship—that is, the thoughtful apprehension of the conditions of one's endeavors. Miller's interest was in educating responsible citizens who would bring philosophy to life in the worlds of art, business, law, or politics. Thus it was that his own academic scholarship declined while his energies were poured into class notes, philosophical correspondence, and philosophical essays. As Miller's bibliography illustrates, little of his writing was published prior to his death and the majority of the works that have appeared posthumously are *occasional* pieces in the best sense of that term—that is, philosophical writings directed toward a specific individual or that deal with philosophical questions apropos of some matter bearing on personal action. Abstract philosophy—written for no one in particular and cut off from action—became anathema to Miller. If at Harvard University he was steeped in *philosophical issues*, at Williams College he was steeped in an *educational culture* that profoundly influenced his philosophy.

In light of this account of Miller's philosophical life, there is no doubt that this book runs the risk of being too *scholarly* (in the pejorative sense of the term). This risk is unavoidable. One basic claim of mine is that Miller is a *systematic* thinker. Actualism is not just an insight into the disclosive and constructive functions of action but is also an articulate philosophical whole that can be understood as a *metaphysics of democracy*. While Miller left behind no finished philosophical system, his published and unpublished writings provide more than the rudiments of a philosophy that does conceptual justice to the matter of metaphysics while maintaining the existential integrity of the active, democratic life. If Miller's writings were occasional, the occasional style of an essayist is inappropriate to composing a philosophical whole out of the brilliant essays, letters, notes, and single dissertation penned by Miller. If these pages do not quite capture the flavor of Miller as a teacher, essayist, and letter writer, I hope this deficiency is more than made up for by the scope and detail of the philosophical argumentation.

What follows is forthrightly a work in philosophical construction. While it is a study of Miller's actualism, this book is also a creative venture that forms a philosophical whole out of what are rich and suggestive fragments. Here I act as Miller's interpreter and advocate—putting together a cohesive account drawing from arguments spread throughout his published and unpublished writings, elaborating on concepts where he was philosophically terse or opaque, and sometimes speaking for him in areas of political philosophy that he alluded to often in his writings but never addressed in detail. Readers will not find much in the way of criticism here. To others I leave the task of detailing Miller's philosophical blindspots. Weaknesses in any one of Miller's arguments, whenever noted, have been buttressed by stronger arguments and examples drawn from another essay. If one of Miller's accounts was thin, I have done what I can to provide a richer and more compelling version. No clear line of demarcation can be drawn indicating where Miller's thinking ends and my thinking begins. Yet I assure readers that in every instance they are meeting with Miller's thought. (Ample citations lead back to the source materials.) My goal is to highlight, amplify, and unify his philosophical outlook by organizing it around the ideas of the *active life* and *a metaphysics of democracy*. In doing so, I have not substantially changed Miller meaning or tortured his thought to serve my own aims. As far as I understand them, Miller's and my own philosophical interests are one in the same.

The book is organized in the following manner.

In the introduction I frame the argument in terms of the long and conflictual career of the paired concepts of the active life and the contemplative life. After a review of the history of this conflict, I find that in the late twentieth century a polemic has been undertaken on behalf of the practical life that has served to undermine the contemplative bases of responsible action. This has been done by attacking all forms of theory, reflection, and abstraction. As a correction to this trend, I propose Miller's actualism because it provides us with the conceptual resources for affirming the fundamental connection that exists between the practical and theoretical lives.

Over the course of chapter 1 I assess the appropriateness of venturing a metaphysical interpretation of democracy. This assessment is undertaken in light of the antimetaphysical tradition of American political thought. Richard Rorty's pragmatism is situated within this tradition and then used as a foil for clarifying what *metaphysics* does and does not mean, as well as what it does and does not contribute to our understanding of democracy. While I find a substantial amount of agreement between Rorty and Miller on the limitations of ahistorical modes of metaphysics, I find Miller's actualist metaphysics to be more adequate for articulating the sort of responsible, critical, and autonomous agency that is central to a democratic identity. This conclusion founds the project of rehabilitating metaphysics as well as integrating the contemplative life with the active life.

A developed concept of action is basic to articulating a metaphysics of democracy. Chapter 2 analyzes Miller's sense of action so as to distinguish it from reductive empiricism as well as airy voluntarism. I focus on the arguments Miller puts forward in *The Definition of the Thing* and develop an understanding of action as a principle of disclosure and organization. Action is revealed not by a direct empirical reference but rather in the form of our world. These descriptions of action in terms of processes of definition are then linked to the practical need of persons to establish local-control. Action thus connects (and is connected to) the universal as well as the radically first-person elements of our experience.

In chapter 3 I turn to Miller's concept of the symbol. Symbols are embodiments of action by which the organization implied by action becomes durable and, ultimately, an object for reflection and criticism. In order to understand the symbolic function I turn to Miller's idea of the *midworld* and articulate not only the basic difference between signs and symbols but also the more subtle qualities of the different types of symbols. As persons we live in a symbolic environment—surrounded by, shaped by, and shaping the enduring forms of our actions and those of our predecessors. This environment is itself a process of interpretation in that symbols, as means of definition, are bearers as well as objects of interpretation. In this interpretative process a communal and historical conception of agency comes to the fore. Moreover I argue that, because of this interpretative process, symbols function as *res publicae*—that is, means of expression, representation, and reflection joining the practical and theoretical.

For Miller the career of the midworld of symbols is nothing other than history. Chapter 4 establishes a series of connections that shows why history is fundamental for understanding the meaning of action, the import of symbolism, and the form and possibilities of democracy. To this end I explore the paradox that history, so often considered the antithesis of metaphysics, is the basic metaphysical category in that it is the condition of all disclosure. Following on that I describe important features of historical experience with an eye toward how each aspect contributes to the connection between history and the exercise of autonomy. The equation of history and philosophy is, as I show, the end at which Miller's reflections arrive. Both history and philosophy address and support what is most important to democratic agency—that is, self-control. History is thus where the practical and theoretical are reconciled.

In chapter 5 the matter of the preceding chapters is revisited and given a new reading in order to establish a metaphysics of democracy. I begin by developing Miller's account of morality (undergirded by identity, agency, and history) as the condition for a *community of power* found in the liberal democratic state. The liberal democratic state is the condition not only for the expansion of individual agency but also for the sort of self-control exercised by free persons. Important features of the state are described in order to show how the liberal democratic state provides the conditions of and is a model for an autonomous and self-reflective will. It is here that democracy and philosophy coincide. Democracy is the model for all communities of power in that democratic communities recognize, engage, and augment the will of persons. This creates the possibility for an engaged philosophical life. Moreover in such communities of power not only is the ancient antithesis between the practical and theoretical dissolved but so too is the equally ancient division between democracy and philosophy.

The epilogue condenses the foregoing account of Miller's metaphysics of democracy into two representative figures—that is, the scholar and the citizen. The scholar and the citizen exemplify two key aspects of the active life. The scholar is the figure of reflection while the citizen if the figure of action. However, as I show, scholarship and citizenship meet in the paradigmatic activity of criticism where thoughts and deeds flow together. The aim of philosophy is the aim of democracy—that is, to encourage people to take account of the conditions of their endeavors and to lend a hand in the reshaping of those very conditions. Action of this sort cannot proceed without reflection and reflection of the sort that Miller recommends is always a mode of action. The scholar and the citizen are, effectively, one in the same.

Several people and institutions deserve my thanks for their contributions to this book.

I extend my greatest thanks to the John William Miller Fellowship Fund for its contribution to my scholarship in the form of the Miller Essay Prize and the Miller Fellowship. These awards provided material support as well as significant encouragement during the researching and writing of this book.

Joseph P. Fell, now chairperson of the Fund Committee, deserves particular mention among the members of the John William Miller Fellowship Fund. Across the whole writing process I have received from him support, generous editorial comments, and philosophical criticisms that have been invariably helpful. This book has been significantly improved by his contributions.

The late George P. Brockway, Vincent Colapietro, Christopher Gowans, and Judith Green all offered commentary on earlier drafts of this book and each added to my thinking regarding Miller.

Peter Hare provided important criticisms of the penultimate draft of the book and previously, in his capacity as editor of the *Transactions of the Charles S. Peirce Society*, kindly considered and published two of my essays on Miller. (Sections 3.2 and 3.3 were originally published in a different form, in the *Transactions* [vol. 34, 1998] as "The Midworld: Clarifications and Developments.") I thank Hare and the Charles S. Peirce Society for maintaining a forum in which the ideas contributing to the American philosophical tradition can be shared and explored.

Much of the research that contributed to this book was undertaken in the John William Miller Papers that are preserved in the Williamsiana Collection of the Williams College Archives. College Archivist Sylvia Kennick Brown made great efforts to facilitate my archival work and I am indebted to her for assuring that my trips to Williams College were always fruitful. Lynne Fonteneau-McCann and Linda Hall also assisted me in the archives and both deserve my thanks.

A final word of appreciation goes to my editor, Jane Bunker, for entertaining my book proposal, shepherding the manuscript through the review process, and, along with her editorial staff, overseeing the editing and production of the book.

Michael J. McGandy
Brooklyn, New York
February 2005

Abbreviations

Abbreviations will be used when citing the writings of John William Miller.

PUBLISHED BOOKS

DP   *In Defense of the Psychological.* New York: Norton, 1983.
DT   *The Definition of the Thing with Some Notes on Language.* New York: Norton, 1980.
MS   *The Midworld of Symbols and Functioning Objects.* New York: Norton, 1982.
PC   *The Paradox of Cause and Other Essays.* New York: Norton, 1978.
PH   *The Philosophy of History with Reflections and Aphorisms.* New York: Norton, 1982.

PUBLISHED ESSAYS

AH   "Afterword: The Ahistoric and the Historic." In José Ortega y Gasset's *History as a System* (Trans. Helene Weyl), 237–69. New York: Norton, 1961.
CRW   "On Choosing Right and Wrong." *Idealistic Studies* 21 (1992): 74–78.
FI   "For Idealism." *Journal of Speculative Philosophy* 1 (1987): 260–69.
TO   "The Owl." *Transactions of the Charles S. Peirce Society* 24 (1988): 399–407.

UNPUBLISHED ESSAYS

CB   "Communication in Beauty" (1933). Miller Papers, Box 9: Folder 10.
EC   "Ethics and Cosmology" (1955). Miller Papers, Box 52: Folder 12.
EPE   "Economics, Politics, and Ethics" (1949). Miller Papers, Box 3: Folder 6.
IH   "Sources of Interest in the Idea of History" (undated). Miller Papers, Box 7: Folder 11.
MM   "Moral Man" (undated). Miller Papers, Box 6: Folder 13.

NL   "The Natural Law" (1956). Miller Papers, Box 4: Folder 21.
NS   "The National State" (1945). Miller Papers, Box 3: Folder 3.
OES   "Obstacles to Ethical Study" (undated). Miller Papers, Box 6: Folder 13.
RMF   "Rejection as a Moral Factor" (1957). Miller Papers, Box 4: Folder 24.
RPR   "How to Render Passion Responsible?" (1942). Miller Papers, Box 12: Folder 3.
SC   "Solitude and Community: A Meditation" (1973). Miller Papers, Box 26: Folder 17.
SF   "History and the Sense of Fate" (1955). Miller Papers, Box 4: Folder 15.
TI   "The Individual" (1972). Miller Papers, Box 24: Folder 21.
TR   "Translation" (1956). Miller Papers, Box 4: Folder 19.
TS   "The Symbol" (1950–52). Miller Papers, Box 4: Folder 13.

PAPERS COMPILED BY EUGENE R. MILLER

PL   "Papers and Letters of John William Miller," edited and transcribed by Eugene R. Miller. This unpublished compilation of papers will be cited according to the pagination of Eugene Miller's typescript. The typescript is available in the Miller Papers (Box 55).

MISCELLANEOUS UNPUBLISHED WRITINGS

MP   John William Miller Papers, Williamsiana Collection, Williams College. Writings contained in the Miller Papers but not listed above will be cited by means of their location in the box and folder system of the collection; the box number will precede the folder number separated by a colon. For example, MP 3:1 indicates that the cited writing came from the first folder of the third box of the Miller Papers. See the bibliography for a more complete description of the Miller Papers.

STUDENT NOTES

PH 5, 1931   "Philosophy of the State." Philosophy 5, Williams College, 1931. Transcribed by M. Holmes Hartshorne. Miller Papers, Box 22: Folder 7.
PH 7, 1933   "Philosophy of History." Philosophy 7, Williams College, 1951–52. Transcribed and edited by Joseph P. Fell, 1993. Miller Papers, Box 53: Folder 2.
PH 1–2, 1950–51   "Types of Philosophy." Philosophy 1–2, Williams College, 1950–51. Transcribed and edited by Joseph P. Fell, 1991. Miller Papers, Box 53: Folder 1.

PH 8, 1951   "American Philosophy." Philosophy 8, Williams College, Spring 1951. Transcribed and edited by Joseph P. Fell, 1997. Miller Papers, Box 53: Folder 2.

PH 19–20 1952–53   "Maintaining Criticism: The Metaphysics of Ethics and Epistemology." Philosophy 19–20, Williams College, 1952–53. Transcribed and edited by Joseph P. Fell, 1998. Miller Papers, Box 52: Folder 16.

Student notes are cited by the class taught by Miller (e.g., PH 8 was American Philosophy in the old Williams College system), the year in which the class occurred, and the page number of the cited passage as it appears in the transcript maintained in the Miller Papers.

THE ACTIVE LIFE

Introduction
The Active and Contemplative Lives

> It is therefore not so trivial a matter, as it seems to some, whether philosophy
> starts out from a fact or an act.
> —Fichte, *Foundation of the Entire Doctrine of Scientific Knowledge*

John William Miller provides us with a *philosophy of the act* that is the basis for
and ingredient to the active life.[1] This is a life of deeds and legislation, power
and responsibility, as well as originality and fate. It is a way of life that looks
askance on the divine and the eternal and elevates the political and mortal. The
active life is inseparable from history and various modes of historical understanding including remembrance, fabrication, and narration. A philosophy of
the act, or *actualism*,[2] necessarily takes up all of these elements. It is a form of
metaphysics that, in seeking a reflective apprehension of the conditions of one's
endeavors and the order of one's world, turns not toward the eternal but rather
to the temporal. Actualism is a philosophy of persons, a philosophy interested
in making the actual "shine" and establishing the "eloquent presence" of the authoritative individual (MS 191). "The acknowledgment of the actual," Miller
writes, "is also the recognition of the individual" (DP 160).

The concern with the active life is of course an ancient one. The term
descends from Aristotle's distinction between *bios politikos* and *bios theoretikos*.[3]
Yet the difference between the life of shared words and deeds enacted in the
political community and the life of intellect and wonder exemplified in the life
of the mind was noted prior to Aristotle's naming of these two lives. Presocratics such as Parmenides considered the qualities and aims of these two lives. Plato
assessed democracy in the *Republic*, found it wanting, and supplanted it with the
autocracy of philosophy. Following on the Greeks, the Romans picked up on the
current of Platonism and appropriated the distinction stated as a difference
between *vita activa* and *vita contemplativa*. The Fathers of the Christian Church
and their medieval descendents adapted the distinction to suit their monotheis-
tic interpretation of the origin and aims of human existence. With the advent
of modernity, the terms themselves began to fall out of use but the importance
of the distinction was preserved as its logic, fraught with tension, was worked out

1

over the centuries with contemplation giving way to action even as the meaning
of action itself was redescribed. The development of that logic determined the
proximate heritage of our contemporary period of historicism, naturalism, postmodernism, and skepticism.

The active life and its complement, the contemplative life, establish a basic
system of concepts and distinctions forming the texture of our contemporary experience. As Hannah Arendt has masterfully shown,[4] not only can the history
of philosophy be written in their terms but an examination of the contemporary
mind also can be fruitfully undertaken by considering the tensions and implications of these two modes of human being.

The fact that the terms *active life* and the *contemplative life* have now fallen
out of use is important. For Miller's interest in appropriating a distinction that
has long ceased to flourish in our explicit discourse might suggest that his philosophical project is an exercise in antiquitarianism. Nothing could be further from
the truth. In crafting a philosophy that sets the human deed in the place of prominence, Miller is, certainly, undertaking a work of philosophical *retrieval*. Just as
was the case for Arendt, however, Miller's interest in the ancient heritage of the
idea (and the actuality) of action is neither nostalgic nor scholarly. The aim is to
reanimate a concept that has never ceased to function in our basic understanding
of our world and ourselves. It is a gross misunderstanding to suppose that, if an
idea or term has ceased to be current, its *existential logic* has also lost energy or even
become moribund. It is not too large a claim to state that the idea of the active life
cannot be dissociated from Western civilization. Moreover the idea cannot be separated from the practices and institutions of democracy. There may be no greater
irony, then, in a day when democratic institutions have achieved such prominence
and influence, that the concept of action receives relatively little attention in
strictly philosophical discourse as well as broader public debate.[5]

The active life presupposes the irreducible originality of words and deeds
(MS 69-70). They are principles of order, revelation, and self-expression. Miller
refers to the original principles in many ways—*act, discourse, res gestae, talk, utterance, verb,* and *vox*. The appeal and force of the concept of action draws on its
deep historical roots in animism (MS 56) and points toward our interest as
democratic citizens in understanding our energies to be fundamental to the
form of our common world (MS 86). In action persons establish a world that is
distinct from the neutrality of nature and eternality of the divine, a world in
which persons are guided by the monuments of the past and in which they
claim the authority to reconsider those monuments and thereby shape the future conditions of action. The actual world is born in original acts and it is the
condition of an existence that is both free and authoritative.

When describing what it might mean for the human word to be, as Miller writes, "its own warrant" (DP 161), it is useful to consider the Greek sense of action and the political life. Arendt made the important assertion that, for the ancient Greeks, *bios politikos* was closely attached to the ideas of originality and birth (1959, p. 10). Her claim is both compelling and perplexing. The political life is, of course, the life of mortals par excellence. It is the life of those who, different from nature and the divine, must die. The mortal is, as we read in Homer, equated with the futile—his actions, his artifacts and monuments, and his life are all passing phenomena. Death and futility thus seem to be the hallmarks of the political life. Yet even as *mortality* is underscored as the defining trait of humanity so too must the idea of *natality*. Humans must perish but, as the chorus of *Antigone* reminds us, "numberless wonders, terrible wonders walk the world but none is the match for man." Persons are unique and astonishing. Nature, as the Greeks understood it, endures and is ever the same. Human existence is defined by the tumult of novelty in which one always begins anew and acts in unexpected ways with unknown consequences. Natality and mortality form a pair.

The common political life of the polis was organized around the union of natality and mortality. Indeed the political life embraced the fragility of human life and, as fragile, ennobled and immortalized it. The reason for the polis was not then simply the management of human affairs—management was more properly the concern of the household—but rather the creation of a space for deeds, remembrance, monuments, and, ultimately, history (Arendt, 1959, p. 176; 1968, p. 71). The polis was the condition of that form of immortality allotted to the mortal—the doing of great deeds and saying of compelling words that become part of the collective memory of the community (p. 19). That is to say, the polis fostered and preserved natality. The political life extolled that which, under other considerations, seemed to determine human existence as humble and pathetic. Its concern was not with memorializing labor or craft (two other modes of human action) but with the most pointless of human actions—words and deeds. The polis was the product and the condition of the impractical expenditure of human energies. In the political life, however, the futility of human existence was transcended and the ephemeral character of actions was transmuted into freedom and authority.

The relationship between natality and mortality marks, in Arendt's estimation, the enduring difference between political and metaphysical thought (1959, p. 11). In political thought action is authoritative. In metaphysical thought action is futile, distracting, and misleading. This old story of the philosophers and the contemplative life will be addressed in a moment. Here it is important to assert that in harkening back to this heritage of political thought, Miller is allying himself with the very source of *humanism* and the origin of *the*

valuation of that which is intrinsically human. Action in the form of words and deeds
is the expression and revelation of the human as human. Similarly the political
life is the condition for the valuation of the human as human. By contrast, in the
necessities of labor the human sinks to the animal and becomes immersed in an
unthinking cycle of natality and mortality. In the rhapsodies of contemplation
the human transports herself beyond the human and comes to disparage natality and mortality. In the political life, however, persons embrace the complex pair
of natality and mortality and thereby transfigure human existence in daring acts
that both call attention to themselves and start something anew. Action is heroic
futility and the political life the condition of its ennobling.

   This ancient Greek sense of action is ingredient in Miller's idea of the
active life. In revising these traditional distinctions Miller essays two things. First
he proposes a broader and inclusive definition of action that encompasses the
threefold categorization of labor, fabrication, and political action.[6] Second he
brings semiotics to bear on action so as to provide a metaphysical description of
the conditions of the possibility of action. In each case, the core notion remains
the same—a basic affirmation of the natality of action. These developments have
important consequences for the meaning of action, history, and politics.

   Miller's tendency is to ignore the distinctions among the types of action that
Arendt so patiently described in *The Human Condition.* Miller finds all action, in
any mode, to be a form of disclosure and all instances of disclosure to be original
exertions of authority. Thus *disclosure is action* and subsumes individual forms of
disclosure in bodily activity, fabrication, and speech. Disclosure itself is given a
systematic semiotic and, finally, metaphysical treatment in the idea of the *midworld.* Here it is good to quote Miller at some length:

   The act *declares* the environment and articulates it. The act is *unenvironed.*
   Functioning does not appear where something called "environment" has
   been *assumed.* Treat the eye as an object, and there is no looking and no eye
   to do it. No clock as another object measures time, and with no clock there
   is no time to measure. It is the barbarian who treats the functioning object
   as another content of consciousness. If words are "tools," why not burn
   books? (MS 14)

   To such functioning objects I gave a name. It was the "midworld." The midworld meets the two conditions: it is not cognitive, and it launches, spurs,
   and controls all cognition. It is actual. It is not "real." It is not "apparent."
   Unenvironed, it projects the environment. (MS 13)

The scope of Miller's sense of action is apparent. In these passages one finds
action described as the property of an eye, a clock, and a book. The eye in seeing

is a form of bodily disclosure of the visible. The clock is a form of fabricated disclosure of time. The book is a form of written disclosure of the intelligible. In each instance, the act reveals a world or a part of a world. The fact that each reveals something different and has a different import does not override this basic disclosive function. Moreover one finds that action is always embodied, it always has a vehicle. These vehicles are *functioning objects* and the systematic organization of functioning objects is the *midworld* that is at the center of Miller's semiotic metaphysics. Thus while for Miller action is energy and has all of the traits of natality that the Greeks ascribed to it, that energetic expenditure is systematically linked with the discipline of form and structure (MS 65). In actualism, the premises of the active life become principles of metaphysics—that is, the order of one's world.

The active life transpires in a middle ground between the natural and the eternal. The glory of this life is that it makes a virtue of what, from other perspectives, are its manifest limitations. Arendt summarized the "frustrations" of action as follows: "the unpredictability of its outcome, the irreversibility of the process, and the anonymity of its authors" (1959, p. 197). Human acts build on one another in such a way that individuals apparently have little control over the career of action. In this light, individuals appear to be carried along by the forces of history and their agency diminished if not canceled. It is a paradox that another of the frustrations of action arises due to the fact that individuals also appear to have too much agency. The capacity for novelty becomes unruly and human affairs, organized around and directed toward novel acts, become confusing. Thus it is that Arendt stressed that the active life necessarily occurs in a condition of plurality—that is, a community of individuals in which each is free and authoritative (1968, p. 61). This plurality is compounded when one considers that there are not just a plurality of agents but also an indefinite plurality of moments in which agency is exercised. Each moment is an occasion of action, but each moment is itself within a historical environment of actions and their fateful trajectories. The fact of plurality requires, as Miller writes, that a price be paid:

> What I propose is that we consider the price to be paid for enfranchising discourse. Discourse needs authority. It is this concern that lies at the core of the philosophy of history. History deals in what has been done in one way or another. . . . It is concerned, therefore, with finitude and its career. But in this respect, history seems to alienate itself from the traditional concerns of philosophy, which have tended to stress timelessness and the ahistoric, treating time as derivative and secondary. (PC 106–7; see also MS 66)

Each act begins anew, but there is no single, clear beginning (MS 8). Rather there is a complex historical context of actions that both constrains and makes possible individual acts. And even as each act claims authority for what it has initiated, no agent is fully aware of the consequences of her deeds (TO 400). This uncertainty of origin and outcome, this fragility of existing orders, this partially blind and limited freedom—these all tally in estimating the price for enfranchising action.

We have been reluctant to pay this price.[7] Indeed plurality, with its necessary confusion and unpredictability, has ever been a source of philosophical and practical discontent. Miller describes this discontent as a dissatisfaction and distrust of historical time (PC 130-60, PH 44-60). And while the forms and phases of this discontent are many and varied they are adequately summarized as a quest for "the ahistoric ideal" or, after José Ortega Gasset, the "Eleatic ideal" (PC 135)[8]— a form of order, a mode of value, and a type of knowledge not subject to the vagaries of history. It is from this fundamental mistrust of action and its historical environment that the contemplative life sprang. Parmenides, Pythagoras, Plato, and Aristotle each made a case for the superiority of unity over plurality as well as for contemplation over active engagement in the world. Important differences among the Eleatics abound, yet the lineage of Father Parmenides makes it clear that as a matter of metaphysics, the constant and singular supersensible (e.g., the One, the Forms, Thought) takes precedence to the sensible, plural, and changing that define history. Further, as a matter of ethics, for Parmenides and his descendents the contemplative life of the philosopher is valued over the active life of the political person.

In sum: The life of considering eternal objects has been considered to be superior to the life of words and deeds transacted in public life. This priority was appropriated by the Romans and, later, by the Christian Church which found it to jibe well with the spiritual interest that set eternal life and the world in opposition.[9] In this vein, *vita activa* was given a broader definition than *bios politikos* such that the active life came to pertain to all worldly activities and not just political action. Here the apoliticism that spanned the Hellenic and Christian worlds—the essence of which, developing earlier Platonic notions, is the idea of the afterlife—moved immortality completely out of the realm of deeds and into the realm of contemplation. Political freedom in words and deeds was supplanted by a theoretical freedom—that is, the inner freedom of thought and will divorced from action (Arendt, 1968, pp. 157-58).

This hierarchy of thought over deed remained in force until the rise of modern, experimental science. At this juncture action underwent a resurgence but, as Arendt noted, the form of action in question was not political action but rather *fabrication* (1959, pp. 205-7). Science was then and remains a goal-oriented and instrumentalized form of action that wrests certain results from nature. Scientific knowledge is the result not of passivity but of activity, and the object of knowledge is nature and not the divine. Yet this form of action does not share in the same sort of uncertainty, plurality, and fragility that typifies political action. Fabrication as craft has enduring results in the form of objects made. Fabrication as modern science is a controlled process that provides enduring results in the form of nature, including human being, interpreted as object or process (1959, pp. 206–11; 1968, pp. 61–63). Indeed Arendt made much of the fact that when confronting the disorder of action, both Plato and Aristotle brought the model of fabrication to bear on the political process and proposed statecraft as the cure for the unruliness of political action (1959, pp. 197–206). Understood in this way, fabrication does not embrace action in its political mode. It is another form of protection against, if not escape from, history.

Modernity, even as it derided the traditional objects of contemplation, continued to subordinate the active life of words and deeds (Arendt, 1959, p. 21). What had changed was the remedy for the suspicion of action. The common thread is the priority of *knowledge over action* (MS 20–35). Action is uncertain. Knowledge is the cure for uncertainty. What modern science achieved that the contemplative life of the ancients could not was the removal of uncertainty from the world itself. Philosophical contemplation was an escape from the world that was by definition plural, disorderly, and uncertain. Modern science took a different tack and cut off this route of escape by denying empirical standing to the objects of contemplation and then went on to redescribe the world completely in terms of empirical knowledge. With *person* and *act* described in terms of objects and processes, what uncertainty remains in the world in the wake of modernity is not the recalcitrant uncertainty of natality but the ever-decreasing (toward an eventual vanishing point) uncertainty of controlled inquiry in pursuit of determinate objects of knowledge. Persons are vanquished, and their words and deeds become subject to scientific description. The world, as Miller writes, falls silent (MP 25:22; see MS 126, 191).

For Aristotle, the life of contemplation was the life of the stranger.[10] The stranger is a person outside the polis, who is neither known nor remembered, and who does not share in the words and deeds of the community. In sum: The stranger is not in history. From the ancients to the moderns, from philosophical contemplation to science—the idea of the stranger has been the operative ideal. We have aimed to step out of history and be objective spectators (MS 36–47). What accompanies this centuries-old search for knowledge in isolation is, of course, alienation (Arendt 1959, pp. 225 ff.). The overall tendency is one of nihilism—that is, a move away from history and a suspicion of all that is individual and authoritative (PH 21), or "the interpretation of experience without any center of existence" (PC 151). This tendency is also fundamentally antidemocratic in that it rids the world of originality, it denies that men and women are agents and thus free, and it replaces the responsible and authoritative confusion of political action with the autocratic rule of knowledge and science. As ever, political freedom remains at odds with freedom as it has been traditionally defined in contemplation and theory (Arendt, 1968, pp. 157–58).

The modern turn from contemplation to action, from the eternal to the secular, did not then result in a *return* to the active life. Built on the ashes of speculative metaphysics, the new political philosophies—such as those of Thomas Hobbes, John Locke, and Jean-Jacques Rousseau—instituted political *science* and not political life. Similarly G. W. F. Hegel reasserted the importance of history but it was history as *process* and *system*, not that history that is the field for and product of the words and deeds of individual actors. And even as Karl Marx appropriated the language of action he construed action as labor and interpreted the human form of being on a purely *natural* model that pointed not toward the revitalization of politics but rather its withering. Modernity installed action as fabrication and labor—that is, action that is productive and goal-oriented. Philosophical contemplation was eclipsed but only by the shadow of the active life, a form of the active life that was but the contemplative life (the life of knowledge) in another guise.

What followed in the wake of modernity was a rebellion against the world and person interpreted in terms object, process, and system. As Miller and many others have noted, modernity and specifically modern science pretended to free persons from dogmatism and the domination of the eternal but, in fact, established a new form of subjugation in epistemological and ethical skepticism as well as a culture of technology and mass values. The world and the person stand or fall together. Miller writes:

> What is happening before our eyes is that adjusting to the environment has brought about the *abolition* of environment. The other end of environment is the individual, and he has vanished with the environment. Where the world has no energy, neither has the person. It is a matter of record. Without persons, no environment, for it is the organization of their acts and utterances. (MS 88)

The person *and* the world were eclipsed as sources of value. Skepticism gave birth to nihilism. Confronted with the results of the fabrications of modernity, postmodernity undertook to destroy those very same constructions. This work of destruction began with the promise of returning us to the active life; it embraced plurality, attacked system and uniformity, deconstructed metaphysics, and sought freedom. Yet it has become clear that this project of dismantling was no more interested in political action than were the moderns and the ancients. It was another phase of nihilism. The modern world was set on its head (plurality chosen over unity), but the qualities ingredient to the active life were treated with the same skepticism and contempt.

The paradox is that postmodernity both plumed itself as and was disparaged for being political. Contra modernity, postmodernity embraced the vagueness and uncertainty of human existence. It made the individual person, in all his specificity and historicity, central to philosophical thought and political action. Indeed, seeing in the Eleatic ideal all that was dangerous to historical action and thought, many brave souls undertook to cease philosophizing altogether and to bring speculation, metaphysics, and systematic philosophy to an end. Yet postmodernity missed the mark. The plurality it encouraged was speculative and not political. Indeed postmodernity was fully internal in its significance and wholly theoretical in its assumptions and tendencies—an example of the contemplative life in disguise. (This time it was a life spent contemplating sheer difference, plurality, and change rather than sameness, unity, and constancy; it was a metaphysical theory about the *absence* of the real and the permanent.) The Eleatic (Parmenidian) and the Ionian (Heraclitean) lineages differ over much but when the matter is the active life they are effectively the same. By working strictly in terms of this ancient dualism, postmodernity failed to address the hybrid forms of action and order that define the political—that is, the search for mortal immortality, orderly disorder, and obedient authority. That is our common world of action. The theoretical chaos of unlimited freedom, unrestrained criticism, and indefinite plurality—this constitutes as much a flight from actuality as the search for the Forms.

Postmodernism underscores Arendt's point that the active life has been so thoroughly disparaged in the course of history that what passes for action is only its appearance (1959, p. 21), be it fabrication, labor, or, most recently, theoretical action in the form of postmodernism. Individuality, freedom, authority—these are the hallmarks of democratic personhood and necessary qualities of the active life. Politics cannot be recovered simply by opting for Ionianism over Eleaticism. The retrieval of the active life will require a new outlook on the history of thought as well as a new perspective on our contemporary actuality.

Miller crafts a democratic metaphysics, a philosophical understanding that comports with, supports, and enlivens democratic sensibilities and institutions. The retrieval of the active life is basic to this project. As we have already seen, however, Miller is not undertaking a simple appropriation of an ancient idea; the active life is substantially revised in terms of both its form and content. Further Miller is not a proponent of the active life and an opponent of the contemplative life. While he criticizes the Eleatic ideal, Miller considers action and contemplation inseparably paired. Contemplation thus needs to be reinterpreted as a mode of action and action needs to be reappraised as a mode of contemplation. Actualism is a thorough development of the active life, the contemplative life, and the dialectical relation between these two fundamental aspects of human being. Thus the appropriateness of the expression, *a metaphysics of democracy*. In this metaphysics the active and contemplative are joined and revised.

In providing a preliminary assessment of the viability of Miller's aim, we can note that the history of thought, up and through postmodernism, has not been wholly antithetical to the active life. As Arendt remarked in various places, the rise of secularism, historicism, science, and politics all have turned us, however incompletely, *toward* the active life. The growth of secularism has decreased our interest in speculative immortality and increased our concern for our earthly posterity (1968, pp. 70–71). The separation of church from state has freed the institutions of politics from the apolitical premises of religion (p. 73). Science, in opening up the cosmos and showing us the indefinite extent of space and time, has deprived us of ultimate ends and forced us to address the flux of historical time (p. 75). Furthermore, as a result of the decay of the contemplative life, we no longer accept the strict duality of philosopher and mere man and no longer regard thinking as a specialized activity (1978, vol. 1, pp. 13, 191). In sum: No matter how inimical modernity and postmodernity have appeared to be to the active life, these trends have established the conditions for a creative revival of the ancient sense of politics and action.

The conditions of a new humanism are arrayed about us.[11] Organized around action, history, and democracy, actualism eschews the tradition of setting the internal and external in opposition. Person and world are in dialectical relationship such that the conditions of interiority are found and maintained in exteriority. "Presence and totality stand or fall together," Miller writes. "The anti-metaphysics of our day masquerades as an assault on any totality; what it is equally attacking is presence, the other side of totality" (MS 13). Actualism seeks a viable humanism and a durable form of human identity in the *interchange* of acts and things, words and objects, self and world that is the *historical career of the midworld*. Miller's semiotic metaphysics shows interiority and exteriority to be aspects of action, its instruments, and its institutions. If we seek the person, we would do well to go out into the world as described and built by action (i.e., the midworld) and look for his controlling actualities in the form of functioning objects (DP 156–57). One must go to the career of actuality—that is, history.

Action and the person are not hidden but rather available in the public life. Just so, authority and freedom transpire in the public domain and the ever-resurgent natality of political action occurs in terms of the record of past actions and the claim to establish new conditions of action. The revival of the active life proposed by actualism is premised on a form of metaphysics that seeks a "reconciliation with the conditions of our endeavors":

It is by action that we establish history. We take into account what has been done. What we say or do thereupon reflects that artifactual world.

This is a central quality of historical reality. If there is any human world at all, it is found in our true deeds and in their implications. History is the endeavor to be accountable to the record of actions. . . . It is a question of what men have done with their own world, such as it may have been at a given time and place.

History looks to the past, but this is only the necessary corollary of its concern with deeds. . . . Show me an act, and I will show you that what has been done is being taken into account in this new actuality. It is not true that one can concern oneself only with present deeds, or with a future activity, leaving the dusty past to historians. . . . There is a deep impiety in all novelties that purport to ignore or to scorn what has been done, no matter how enthralling the vision of the future that they may summon. . . .

History, in this respect, is an attitude of piety. It is our reconciliation with the conditions of our endeavors. It is the story not only of acts—*res gestae*—but of their condition. (PH 149-50)

The basic affirmation is that action must always look to the public and historical career of words, deeds, and institutions. Action must affirm its own history if it is to make history. Novel action must authorize other actions and what those actions have wrought if it, too, is to claim authority. The *reconciliation* of which Miller writes is not, however, mere recognition and acceptance. It is a mode of active, reflective, and critical engagement. It involves what Miller calls *scholarship*—that is, the reflective illumination of the world of thought and action by considering its basis in action, the fateful career and conflicts of its authoritative orders and institutions, and its implications for responsible action in the future (PC 174-92). Scholarship is thus a mode of heroic citizenship in which one dares to act both with knowledge of the conditions of action and an appreciation of the unknown and fateful consequences of each act.[12] Even as the contemplative life without action is a fiction, the active life is naught without reflection and criticism.

The active life and the contemplative life fuse in the political life of democracy in which one acts with authority and takes responsibility for the conditions of action. It involves the reflective identification of historical limit as well as the critical maintenance and revision of those limits. This is the political center of actualism. "The idealism of the future [i.e., actualism] will be a philosophy of history, of action, of self-generating, lawful finitude," Miller writes. "Such are the conditions of a metaphysics of democracy" (PC 74).

ONE

A Metaphysics of Democracy?

It is no news that metaphysics is in disrepute. Metaphysics has been on the defensive since the advent of modernity, as has talk of ontology, teleology, and utopia. Whether one attends to the Anglo-American or Continental traditions, it is understood that respectable philosophizing should avoid metaphysics—its terms and concepts only allowed to appear under the ironic protection of inverted commas. It is also not news that liberal democracy has regularly been the foe of grand theories and ever the friend of plain, enlightened thinking. Far from being associated with speculation, as John William Miller aptly notes, democracy is considered "the triumph over such fantasies" (PC 73). The democratic cast of mind, so influential during the past three centuries, promotes individuality and autonomy while resisting totalitarian politics and the dogmatic ideologies that lend them support. Not only is metaphysics philosophically dubious but it appears to be politically dangerous as well. Nothing then could be more unlikely than offering a metaphysical account of democracy. Opposition comes on all sides.

In terms of this assessment Miller's statement that the democratic person needs a metaphysics sounds paradoxical (MS 191). For this claim is not the weak one that a democratic polity can abide metaphysics or grant it toleration when contained to the private lives of its citizens. Miller insists on a thoroughgoing, and even practical, connection between the two:

> Yet, even the democratic man must have dignity. Sovereignty, whether monarchical or democratic, needs sanction. This sanction turns on the responsibility of the sovereign, and on reverence for his pronouncements. One does not escape tyranny by multiplying irresponsible and subjective arbitrariness. Every man may be a king; but in our time a king must be a constitutional authority. (PC 73)

Any affirmation—either theoretical or practical—of the dignity of persons must address their authority and the constitution of that authority. The alternative of supposing that dignity is found in the rejection of all authority is a blind alley; once authority is dismissed arbitrariness takes its place. This recognition leads to the reaffirmation of the significance of metaphysics to the practice of liberal democracy insofar as it provides insight into order and, thus, authority. It also draws one toward a reconsideration of conceptions of ontology, teleology, utopian thinking, and even democracy's own status as an idea—that is, a term of systematic control (PL 495).

Metaphysical language is neither a vice to be abhorred nor an accident to be avoided. On the contrary, it is inevitable (PC 30). Metaphysical concepts pervade the experience of persons. Returning to metaphysics means nothing other than coming to terms with the structure of experience. It is also the necessary manner for addressing authority and the fragility of its constitution. Miller's strong claim is that one can only find the person via metaphysics.

A brief statement cannot silence the dissonance that arises from the claim that we must unify democracy and metaphysics, the active life and the contemplative life. If anything it is heightened. This opposition, however, is instructive because it reveals important aspects of the relationship between democracy and metaphysics concealed in the habitual and unproblematic usage of these terms. It is a relationship that is worthy of exploration. This work is an essay in examining such connections, and these insights serve as a basis for reconfiguring democratic political thought so as to comport with the active life.

With these larger aims in mind, the present chapter frames the issues and concepts at play in Miller's retrieval of the active life and his attempt to forge what, following Walt Whitman, he refers to as "a metaphysics of democracy" (PC 73; cf. Whitman 1867/1982, p. 984). This is a challenging task. Addressing democracy is difficult because of its familiarity and the ubiquity of its terms. In addition there is such an immense literature, reflecting the great variety of theories of democracy, that any attempt at interpretation runs the risk of losing its way. Miller's philosophy is also a challenge for the interpreter. First there is the exacting nature of the thinking involved, thinking that resists the well-trodden paths of realism, idealism, and pragmatism. The second difficulty is that, unlike the idea of democracy, actualism is burdened by a lack of conceptual familiarity not to mention a relative paucity of scholarly literature.

It is such challenges of interpretation and presentation that recommend an unusual starting point for this work—that is, the pragmatism of Richard Rorty. Although unlikely, Rorty's thought serves as a helpful entry into and instructive foil for actualism. Because it is rooted in the American political tradition, Rorty's presentation of the political enterprise highlights not just the tradition of thought in which Miller himself stands but also stresses those particular political tendencies that actualism must address if it is to be persuasive. Moreover, despite a gap of two generations, Rorty's position within contemporary philosophical debates matches surprisingly well with Miller's own situation amid the contending forces of idealism, positivism, and pragmatism. Rorty's well-known variant of pragmatism thus serves as a *point de repère*—it not only usefully focuses the discussion of democracy but also establishes a set of ready comparisons with Miller's philosophy.

§1.1   SENSES OF DEMOCRACY

Prior to considering Rorty, the work of stage-setting requires a preliminary estimation of the meaning of *democracy*. As a term of philosophy, *democracy* both benefits from and is hampered by its familiarity to the contemporary mind. The benefits are obvious in that familiarity keeps it clear of abstruseness and readily assists in connecting the concept with actual practices such as deliberating, voting, and enacting the law. This familiarity can hamper a philosophic examination of democracy, however, to the extent that democracy, because of its mundane aspect and widespread acceptance, hardly seems worthy of examination, puzzlement, or speculation. Given this difficulty, it is worthwhile to devote a few paragraphs to sketching Miller's own sense of democracy and provide a more refined description of its liberal variant that is at the center of his metaphysics of democracy.

Miller's approach to political philosophy comes via the idealist tradition and, more precisely, British and American idealists such as Bernard Bosanquet, F. H. Bradley, T. H. Green, William Ernest Hocking, and Josiah Royce. At the root of this tradition is the influence of J. G. Fichte, G. W. F. Hegel, Immanuel Kant, and Jean-Jacques Rousseau, all of whom defined the ethical and political enterprise as a search for freedom in and through a community. Miller follows closely in this tradition insofar as he emphasizes freedom as a state of reflective and conscious control. This freedom, while it resides specifically in individual persons, is made possible by organized associations and, most effectively, the state. Just so, Miller criticizes conceptions of autonomy organized around the pursuit of desire, laissez-faire, and no-harm principles of action. In contrast to these popular estimations, he claims that freedom is actualized in conscious self-composure at the level of both the person and the community. "It is a great illusion to suppose that government will protect rights when actual individuals display nothing but desires in their wills, and nothing but opinions in their minds," Miller states. "Such doctrines paralyze resolve. They are degenerate, and they invite the conqueror and the despot" (PC 73). Freedom is not merely unrestricted action. Freedom is also not something managed by democratic institutions. To Miller's mind, freedom involves self-control, and democratic institutions function to reveal, maintain, and expand self-control. Political participation is, even if unnoted by oneself, a philosophical education.

Despite sharing this positive conception of the state, Miller is wary of the ethical and political philosophies of the idealists. Inclining either to thin abstractions from concrete life (e.g., Kant) or veering toward all-consuming systems (e.g., Hegel, Bradley), idealism often purchases its reflective composure at too high a price. Because it sets up freedom as a regulative ideal or describes it in terms of a process where the person is effectively obliterated, idealism tends to resonate poorly with the sort of self-control sought by actual persons. Thus Miller remarked late in his life that his metaphysics required Main Street and "not some unanchored idealism" (PL 514). No metaphysics worthy of democracy can avoid the local and individual. In this respect Miller's sense of democracy is equally rooted in the liberal, democratic tradition of the United States. Borrowing from empirical and legalistic strains in the political philosophies of Richard Hooker and John Locke, this tradition emphasizes the equal authority of persons and insists on securing rights via legal protection. The state takes on a more negative and operational aspect—that is, the state is not the source of personhood but rather the ensemble of means that persons employ to effectively establish autonomy. This principled respect for persons, ingrained in our institutions and moral sensibilities, precludes theoretical conceptions of freedom (no matter how high-minded) that do not match up with the actual lives of persons. "Respect for experience has gone too far to be recalled," Miller notes. "At bottom it is a respect for persons" (PH 173). This is a fundamental axiom of American political consciousness wherein a concern for the private has become a public matter (MP 11:5; PL 105).

Miller's conception of democracy runs between these two traditions of Western political thought. Freedom cannot be described in terms of a speculative ideal or located in an absolute state of affairs. Freedom also cannot be a power invested in each individual such that democratic institutions are merely the neutral medium, or modus operandi, for regulating relations among self-possessed individuals. Reconciling the tension between these two extremes—particularly between freedom and authority (PL 143)—is the task of actualism. Freedom must occur in what is shared among persons, in those "over-individual" elements such as laws and institutions.[1] That freedom will, however, be the property of the person and the authority will be articulated in the first person singular and plural. Personhood is that form of individuality made possible by membership in the political whole.[2]

The key is connecting personal will to its institutional embodiment. The formal element noted by idealism needs to be joined with the concrete actuality highlighted by empiricism. This is achieved by thematizing *action, symbolism,* and *history* as structural and mediating elements in this struggle between particularity and form, person and institution. Providing some flavor of his philosophical approach, Miller remarks:

We are demoralized today because we proclaim liberty but no actuality as local control and as revelation. Nothing is to be revered. There is no

eloquent presence. . . . Intellectuals have no verbs; the common man does.
I am joining that common man. And if this is a free country, we'd better get
ourselves a metaphysic that has respect for the man on Elm Street. As it is,
he is treated with patronage and disdain. Nor does he quite know how to
stand in his authority because he is there and therefore projects a world in
his doing. (MS 191)

The *world* that is the basis, medium, and consequence of action is what Miller
refers to as *the midworld*. It is a region composed of such human actions and fabrications as words, tools, instruments, institutions, and laws. They are objects as
well as practices—that is, *functioning objects*—disclosing and articulating experience.
As such, functioning objects are also vehicles for disclosing the *authoritative* person. The person and her authoritative forms are in constant and dialectical interaction. Form neither reigns over persons nor do persons stand independent of
form. The process animating their mutual dependence and constitution is what
Miller refers to as *history*, the basic form of the active life.

Mere idealism or simple empiricism—each for its own separate reasons—fails to
reveal the authority of the person. Miller's metaphysics of democracy addresses the
historical person amid the career of these acts, practices, and institutions. How then
to describe these active forms of democracy? Although it owes much to its origin in
Athens and development in Rome, the intervening span of historical revision must
be taken into account when defining *democracy*. To this end, the state of democracy
can be delimited by using C. B. Macpherson's genealogy of liberal democracy.

Setting aside Macpherson's basic, and somewhat dated, classification of
types of democracy articulated in *The Real World of Democracy*, one can concen-
trate on three types of democracy—protective (e.g., Jeremy Bentham), developmental (e.g., John Stuart Mill and John Dewey), and equilibrium (e.g., Joseph
Schumpeter). All three types have arisen since the beginning of the nineteenth
century and thus coincide with the downfall of popular conceptions of democracy that decried the economic relations of capital (e.g., Rousseau and Thomas
Jefferson). Each of the three types in question integrates the capitalistic mode of
economic relations into its conception of democracy: Protective democracy sup-
plements the participatory liberal marketplace with a corresponding form of political participation; developmental democracy sees economic and political
participation as preeminent ways of actualizing human potential; equilibrium
democracy describes politics in terms of market models and envisions government as a provider of political goods to political consumers who register their
preferences with votes. Of these three, it is the equilibrium model that is both
contemporaneous to and most descriptively adequate of our current state of

affairs. A cursory glance at the American political scene—for example, its use of polling, focus groups, and service-sector language—suggests the ways in which market models and marketing practices have come to determine politics.

Macpherson's genealogy shows that the significance of market relations, strong intuitions regarding the integrity and freedom of persons, and goals such as providing the conditions for full human development have for any discussion of democracy. They also suggest a strong antimetaphysical bias—that is, a predilection for the individual and concrete (action) against the general and speculative (contemplation). In adopting Macpherson's sense of liberal democracy one sees that the current practice of democracy is decidedly informed by the legalistic strains of the empirical tradition. The idealist tradition, and particularly Hegelian thought, has been clear that economic relations are, at best, a stage in the development of the person and the community as a whole. The liberal democrat, by contrast, is inclined to see market relations as the model for politics par excellence. In the degree to which Schumpeter's idea of a political marketplace reigns, politics is inevitably conceived of as a modus operandi by which isolated individuals maximize their personal goods. (Process and system trump action.) Politics is, in this light, not understood as a constitutional form of relations. The sense of authority that resonates most in contemporary society is that outlined by Macpherson's notion of *possessive individualism* in which economic and political terms coincide.[3]

This definition of the contemporary liberal variant of democracy is primarily descriptive. Quite simply: This is where one is. This description also establishes the object of the examination, criticism, and revision proposed by this book. Like Macpherson in *The Life and Times of Democracy*, Miller foresees a model of political association achievable beyond the current stage of equilibrium democracy. Yet, in Miller's case, liberal democracy properly understood cannot be construed just as a stage to be surpassed. Liberal democracy has a normative force. The most critical insight gleaned from market relations regards the autonomy of persons and their unavoidable responsibility for making their own lives. Liberal democracy is described by Miller as "a school of the will," "the only condition under which [persons] could assert a social or moral will" (PC 41). Balancing this assessment of individualism with a healthy estimation of the *form* of political association we find common authority, fairness, and the rule of law to be necessary for the development of the individual. This richer conception of liberal democracy is not just a de facto description of a political state of affairs but is also an outline of a regulative conception of democratic community. Miller's aim is not to overcome liberal democracy but to deepen one's understanding of what is requisite for and implied by liberal democracy—that is, the active life.

§1.2 AMERICA'S ANTIMETAPHYSICAL TRADITION

There is no doubt that the current state of democratic theory and practice is clearly antimetaphysical. Miller's philosophy of the act and his interest in clarifying liberal democratic practice runs counter to *la couleur du temps* that Jean Lyotard identified as the declining credibility of grand narratives (1988, p. 46). Following on the skeptical tradition of modernity, the influence of Friedrich Nietzsche, Martin Heidegger, and Ludwig Wittgenstein—just to name three self-described antimetaphysicians—has thoroughly undermined metaphysics in the conceptual sphere even as liberalism has threatened it in the practical sphere. As stated earlier, opposition comes on all sides.

Although much of the contemporary skepticism and ironism regarding metaphysical terminology is owing to the work of these three Europeans, this examination looks toward another source of philosophic discontent. The dubious status of metaphysics, and one's hesitancy to link it with democracy, is most profitably understood as deriving from another, native, source: American philosophical and political theory. It is for this reason that it is Rorty who poses a truly provocative challenge to Miller's claims regarding the pertinence of metaphysics to liberal democracy. More so than any other contemporary philosopher, Rorty clearly expresses this fact: Metaphysics, understood as an overarching theory of the real, is suspect to the modern democratic mind. As much as he has been influenced by Nietzsche, Heidegger, and Wittgenstein, the roots of Rorty's thought have a deep hold in a modern and liberal American philosophical and political tradition that has always been wary of metaphysical speculation.

A keynote of this American tradition to which Rorty subscribes is its antiabsolutism. One can already note the general contours of this tendency in the ideas of Jefferson and Thomas Paine—both foes of dogmatism and enemies of those metaphysical statements propping up dogmatic authority. Jefferson is well known as a proponent of religious toleration and as the author of various documents challenging the arbitrary authority of kings. As an apologist for the revolutionary sentiment in America and France, Paine for his part warned, in *The Age of Reason*, against the "moral mischief" that "mental lying" and irrational obedience produced in society (1794/1995, p. 666). More significant than establishing any definite doctrine, Jefferson, Paine, and other figures of the American Enlightenment set a tone emphasizing the liberty of reason and the experimental character of experience. This description of our human faculties, and correspondingly of reality, resisted dogmatism in science, religion, philosophy, and politics. Each individual, relying on his intellectual powers and without the support of royal or ecclesiastical authority, was adequate to the task of discerning truth from falsity and charting a course through the world. The founding of the American Republic was a practical enactment of those sentiments.

Although there are elements in this outlook peculiar to the early Republican period, there is no mistaking the antiabsolutist note resonating through the two centuries since that period. In the nineteenth century, particularly in Ralph Waldo Emerson's essays "The American Scholar" and "Self-Reliance," American antiabsolutism found articulate expression. In the twentieth century this heritage received a vital reinterpretation through the work of two philosophers from whom Rorty draws considerable support—Dewey, whom Rorty describes as his intellectual predecessor, and John Rawls.

Speaking in an idiom more familiar to the contemporary ear, Dewey criticized a pervasive form of "confused metaphysics" embodying some of the worst habits of thought (1929, p. 88). These bad habits are displayed in a tendency toward establishing hierarchies of objects and types of experience. Moreover these habits often collude in schemes that systematize experience in terms of these fixed hierarchies. Human intelligence strives to organize, Dewey recognized, and these attempts give birth to metaphysical ideas. Yet intelligence often forgets that it is, at one and the same time, describing *and* plunged into experience. Descriptions cannot stand aloof from the ongoing process of experience and its future redescription provoked by the demands of the environment and the exigencies of inquiry. In keeping with the American tradition, Dewey sensed that the greatest urgency for attacking this brand of metaphysics is not theoretical but social and political. As Jefferson and Paine believed, bad philosophy is an apologist for political, cultural, and theological absolutisms stifling social and political innovation. The very possibility of democracy, as well as social progress, demands just the opposite. Dewey's recommendation was that philosophy assist progressive tendencies in art, industry, and politics by criticizing not only absolutist philosophy but also those dogmatisms embedded in everyday practice. Speaking not just for himself but for a whole tradition, Dewey held that scientific inquiry, critical reason, and reformist politics are hallmarks of the democratic character.

What transpires in the work of Rawls—forming, in this account, the last bridge to Rorty's own philosophy—is the further abandonment of the metaphysical for a practical or political conception of the person and sociability. (Indeed a 1985 essay of Rawls's was titled "Justice as Fairness: Political not Metaphysical.") The articulation and organization of a just society is not, Rawls claimed, in any way dependent on "claims to universal truth, or claims about the essential nature and identity of persons" (1985, p. 223). Rather, as he stated describing his own position:

[S]ince justice as fairness is intended as a political conception of justice for a democratic society, it tries to draw solely upon basic intuitive ideas that are embedded in the political institutions of a constitutional democratic regime and the public traditions of their interpretation. Justice as fairness is a political conception in part because it starts from within a certain political tradition. We hope that this political conception of justice may at least be supported by what we may call an "overlapping consensus," that is, by a consensus that includes all the opposing philosophical and religious doctrines likely to persist and to gain adherents in a more or less just constitutional democratic society. (1985, pp. 225–26)

Political practice has a distinct priority over philosophy. Indeed philosophy is ultimately trumped by the exigencies of arranging a practical consensus that fits with the basic cultural intuitions of members of a democratic society. Political practice and institutions are basically constructive and not the result of any philosophical deduction from foundational truths (Rawls, 1993). Yet, because all construction occurs according to these fundamental intuitions, the political process does not, Rawls claimed, reduce to a mere modus vivendi, a convenient way of getting along in life; it is a sound development of a stable and, from a practical point of view, necessary outlook. It is the stability of that outlook, however, that philosophical metaphysics continually sets in question by claiming that cultural intuitions are not sufficient guides for action. Because it insists on claiming authority over the practical, metaphysics finds itself at war with politics. Despite this basic antagonism, Rawls did not considered philosophy to be anathema. He also did not regard it as completely irrelevant. Instead Rawls stated that philosophical beliefs and principles are "too important" to be adjudicated and regulated by political institutions (1985, p. 231). Thus, like religion in the early days of the American Republic, an antiestablishment clause must now be crafted to separate metaphysics from politics. It will be tolerated as sovereign in its own sphere but rendered effectively null and void in public discourse. Only by affecting this separation, Rawls argued, does a plural and democratic society have a chance at achieving a consensus that will respect the liberty and equality of persons.

This is but a sketch of a political and philosophical tradition that is, truly, multifaceted and contentious. It remains a reasonably accurate depiction of a major tendency within American thought and a portrait of the transition from contemplation to action as fabrication (cf. Arendt, 1959). It also charts a line of philosophical descent to which Rorty proudly appends his own name. And if he is not as zealous an opponent of speculation as his intellectual forebears, Rorty certainly thinks, like Rawls, that our current form of liberal democracy can benefit from the further clarification of its unfortunate relationship to metaphysics. His work in this regard shows him to be both an inheritor of, and reformer

within, this antiabsolutist tradition. Furthermore, Rorty's pragmatism is of
importance insofar as it represents what might be considered a near-culmination
of the contemporary movement leading away from the contemplative life and
toward the active life understood in terms of fabrication and science.

The contemporary flood of antimetaphysics represents a final assault against
Plato's reversal of the order of life when, in the *Republic*, he set the philosopher up
as king and made the citizenry subordinate to contemplation. In that book, the *poli-*
tikos denigrated and finally undermined politics. Since then there has been an in-
termittent struggle to set life back on its feet via the reestablishment of the proper
relationship between action and contemplation. Contemporary philosophy (or an-
tiphilosophy) has joined this fight with more vehemence, and perhaps success, than
any previous moment of Western thought. Theory has been denigrated as dead
thought or, at best, thought that arrives at the twilight. Contemporary antimetaphysicians have pointed out the incapacity of theory to organize the plurality of actuality and, indeed, its inability to control its own internal contradictions. In light
of this general movement, Rorty and the other antimetaphysicians can be seen as
fulfilling Jefferson's admonition that "'life belongs in usufruct to the living'; that the
dead have neither powers nor rights over it" (1789/1984, p. 959). What will be discovered, however, is that the route of return to the active, political life is far more
complex than any antimetaphysician, American or European, could foresee.

§1.3   RORTY'S CHALLENGE

For Rorty, democratic politics is a process of creative coping in an often hostile, and
always uncertain, environment. The political process is established to attain those
aims that a community sets for itself. It is the intersubjective exercise of prudence.
Liberal democracies distinguish themselves from other communities by their effective desire for the reduction of suffering and humiliation (Rorty, 1991, p. 91). The
prudential calculations of liberal democracies are crafted with these goals in mind.

This is far from a lofty pronouncement. Yet, as Rorty states in "The Priority of Democracy to Philosophy," it is the "light-mindedness" of this version of
democracy that recommends it (1991, p. 193). In this regard Rorty's position is
in line with a tradition reluctant to engage in metaphysical speculation (understood as "a search for theories that will get at real essence" [1990, p. 88])[4] and
wary of philosophical hubris. This understanding of democratic practice still differs, however, from its predecessors in two important ways. First it does not, contra the Enlightenment, justify itself in terms of some conception of Nature,
Divinity, or human essence. Second it does not, contra Dewey, seek the perfec-

tion of either the individual or the community. The recognition of suffering and humiliation requires neither metaphysical postulates nor ideal goals. These phenomena define, Rorty claims, the atheoretical and experiential substrate of contemporary democratic societies that Rawls suggested is the appropriate ground on which to base political practice. Because of this, the reduction of suffering and humiliation can be undertaken quite competently by a conception of pragmatic politics emphasizing "instrumental reasoning":

> Some of our ancestors may have required such an account [of the nature of human being], just as others of our ancestors required such an account of their relation to their Creator. But we—we heirs of the Enlightenment for whom justice has become the first virtue—need neither. As citizens and as social theorists, we can be as indifferent to philosophical disagreements about the nature of the self as Jefferson was to theological differences about the nature of God. (Rorty, 1991, p. 182)

Rorty claims that contemporary liberal democrats can live perfectly well without theories of reality and concepts of human nature. Similarly we can set aside any belief that science or politics tracks the truth of the cosmos and, thereby, is an engine of progress toward a perfected state of affairs. Eschewing grounds of any sort fosters the sense of autonomy, and here liberal democracy approaches its limit. Politics, life, and action seemingly break the bonds tying (and thus subordinating) them to metaphysical ideas.

Such a dephilosophized form of politics, for all its spareness, makes a strong claim for being suited to the task of organizing the public sphere. In Rorty's estimation communities are already sufficiently joined by a sense of solidarity that arises from "a lot of small contingent facts" and the exigencies of living in common (1991, p. 188). Liberal democracies, communities concerned with justice and the elimination of suffering, need not go beyond contingency toward metaphysics in seeking their justification. The rise of modern democracy is itself dependent on a set of historical circumstances that has made us "more afraid of being cruel than anything else" and thus has moved us in "the direction of greater human solidarity" (1991, p. 192). The pressing need is not to found a community on philosophical bases—a claim that disingenuously suggests that there is not already an existing pragmatic community. The need is for making existing communities work better. The cash value of *working better* would be a real decrease in suffering and humiliation.

In sum: For Rorty metaphysics is passé. It is unneeded for the work of justice or, secondarily, for making sense of democracy.

This way of putting the matter both captures Rorty's style and shows the real innovation of his work within the American democratic tradition. Unlike Jefferson and Paine, Rorty does not think that bad metaphysics threatens the existence of democratic communities. Supposing that metaphysics, as such, could be a threat of this magnitude only grants it an exaggerated significance. If politics is enveloped in the language of metaphysics, it remains politics that is guiding metaphysics; philosophical vocabularies, as Nietzsche long ago suggested, are covers for expressions of value. What must be resisted are those *practices* that our community finds pernicious. Thus, like Rawls, Rorty is interested in supporting practices and institutions that prevent or adjudicate conflict. Toward this end, however, there is little point to metaphysical disputes. This is perhaps Rorty's main difference from Dewey. Rorty is not arguing that democratic society needs an improved form of metaphysics. (Dewey, on the other hand, was.) The whole way of talking that pertains to metaphysical discourse—even Dewey's naturalistic metaphysics of dynamic experience—is not useful. According to Rorty, philosophical metaphysics at its best can only serve a secondary role in the public sphere. And when it does, it is acting primarily as a form of literature and not as *prima philosophia*. In its average mediocrity, or worse, metaphysics appears to be of no pertinence whatsoever. If one is concerned with political reform or social justice (i.e., being edifying), then it would be better to be a journalist or novelist.

Rorty's stance is that contemporary liberal democratic society has outgrown metaphysics. It is no longer necessary to lean upon it as a crutch or attack it as if it were a dire threat. Metaphysics is not as important as Rawls suggested; it more likely a source of personal pleasure or confusion than a cause of social conflict. Rorty agrees with Rawls, although for different reasons, that metaphysics should not be abolished. Echoing Jefferson's position regarding religion and following Rawls, Rorty holds that in a liberal democratic society metaphysics can and even should be tolerated. Yet Rorty breaks from Rawls by describing metaphysics as primarily a pastime; it is an activity limited to the private lives of citizens, and whereby a person can seek individual perfection if she so chooses. It is important to note, however, that even while liberal democracy makes space for such private pursuits they are neither requisite for nor dangerous to democratic politics. In this sense, philosophical metaphysics has not been abolished but, rather, democratic politics (i.e., pragmatic coping) has been placed prior to philosophy (i.e., metaphysical theory). The value of philosophy—positive or negative—is of vanishing significance to public life.

If he has made a point of giving up the game of justification and argument, Rorty's adaptation of the American antiabsolutist tradition is not unprincipled. Rorty's general trend of thought is both coherent and well-reasoned. That trend is thoroughly historicist: Experience is an interpretative process in which one makes determinations (e.g., of truth, goodness, right) via history's interpretative legacy as well as by comparison to the interpretations of other past, present, and possible future individuals or communities. A historicist of Rorty's stripe believes that experience is primarily hermeneutic, or "conversational," in the sense that the legitimacy of anything he might say can only be assessed in relationship to a possible, and historically situated, community of conversation partners (Rorty, 1979, pp. 315–56). In summarizing this outlook, three important claims can be noted. For present purposes, these claims provide an outline of this version of historicism and a clear basis for comparison with Miller's actualism.

First Rorty claims that for too long philosophy, and Western culture more generally, has been caught in the metaphor of the mind being a mirror of the world. Knowledge, as opposed to opinion, encompasses those allegedly accurate mental representations that present the world as it is independent of the knower. Rorty rejects representationalism and its assumption of a polar relationship between a knowing subject and a known object. He replaces it with a "holistic" approach to knowledge—and experience more generally—emphasizing that knowledge claims cannot escape certain historical and hermeneutic conditions. The very first of these conditions is that an individual cannot get outside of his experience to affirm the claim (basic to dualism and realism) that there are such discrete entities as *subject* and *world* interacting in the epistemological terms of *knower* and *known*. The world representational philosophy sought to mirror, standing independent of opinion and history, is what Rorty refers to as "the world well lost" (1982, pp. 3–18).

On setting aside the mirror metaphor, there is a second and equally urgent need for getting rid of the host of distinctions it makes possible. Most important, the distinctions between *knowledge* and *opinion, science* and *prudence*, and *fact* and *value* must be discarded. The first term of all of these relations is taken to be that which is real and accurately represents the world. The second term is taken to be that which neither conforms nor does not conform to the world but rather is based entirely on relative determinations lacking in truth-value. Instead of cutting up things in this manner, Rorty suggests considering that "there are no constraints on inquiry save conversational constraints—no wholesale constraints derived from the nature of the objects, or of the mind, or of language, but only those retail constraints provided by the remarks of our fellow-inquirers" (1982, p. 165). In science, as in politics, there is no original truth to be tracked; there are no a priori limitations. Each hypothesis or policy is to be assessed only in relationship to a relevant community of speakers and inquirers. In other words, instead of it being a second-class epistemological citizen, prudence should be recognized as basic to all statements and intentional actions. The language of *practice* replaces that of *knowledge*.

Third is the claim that, although the world of the realist is lost and there are no a priori constraints on one's claims and actions, everything does not dissolve into a facile relativism. What sort of justification is possible once the mirror metaphor is abandoned? Prudential or, as Rorty phrases it, "ethnocentric" justifications (1991, passim). That is, a person commends or condemns, affirms as true or false, from the relatively stable outlook and set of aims made possible by her historical community. This is a route between simple relativism and metaphysically founded objectivity. Far from a recommendation for chauvinism, ethnocentricism is nothing other than a confession of human finitude: There is no objective, atemporal position against which to contrast the ethnocentric outlook. To Rorty's mind, this does this foreclose the possibility of being self-critical and open to a cosmopolitan appreciation of different cultures and practices. What it shows are the limits of justification and philosophy.

§1.4 MILLER'S ANTIMETAPHYSICAL SYMPATHIES

Rorty's challenge to metaphysics owes its strength to its basis in the American tradition and its persuasive development of three key claims (outlined above). In his pragmatism the political life apparently regains prominence over the theoretical life. The further suggestion (epitomized in the trivialization of metaphysics) is that the political life can *only* be reestablished at the expense of the contemplative life. What makes this challenge all the more arresting is that many of Rorty's claims, not to mention his sympathies, are held in common with Miller. Yet Miller, working from the same material, is adamant about the *relevance* of metaphysics to democracy.

In order to clarify this seemingly paradoxical disagreement between Rorty and Miller, it is appropriate first to pay heed to the ground they hold in common. The extent of *agreement* that exists between Miller and Rorty is considerable and derives from their common struggle against the dogmatic empiricism of logical positivism. Their most basic point of agreement, and an obvious way of resisting positivism, is the assertion of the importance of history. According to Miller, our ideals and theories have been in continual retreat from history (PC 130–60). How can one speak of possessing knowledge when it is only a temporary hold on experience? How can a person chart his course through life if there are no fixed posts in the moral landscape? How can we hold our ideals in proper esteem if they are not independent of the vicissitudes of history? A preferred way of staving off the skepticism and nihilism suggested by these questions is through an alliance with ahistoric principles. Thinking of Parmenides and quoting José Ortega y Gasset, Miller refers to this contemplative tendency as the *Eleatic temper of thought* (PC 135; cf. Ortega, 1961, p. 192). Miller claims, contra ahistoricism in general and positivism in particular, that "our relations with [historical] time are total and constitutive" (PH 54). The tenuousness suggested by skeptical questions is not precisely a *problem* of knowledge or ontology—that is, something to be solved and set aside. Rather it is a testament to the finite and risky character of historical experience.

The Eleatic temper, the basis of so much of Western thought, depends on an implicit corollary: One can, at least in certain instances and via certain methods, see things as they really are. That is to say, contextual contingencies and perspectival limitations can be completely escaped. This corollary has its complement in the claim that we know that there are definite things independent of human experience and that we can know precisely what they are independent of human experience. This is the objective world that thought aims to represent. Miller is inclined to agree with Rorty when he says that "the realistic true believer's notion of the world is an obsession rather than an intuition" (Rorty, 1982, p. 13), and that the realist's gesture to things totally independent of experience is incoherent (FI 262–65). The language of the realist brings forth all the traditional problems of epistemology and makes *representation* a synonym for *skepticism*. If Miller has a bit more of a taste for these problems—in that he sees them as "necessary" and even revelatory (PC 68–72, 112; see §2.1)—he agrees with Rorty that there is no reason for remaining stuck in the perplexities of cognitive representation.

More generally, both Miller and Rorty take issue with the spectator model of experience. As an alternative, both propose that any conception of experience is closely linked with vocabularies of action (TO 399–400). In this vein Miller writes:

> Perception is never direct. It is something more than a combination of sense data plus the psychological functions of memory and imagination. An object with a name is consolidated. It possesses a unity lacking in passive perception. It acquires that unity through the factor of action. Names are our deeds. (PC 121)

The order of priority between theory and practice is reversed. Action, according to the spectator model, is guided by universals or essential facts discerned by either rational intuition or direct empirical observation. Action has no bearing on such universals or facts; they have a bearing on action. But what if this traditional formulation is disrupted? Miller describes the alteration that occurs on the dismissal of the spectator model: "The universal in all its forms loses its nonhumanity when contemplated through the motives which operated to produce it. . . . The universal lies in the line of action and of function" (AH 268). Human deeds are deeply entwined with, and are revelatory of, the facts and universals guiding action. This sparks the recognition that when a person speaks of acting in light of certain facts, or according to limits marked out by universal principles, she is in fact talking about the dialectical relation of individual actions and generalized forms of action embodied in symbols such as instruments and institutions.

Both Miller and Rorty want to overcome the debilitating humility and corresponding irresponsibility arising from severing the intrinsic connection between human action and the world. Thus near the close of *Contingency, Irony, and Solidarity* Rorty writes that it should be urged "that we try *not* to want something which stands beyond history and institutions" (p. 189). Miller could not be more in agreement. Yet, for Rorty, turning to history and institutions signals the end of metaphysics and the diminished import of philosophy. Miller by contrast believes that it is with this recognition that *good metaphysics* begins and philosophy finds its proper function. Contrary to current understandings, the retrieval of the political life need not result in the denigration of the contemplative life. The retrieval of the political life must, however, lead to the *revision* of the contemplative life.

§1.5 REVISIONS OF METAPHYSICS AND HISTORY

Given the significance of what they agree on, the differences existing between Miller and Rorty must have something to do with what each means by *metaphysics* and *history*. And each one does mean something quite different when he uses these words. It is only by clarifying Miller's sense of these terms that a case can begin to be made for the plausibility of a metaphysics of democracy. On this basis further considerations regarding the practice of criticism and its relationship to autonomy will be addressed in an effort to strengthen Miller's position against Rorty's antimetaphysics (see §1.6).

Beginning with *metaphysics*, it can be said that Rorty's conception of the word is narrow. The general tone of Rorty's discussion shows that the word *metaphysics* designates those hubristic philosophical enterprises that claim to have justified (or must justify) all knowledge, discerned ahistoric principles, and systematized the cosmos. In *Contingency, Irony, and Solidarity* he defines metaphysics as "a search for theories which will get at real essence" (p. 88). (Essence in this case could be either purely material or intellectual; the key thing is that essence would be absolutely determinate—that is, a solid building block.) At two other moments in the same book Rorty expands on the sense of this definition—at one point linking the metaphysician with the Platonic theory of recollection and at another affirming that he uses *metaphysics* in the "pejorative sense" employed by Heidegger and "popularized" by Jacques Derrida as *la métaphysique de la présence* (Rorty, 1990, pp. 76, 111; cf. Derrida, 1967/1973). Thus it would seem that in doing metaphysics one must be searching for the ahistorical data of the empirical world or the eternal Ideas in the mind of God.

Miller, in contrast, considers himself a metaphysician who is *allied* with the contingent, historical, and individual. The sense of Miller's assertion supposes three distinct claims. The first claim develops a phenomenological point about the character of experience. The second suggests a broader understanding of metaphysics in which history has status as a category. The third elaborates the connection between autonomy and historical metaphysics understood as a reflective apprehension of "the conditions of our own endeavors" (PH 149). Taken together, these three claims not only disentangle the theoretical life from Plato's attack on the political life but they deflect Rorty's strike against the contemplative life. The result is a simple but strong basis on which to recompose both the contemplative life and the active life.

First, the employment of universals and metaphysical categories is a compulsive—that is, constitutional—aspect of human experience (PC 30). If one can agree with Rorty, as Miller does, that individual metaphysical vocabularies are formed around contingencies, there is still the question of the contingency of metaphysics itself. Criticizing metaphysics as Rorty does—suggesting that it is passé—supposes that it is optional. Miller disagrees:

> We need not take too seriously the current objections to metaphysics. Anyone who looks farther than his nose may find himself wondering what lies over the horizon. No one takes satisfaction in the narrowness of his outlook nor could he appear to do so without a disguised pretentiousness like that of Antisthenes the Cynic, to whom Socrates commented that his pride showed through the holes of his ostentatious rags. We like to inhabit a world, and indeed are sure to do so if we enjoy so much as a local habitation and a name. (AH 237)

There are unavoidable practical questions for which only metaphysical answers are appropriate. Another way of putting the matter is to say that metaphysics is part and parcel of practical assurance and insofar as assurance is a necessary ingredient in experience then metaphysics is itself a constitutional aspect of experience. It is not an exaggeration to say that even in one's most mundane and immediately practical activities metaphysics is always involved. For metaphysics in its barest sense is equivalent with the presence of order (MP 4:1). Over the course of the day, for example, one might make a measurement, tell the time, appear in court, and play billiards, all the while thinking himself an ordinary person and by no means a metaphysician. Yet what is the status of *time, space, law,* and *causality* operative in the foregoing endeavors? Indeed, what is the status of the *self* who is said to have done all of these things? As David Hume demonstrated, they are not empirical and cannot be established, as G. E. Moore challenged, by some form of ostensive reference. Rather they are all testimonies to and assertions of order. Which is only to say, along with Miller, that a person does "inhabit a world," and because he inhabits a world and is not a mere fragment of consciousness metaphysics is inevitable (PC 174-92). Far from evading personhood and immediacy, then, this inchoate metaphysics establishes them (AH 239).

Moving to the second point, it can be said that metaphysics is by no means antithetical to a fine-grained appreciation of history. Platonism may reduce history to a function of the ahistorical.[5] And, unquestionably, metaphysical categories and entities have become suspect because they carry Eleatic assumptions. Yet a metaphysics of the act, and its categories, need not be ruled out of court by a historical sensibility. This is because, as Miller affirms, these metaphysical categories have their origin in history. Moreover these categories disallow the sort of simplicity and cognitive self-evidence characteristic of the metaphysics of presence that Rorty rejects. Given this, is it still beyond the pale for philosophy to claim that causality and law are thoroughly historical concepts that have metaphysical status? Must philosophy be either Eleatic or nothing at all? What Miller's philosophy suggests is that one can be a metaphysician without evading history. The trick is making history—emphasizing contingency, individuality, finitude, and action—a constitutional mode of experience and thereby making it a metaphysical concept (PC 107). One cannot be a good metaphysician without also being a historian.

Finally, metaphysics is a practice that maintains autonomy in its democratic sense. Metaphysical discourse is primarily self-maintaining discourse. This assessment draws on the point made in the first argument for the legitimacy of metaphysics—that is, metaphysical categories are operative throughout experience. Universals articulate a person's world and self-conception, and thus provide the conditions through which she acts with control in that world. Universals are not the matter of mere speculation but rather "the sole evidence of our self-possessed finitude" (AH 259). Metaphysical examination is a way of bringing those conditions of action to light.[6]

The point of a metaphysics of democracy is not to demonstrate the truth of democratic principles or practices. (Miller is himself skeptical as to the force of argument regarding fundamental matters [PH 10].) Rather, as Rawls and Rorty recommend, what is sought is clarification from the inside of engaged and historical practice. Via such clarification autonomy is glimpsed, and it may be achieved and further maintained in the responsible engagement with the conditions of one's endeavors. Metaphysics supports democratic individuality and autonomy (see MS 189-92; PC 72-74).

Given these three claims why would one assert that our current liberal democracies have outgrown metaphysics? In Rorty's case this insistence is justified by an uncharacteristic reliance on the authority of Heidegger's use of the

term. By making *Platonism* and *positivism* synonymous with *metaphysics*, Rorty
has stacked the philosophical deck—by offering a plausible but quite narrow
definition of what is truly a vague and unruly human tendency he enables himself, *tout court*, to dismiss everything associated with metaphysics. There is no
question that in Platonism, say, there is a compulsive drive for organizing
experience in terms of an abstract framework as well as an exaggerated insistence on the permanence of the resulting organizational systems. Is it fair or
adequate, however, to go on to say that Platonism defines metaphysics? Assent-
ing to this would be difficult. Yet Rorty remains obsessed with Plato and
Platonism.[7] If Plato was too extreme in attacking the political life, Rorty and his
fellow antimetaphysicians respond with an equal excess of vehemence by making philosophy into a mere parlor game or opting for a principled "aesthetic
pluralism" or "nominalist historicism" (Hall, pp. 5, 66 ff.). They are anguished
by and angered with Plato for not fulfilling certain promises—promises that, inci-
dentally, Plato never actually made. The antimetaphysicians are then the true
Platonists, only they now disavow the theoretical insignia and preach philosophical
repentance. The unfortunate result of current antimetaphysics is that it impover-
ishes our fund of conceptual resources and narrows our range of critical thought.

This last point will taken up again when it can be more fruitfully explored in
light of a discussion of criticism. Before doing so, however, one can note in summary that the three-pronged constructive argument sketched does a fair job of
reestablishing the plausibility of metaphysics. If one connects having a metaphysics
with having a world—a conception that, because of his indebtedness to Dewey and
Heidegger, Rorty cannot discard—then metaphysics is a long way toward being re-
habilitated. If one further admits that the grotesque pride of some metaphysicians
has unwittingly been mirrored in the pretensions of those who wish to get beyond
metaphysics and cease doing philosophy altogether, then surely there is good reason for giving a more modest, historical sense of metaphysics a fair hearing. Finally
if the very concepts of *autonomy* and *personhood* are bound up with metaphysics,
metaphysics can hardly be inimical to democracy. Metaphysics or philosophical
contemplation once again takes its appropriate place and exhibits its necessity. As
important as it is to take our finitude seriously (as Rorty would agree), one must
recognize what both supports and is at stake in finitude.

Finding a synthetic and dialectic alternative to Rorty's all-or-nothing formulations
is Miller's express purpose. The option is not between a concrete nominalism
(i.e., positivistic Platonism) and a speculative universalism that theoretically
organizes the concrete (i.e., the Eleatic ideal). Rather one begins with history—that
is, finite temporality and conscious action—as the process generating appearances
and consequences. History is not the playing out of one absolute order. It is the

provision of orders, systems, and logics in all their fragility, plurality, and tenacity. Once one begins counting, telling time, or making systematic judgments consequences follow (MS 19). Yet because each of these orders is fully historical its course is both tenuous and unpredictable (PH 29); any necessity, because it plays itself out in and through human acts, undergoes what all that is mortal must undergo—birth, growth, decay, even death.

Miller gives this broad account of his sense of history:

> We cannot escape history, and we cannot escape the study of history. Nor is there any history at all apart from the thrust of present meanings into their yesterdays. History is a category because it is a necessary condition of the present. In history time is efficacious. . . . In summary: history avoids finality, establishes finitude, defines the relatively static, emerges from commitment and conflict, allies us with evil, and presents the universal as self-revision in terms of the necessary. . . . It is the most concrete of all categories, and one of the latest to emerge. (PC 92)

History is neither fact nor abstraction. It is a *constitutional process* whereby the very shape of the world is developed. History provides the conditions in which chance, accident, and the unique can appear but is not reducible to any of these three. It is where the universal and absolute arise but simultaneously lose their pretension to ahistoric sovereignty. It is the source and field of the relationship between the poles of nominalism and universalism with which thought has preoccupied itself—for example, the ongoing battles between the Ionians and the Eleatics. History is the category of all other metaphysical categories (see §4.1).

Historical thinking is the reorientation of how one attends to concrete experience. Rorty is still touched by the legacy of Hume's skeptical reversal of Platonism that assumed that the discrete was real and the universal mere superstition. This empiricism is as ahistoric as is Platonism—neither the forms nor the qualia of sensation are in historical time. (In this respect, the following statement by Miller might well apply to Rorty: "How often we have heard that man is finite, that he dwells in time and is subject to its limitations. We have heard this, but we have not believed it" [MP 17:5].) Miller rejects the Eleatic ideal but also cuts off the empiricists by proposing that "history is radical empiricism" (PC 94).[8] Historical experience does not reveal a plethora of discrete entities but rather fragile continuities and orderly forms of finitude. Miller makes a case for an empiricism that addresses the *conditions* of the empirical, factual, and discrete. Miller's empiricism concerns itself with action as well as the media or vehicles of order—that is, symbols (see §§3.2 and 3.3). A symbol can be an object (e.g., a yardstick, scale, building), practice (e.g., swearing oaths, keeping promises), or formal law (e.g., the United States Constitution, rules of grammar, the Laws of Thermodynamics). These objects, practices, or laws appear discrete; they are particular in the sense that one can either identify them through ostensive reference or distinguish them in a historical moment (MS 43). Yet such symbols are as universal and structural as they are particular. They are elements of what Miller refers to as the midworld, that *actuality* that discloses and organizes the subjective and objective, the real and the apparent (see MS 13). Without the particular object and its employment, without the specific deed, the universal falls out of sight. Similarly, lacking universals the particular cannot be distinguished (see §2.2). The mutual dependence of the particular and the universal is embodied in the symbol. The relationship is basically dialectical; it appears in action and nowhere else.

Rorty's considerations strongly suggest that the disrepute that metaphysics has fallen into is primarily a function of a limited conception of what metaphysics can mean. This limited conception is based on a narrow empiricism that dismisses all form and universality as mere illusion. There is more discontent and, indeed, philosophical ressentiment here than good thinking. It would be foolish to foreclose the possibility of a historical form of metaphysics. What the foregoing examination also suggests is that the contest between the contemplative life and the active life has been cast in misleadingly antithetical terms. The strict division of theory and politics—exploited by both sides in the contest—results from what Miller would argue is a misunderstanding of the form and import of history. Any project aiming at the recuperation of a philosophical life amenable to politics—not to mention a political life amenable to philosophy—necessarily leads through history.

§1.6   REINVIGORATING CRITICISM

Miller is fully in agreement with Rorty when he urges "that we try *not* to want something which stands beyond history and institutions." Yet Miller offers a *metaphysical* way of maintaining and fortifying this relationship with our actual institutions and practices. The challenge to metaphysics must be pursued one final step further, however. As noted at the outset, democracy is grounded in an estimation of the integrity of personal experience. Metaphysics, by contrast, is assumed to move away from the individual and toward the universal in a manner that ultimately compromises personhood. With this in mind, can it not be asked if Miller's rejection of simple empiricism and his affirmation of historical universals and overindividual elements that structure experience amounts to some loss of nerve, some fleeing from finitude? Stated in other terms: Does not the appeal to these environing, symbolic conditions result in a loss of self-control or autonomy?

In this vein, Rorty can be seen as announcing a final warning when, in his essay "Pragmatism Without Method," he speaks against "philosophical depth":

The idea of "philosophical depth" is in the air once again, and this means, inevitably, a trip back to the Continent. This trip is by no means a bad thing in itself, but it has become associated with the idea that liberalism is both intellectually lightweight and in need of being "diagnosed." So we now have the dismal spectacle of what [Sidney] Hook used to call "knee-jerk liberalism" (i.e., trying to figure out how to blame anything bad that happens on American ruling circles) combining with specifically philosophical *Tiefsinnigkeit* in the claim that we need "new philosophical foundations" for criticism of "contemporary bourgeois society" (i.e., the surviving parliamentary democracies). (1991, pp. 76–77)

Encouraging such deep thinking on the matter of democracy, Rorty holds, betrays not just an adherence to the sort of philosophical fantasies diagnosed in *Philosophy and the Mirror of Nature*; it also reveals a profound lack of confidence in one's local community. The search for principles and foundations could be just a sophisticated way of testifying to one's distrust of finitude. And even if this self-styled metaphysician of democracy is not retreating all the way back to the Eleatic ideal, it is plausible to wonder whether history and institutions are, in the end, not enough for Miller.

Rorty recommends the cultivation of a certain "light-mindedness" as an antidote to metaphysics. Instead of becoming engrossed in metaphysical speculation about transcendent structures of experience, the light-minded are more pragmatic, more tolerant, and more liberal. Light-mindedness promotes action not contemplation, democratic solidarity and not metaphysical unity. Light-mindedness is autonomy taken to its limit; it is the final blow dealt to metaphysics, contemplation, and absolutism.

Does actualism fall prey to these criticisms? Is actualism, finally, at odds with itself? The response must be negative. Yet actualism is liable to this misunderstanding. For, as stated earlier, the key to Miller's philosophical approach is finding a middle route between Parmenides's Eleaticism and Heraclitus's Ionianism. This *via media* is, of course, attacked from both sides—that is, the Eleatics will see actualism as succumbing to relativism while the Ionians will judge it as unduly wedded to the absolute. Rorty's assessment of *Tiefsinnigkeit* only attacks a misinterpretation of actualism. An interest in universals and formal structures is not necessarily contrary to the democratic impulse toward autonomy. It is rather the flight from universals and formal structures that undermines the search for autonomy. This is an interesting and paradoxical turn—those laboring to reestablish the dignity of the active, political life have actually compromised politics by ridding it of all elements of contemplation.

In Rorty's case this wayward search for autonomy has led him to latch onto a largely instrumental conception of reason in which action is a mode of fabrication and calculation.[9] Organized around the key metaphors of *coping* and *web weaving*, this version of pragmatism reduces all reason to calculation and makes all imperatives hypothetical in character. Life is a continual process of dissolving confusions toward the end of increasing local-control and decreasing psychic confusion. Once present difficulties are resolved, instrumental reason has fulfilled its task and thought remains at rest until presented with a new difficulty. What this suggests is that all problems, and thus all instances of reasoning, are essentially accidental—that is, contingent upon conditions of one's environment and the demands of one's hypothetical plans of action. Rorty's approach is that of a person who wants to get *beyond* a problem rather than one who realizes that she must live intelligently and responsibly *with* a problem. Miller proposes, by contrast, that certain problems are *constitutional*—that is, a condition of having a world and an identity. And even those problems that are not in themselves necessary are still important ingredients in the structure that articulates a given person's sense of self. Problems are then critical—and subject to thoughtful criticism—in that they are part of the very contour of one's ordered experience. Each person must not only find the instrumental means for addressing the problems that life tosses her way. She must also find the philosophical resources to compose and reflect on her inherently problematic identity and world.

Miller would of course concur with Rorty in his insistence about staying on the surface *so long as* the contrast is with the sort of philosophical depth promoted by Platonism. Autonomy requires a modicum of control over both self and environment. Instrumental reasoning may serve well to establish *local-control* via the construction and continual repair of the means of facilitating plans and attaining goods. Yet instrumental reasoning falls considerably short of maintaining *self-control* because it refuses to recognize those symbolic and quasitranscendental forms constituting individual identities. As Miller notes, without a sense of the quasitranscendent—that is, symbolic modes of order—ethics devolves to the management of accidental experience (MP 4:1).

For Miller *criticism* is the activity by which persons attain local- as well as self-control. Criticism is not the rearrangement of certain states of affairs so as to better suit plans of action. It addresses and revises the very form of one's world—that is, authoritative symbolic modes of the midworld. Criticism moves toward that form of freedom wherein "we see the awful, but responsible, spectacle of man's reinterpretations of himself and nature, and reassessment of our heritage" (PC 103-4). In order to participate in this liberating and responsible form of activity one must be prepared to engage in metaphysics. For metaphysics in Miller's sense of the term is not mere speculation. It is a mode of inquiry that, in the vein of transcendental philosophy, seeks after the conditions of one's experience and action (PH 19-20 1952-53, 27).

Philosophy in its best sense is always a mode of criticism (FI 265-67). Criticism, in turn, is always practical. The pretension to criticism without metaphysics does not attain to the level of autonomy in which Miller is interested. Criticism that does not take the form of experience into account is little more than rearranging the pieces that one is given to play with using (although perhaps not cognizant of) the established rules. The stronger sense of criticism means that attention is directed toward the very rules of the game and not a play to be made within the game. Criticism may be revolutionary; coping can never be. Even when it is not revolutionary, and only connotes a reflective maintenance of the conditions of endeavor, criticism still suggests a level of responsibility to which coping cannot attain.

The language of instrumental reasoning is, finally, too blithe to account for those "dark emergencies which are the occasion of desperate attempts to maintain civic order and personal integrity" (PC 123). Democracy requires metaphysical categories and a metaphysical vocabulary:

> It is a great illusion to suppose that government will protect rights when actual individuals display nothing but desires in their wills, and nothing but opinions in their minds. Such doctrines paralyze resolve. They are degenerate, and they invite the conqueror and the despot. What shows men to be free is their capacity to recognize and revise the grounds of their choices and of their opinions. (PC 73)

> What Kant proposed was the capacity of thought to police itself. He did not carry out that idea. Since then it has grown. . . . The idealism of the future will be a philosophy of history, of action, or a self-generating, lawful finitude. Such are the conditions of a metaphysics of democracy. (PC 74)

Becoming aware of, and taking responsibility for, the conditions of one's endeavors—that is, the ideals, principles, and laws guiding action—requires a retrieval of metaphysics. The sense of metaphysics corresponding to this call for responsibility has already been articulated above—that is, the apprehension of the conditions of our own endeavors that Miller terms "the moral universe" (EC 1; see §5.1). It is in terms of a moral universe that action and autonomy make sense, and it is to the midworld and its history that we must look in order to ascertain what such a universe looks like.

§1.7   CONCLUSION

Elucidating Miller's position vis-à-vis Rorty's has been more than a simple exercise of refuting antimetaphysical claims. It has been an opportunity for criticizing and revising the very sense of *metaphysics*. For there is good reason for democrats to be wary of metaphysics and to guard their principal interests with care. The history of philosophy, not to mention the history of political institutions, provides ample evidence of how metaphysical assumptions can be antagonistic to democratic practice. Setting democratic principles against traditional forms of metaphysics proves useful for fostering a reappraisal of the significance of metaphysics. In this manner the question A *metaphysics of democracy?* reanimates metaphysics by saving it from both those absolutely assured of its importance as well as those absolutely assured of its insignificance.

Miller's sense of the pertinence of metaphysics is in line with the democratic concern for the integrity of individual experience, the autonomy of persons, and democratic solidarity. The primary aim of actualism is *not* providing a description of all that is (i.e., a *theory* of the real). The key is the *practical* question of authority. Miller's actualism is guided by the concern for putting persons and political communities in touch with the conditions of their own actions, institutions, and ideals (DT 11, 155). Moreover this assessment suggests that democratic understandings of autonomy require the contemplative life once again be joined with the active life. Considered in its fullest sense as the life of an authoritative and reflective person, the political must be united with the contemplative. Politics gains nothing by rejecting the philosophical inheritance of twenty-five centuries. Rather one must see how philosophy and politics are mutually constitutive: Philosophy is of political significance insofar as it is the activity of criticism and, thus, concerns the conduct of public life, while politics is of philosophical import in that it models and provides a vehicle for criticism.

TWO

Action

The recovery of metaphysics and the illustration of its pertinence to liberal democracy begin with the concept of *action*. For while the reasons for the split between the contemplative life and the active life can be described in many ways, perhaps the most critical formulation addresses the misunderstanding of the import of action. Whether grasped in terms of the sort of noble futility that the Greeks ascribed to human deeds, interpreted according to the pragmatic model of problem solving, or understood on the physical model of causality, our predominant conceptions of action have enforced a division between theory and practice. Action is transient, particular, and insubstantial; it shares nothing in common with the permanence, universality, and reality captured in the Eleatic ideal.

Miller's interest is linking practical authority (a concern of the political life) with ontology (a concern of the contemplative life). In order to have ontological import, action must be an idea—that is, play a constitutional role in experience (PH 181). The allusion to Immanuel Kant and G. W. F. Hegel is intentional. The *constitutional* is synonymous with structure (MP 19:10), and categories born of action are themselves elements of structure (DP 62). Developing this basic understanding, Miller uses the term *constitutional* in two distinct senses. First the constitutional is understood as *the necessary*. An idea can be said to be constitutional in the sense that it is "a control, not just an episode," form and not data (PL 495). Without action there is no definition, no identity, no difference; lacking action there is nothing. This sense of constitutionality will guide the discussion in sections 2.1 through 2.3. The constitutional is also understood as *a constructive element*, as in the gerund constitut*ing*. This sense of constitutionality will be developed in section 2.4 via an exploration of the causal efficacy of action.

Beginning with action in the form of words and deeds, however, does not represent a claim that *act* is absolutely prior to *symbol, history,* or *democracy* in the metaphysics Miller is articulating. Indeed even as it is appropriate to refer to his thought as *a philosophy of the act,* Miller describes his own work as a "historical idealism" whose novelty resides in its uncompromising insistence that the idealist tradition be revised so as to give history categorical status (AH 240; see chapter 4). It is also a philosophy established on the midworld and the attendant claim regarding the centrality of the symbol to any understanding of ontology. It is finally considered a metaphysics of democracy. But what is history but the tale of the conscious apprehension and fateful consequences of free actions? What is the symbol but the vehicle and embodiment of the act? And what is democracy but the institutionalization of the efficacy of action? Action, symbol, history, and democracy implicate one another in such a way that no one aspect can be given strict priority. There remain principled reasons for beginning with action, as well as for describing Miller's philosophy as fundamentally a "philosophy of the act." It amounts to an assertion of the importance of the first-person standpoint.[1] This is the key to the reestablishment of the active life and the authority of persons as authors of unique and history-making deeds. Furthermore, action provides the key to some persistent ontological, epistemological, and political difficulties, and prevents them from remaining unproductive problems. It is fair to say, along with Stephen Tyman, that action is the "knot" of Miller's thought and thus deserves pride of place (1993, p. 66).

§2.1 DISCLOSURE OF ACTION

The shift from the cognitive to the active register is suspect in the context of a philosophic tradition that has been skeptical about the act and its historical categories. It is thus important to address the problematic status of action: How is action possible? How and where does it appear? What are its consequences?

Before addressing these questions in earnest in section 2.2, the possibilities and limitations of this inquiry must be established. What sort of clarity can one expect from such an investigation? Miller warns against carrying a philosophical analysis into every facet of experience because, as he comments, "where any and all statements are to be defended one becomes defenseless" (MP 25:20). Indeed what can be termed the *problems approach* to philosophy has serious limitations. Foremost among these deficiencies is the one to which Miller's statement alludes—the tendency of producing *theoretical* skepticism or, putting the matter in another way, making a *speculative* case for alienation. This results from analyzing experience into discrete elements as well as impossibly stringent forms of cognitive justification. The very methodology fosters skepticism by emphasizing the discrete and looking askance on connections. Furthermore the fact that such analysis can only yield theoretical skepticism points to another serious limitation—that is, its self-imposed divorce from the existential basis of philosophical conflict (PC 72). What at the theoretical level are confounding questions of justification often do not trouble practical experience. Analytical

philosophy often does not reflect our nontheoretical commitments and attendant crises of control and identity.

Miller's interest in philosophical problems and analysis departs from this
sterile method. Actualism shares the pragmatic sensibility that understands problems to be the stuff of life, the means of an articulate and dynamic existence. Yet
Miller also wants to exceed pragmatic insights. The difference between pragmatism and actualism lies in the status given to the problem: Is the problem in question accidental or necessary? A problem that can be set aside without a loss of
basic control and articulation is an accidental problem. (Both analytic philosophy and pragmatism tend to address problems as accidents.)[2] Miller is thus sym-
pathetic with the philosophy of José Ortega y Gasset and his claim that "the life
of man appears essentially problematic" (1961, p. 115). In the very having of a
problem a power arises, a form of conscious control, distinct from the sort of
force and responsiveness that the organism bears in its body (MP 21:13). Here we
meet with the limitations of the naturalistic account. Any particular problem—
for example, a locked door, dangerously cold weather, snarled vehicular traffic—
gives access to the structure of a particular field of activity. The animal cannot
have such access. This is the unbridgeable difference between the simplest types
of conscious learning of structure and the most highly developed forms of responsive training to content.

The access to structure provided in the situations just noted is, however,
accidental, contingent, and nonsystematic. A person's insight into the circumstances surrounding freezing temperatures will not produce systematic results and
revisions in the way that he relates to any environment whatsoever. Miller terms
these problems *psychological*. Here a person learns structure but not fundamental
structure. Yet the concern of philosophy is with "the everywhere" (DT 40). "Some
disconcertments are constitutional, not accidental," Miller writes. "They occur as
a threat to control, not to a detail within the controlling law" (PC 70). So a class
of necessary problems must be added to these accidental ones. What Miller calls
idealism—and is here called *actualism*—addresses such problems, and questions of
structure more generally (FI 267).

The problem of knowledge, and its resultant skepticism, is an important
example of a constitutional problem (PC 111–12). Different from simple error or
frustration, raising the problem of knowledge systematically separates thought
from its object. This separation generates universal consequences. Primarily it
contributes to the discovery of the person and world. It also gives rise to the need
for generalized modes of justification. Knowledge is not a problem pertaining to
a specific environment but, rather, concerns the relation between person and
environment as such. It is only via the problem of knowledge that these two terms
truly come to light as elements of structure, means of control, and objects of

knowledge. A situation without systematic difficulty lacks systematic control. This sense of power is essential to autonomy. The problem of knowledge is necessary for its revelation. This description of the possibilities and dangers of philosophical analysis holds equally for the questions of being and ethics. The inquiry into how there is something rather than nothing organizes ontology while the puzzle of freedom orients ethics. In a necessary problem the world is "transfigured into self-control" (MP 14:7). Actualism makes a case for the revelatory status of these fundamental philosophical issues. The necessity of problems is a defining quality of actualist philosophy concerned with paradox, dialectic, and conflict (all ingredients of self-control). The degree to which a person shows respect for problems—neither explaining them away nor reducing them to the simpler level of pragmatic difficulty—becomes a measure of the character of her philosophy.

The starting place for philosophy, as Miller makes clear, must be necessary (DT 12; cf. Garhringer, 1990, pp. 34–37; cf. Diefenbeck, pp. 51–57). The implications of philosophy must be ontological, otherwise, as most positivists came to think, philosophy is just bad science. If philosophy will traffic in problems, then they cannot be *accidental* or liable to *solution:*

> Any problem about reality must be identical with reality. The problem must be unconditioned if it is to convey an unconditioned answer.
>
> Instead, then, of proposing the unconditioned as an answer let it be considered as the property of a problem. This would be a problem about structure, for it is only there that thought shows its authority. Only in a problem about structure could this authority be seen in its urgency and in its origin. (PC 70)

The necessary problem is not a matter of fact. It is not an illusion or a misunderstanding. It is revelatory and the very possibility of the conscious apprehension of structure (PC 72). The necessary problem reveals the systematic conditions wherein it makes sense (DT 184). These "constitutional conflicts" are philosophical and existential opportunities. "They are necessary," Miller writes, "because only in them is the presence of thought revealed" (PC 70).

For this reason Miller embraces a form of philosophical analysis. He does so under the heading of *dialectic.* The world and its crucial terms are revealed in terms of dyads, questions, oppositions, and conflicts. Yet to speak of dyads is to speak of a third factor; that factor is action. Without an appeal to this third factor problems become mere cognitive impediments. Thus, while it is a problem in its own right, action is also critical for understanding the form and import of other central philosophical questions. This is the clear imperative of Miller's work: Necessary problems, and the structure of experience that they reveal, must be addressed by means other than the cognitive resources most readily available to analytic, epistemology centered discussions.

"Where the human act is not allowed to be absolute, it can have no absolute consequences," Miller writes. "Its consequences will be in the power of those forces which permitted the act to occur" (PH 140-41). The extremes of pure realism and idealism are to be avoided precisely because they place action in a subordinate position. If there could be a nonactive experience as realism and idealism both suppose, if significance were possible without action, then actualism would not only fail but would be pointless (MS 58). Yet, Miller argues, realism and idealism cannot adequately account for either the revelation of being (the problem of ontology) or knowledge (the problem of knowledge), and so they cannot account for the basic contours of active, lived experience.

The fundamental difficulty of both realism and idealism is the assumption that there is an *irremediable* dyadic relationship between subject and object, knower and known (MS 20-35; DT 83-111). The troublesome aspects of this assumption have been well addressed by Josiah Royce in the first series of *The World and the Individual*, as well as by Hegel, Charles S. Peirce, and John Dewey. Miller's criticisms (which will be developed further in §2.2) share enough with these other well-known accounts such that some of this background can be assumed while offering a more pointed assessment.

The general thrust of actualism is this: If one begins with the assumption of the discrete entities of knowing subjects and independent objects then there are three possible results—that is, 1) a pluriverse of absolutely discrete entities, 2) solipsism, or 3) mysticism. The first is the dilemma of empirical realism in which the distinctions between entities—especially between subject and object— are maintained so rigorously that knowledge becomes impossible; relations have no standing if only individuals are real. The second result, solipsism, can arise from either realism or idealism. A rational realism will not claim that relations are unreal. Yet such a realist will hold that the real is wholly independent from mind. This distinction, once enforced, exiles mind from the real. Idealism, of course, results in solipsism by claiming that the difference between the mind and reality is merely apparent. Reality is synonymous with either the content of one absolute mind or the collective projection of subjective minds. The result is the same—everywhere mind only meets itself. The last situation, mysticism, occurs when an overweening desire for eliminating the gulf between person and object results in the total effacement of the distinction. All relations are confounded in an undifferentiated whole. None of these descriptions do justice to the phenomenon of knowing or prove reasonable goals for knowledge. They are, unfortunately, the necessary results of beginning with the simple dyad.

Both realism and idealism are cognitive philosophies of entities and not of action. They effectively destroy the problem of knowledge, and thus knowledge itself, by failing to make it a productive problem. Similarly neither realism nor idealism does justice to the question of being. Independent objects or minds are the unquestioned and, finally, unaccountable starting places for both philosophies. In this sense, epistemology-centered philosophy, in all of its forms, is profoundly dogmatic (FI 260-61); all questions of constitution are avoided as one delves *toute de suite* into epistemological puzzles. The effect of such assumptions is the exclusion of action from philosophy and the contemplative life.

Miller's complaint is not aimed at the subject–object dyad. He is concerned with how that distinction is understood and maintained. The point is preserving the problem of knowledge while not "destroying knowledge in the posing of the problem about it" (MS 24). There is wisdom in both realism and idealism. There must be an object distinct from the person, as realism claims, if talking about knowledge makes any sense (MS 22). Idealism is equally right in stating that thought cannot seek after something wholly alien but in some respect must find itself in knowledge (MS 25). The actualist response to the dilemmas of dyadic philosophy marks a difference by involving a third element—that is, action, verb, and symbol—that establishes relations and enforces distinctions. Neither mental nor material, neither appearance nor reality—action is not reducible to either pole of a dyadic relation. Action has a priority to knowledge. Miller's claim is that only by making action absolute are the problems of knowledge and ontology maintained.

Action, however, is itself problematic. Action is not cognitive in either an empirical or rational sense (see PH 19-20, 1952-53, 15-23). It is not an object of knowledge. Because it is not an object, action is likely to be consumed by the demand that all that can be said to exist must be available to cognition.[3] For this reason Miller warns against proving too much (MP 13:11). This warning, far from being a sign of weakness, is a principled response to the assumptions of cognitive philosophies. If the spectator model chases the active knower out of the world and, finally, makes a mockery of the very process of epistemic justification, then limiting the scope of cognitive reason is required. Resources for resistance are not found in theory. What intercedes is the act. As J. G. Fichte asserted, each person "must present himself as free" (1802/1982, pp. 13–15), as capable of *acting* in the strong sense of the word. Miller takes up Fichte's insight and approaches the primacy of action in a similar fashion: "We can no longer 'save the appearances'; we must save the activity. If you save the appearances you will end up in speculation" (MP 22:14; see AH 265). A careful evaluation of the finite perspective demands the recognition of action as the noncognitive basis for cognition (MS 11).

Miller is aware of the difficulties of *talking about* that which allows one to talk or think about any thing in particular (MS 59–65). If action is the basis of the demonstration and the resolution of other problems, to what proof is action itself subject? A circle, and perhaps a vicious one, is implied in the supposition that one can theorize about action. Miller describes this difficulty by means of the example of language itself, which he understands as the paradigmatic example of utterance. (The spoken word [*vox*] is among the class of things done [*res gestae*].) In speaking a person articulates, arranges, and grasps experience. Any *thing* that resists being articulated in terms of words has a dubious status; it may or may not be an experience but it certainly is not *known*, certainly is not any distinct, cognizable thing. Language, like any action, provides structure; its denotative power depends on a presentational aspect. Language is not just a tool for arranging beings. It has ontological or formal import as well. This is where the difficulty lies:

> We know the difficulties of treating form as a thing which can be represented; form is not a thing. It is not a datum. No way of referring the form of a language to the form of an object is possible unless the object can be defined as already possessing form. And that is impossible, since no form is an object, thing, datum, real or imaginary. (DT 173)

Language "in principle cannot be an object of study" (DT 176; see MS 59–65).[4] The conditions for reasonable discourse, however, appear to require that we make language into an object. Confronted with this dilemma, action can become mysterious; its status in rational discourse, as Fichte noted in the *Vocation of Man*, is tantamount to an article of faith. Another possibility is giving up talking altogether, or at least banning the sort of talk that is self-consciousness and aware of its own conditions. This is the route of the mystic: Forsaking talk paradoxically becomes a way of respecting the ontological status of language. Either way one is led to a dead end.

The very possibility of action or philosophizing about action is problematic. (This is well illustrated by the difficulties of analytic philosophies of action such as Donald Davidson's causal model and Carl Ginet's intentionalist model.) For Miller the problem of action has the status of a necessary problem. Fichte provided clues for clarifying this dilemma (cf. Tyman, 1990). His methodology is an unstable cross between intuition, practical assertion, transcendental inquiry, and rational deduction. These four distinct methodologies are all employed in his systematic treatment of Kant's idealist insight. Intuition, however, may be considered Fichte's primary way of apprehending action. In his Second Introduction to *The Science of Knowledge*, Fichte denied that the active intellect is passive in any respect; it is not mere substance and thus is not capable of being

cognized like other passive objects. Unavailable to discursive reason, this activity
shows itself via an intellectual intuition, "the immediate consciousness that I act"
(1802/1982, p. 36). Both indubitable and nondiscursive, this immediate recognition pervades experience. Yet in the First Introduction Fichte took a different
approach and made a case for the primacy of action based on practical "self-
interest." This self-interest demands that a person think of herself as free. Here
the act is not so much a subjective immediacy as it is a dogmatic principle. Indeed Fichte recognized that both realism and idealism are equally dogmatic in
that neither can prove its own first principles nor disprove the first principles of
the other. What breaks this speculative deadlock in the favor of idealism is not
that idealism gets beyond dogmatism via some form of incorrigible evidence.
Rather the difference is one's practical interest in the dogmatism of freedom.
Despite the incongruence in Fichte's thought across the two introductions a
basic structure prevails: A system of reason unfolds from that which is, in principle, not available to discursive reason.

This sketch of Fichte's methodology in *The Science of Knowledge* is useful for
clarifying Miller's approach. As regards basic methods, Fichte and Miller are in
full agreement: The condition of justification is not subject to justification in the
same sense, or in the same fashion, as that which it justifies. Yet, as to how one
gains access to that first condition (i.e., action), there is some disagreement
between Miller and Fichte. Miller himself makes much of immediacy when
describing the role action plays relative to cognition. Describing that sense of
immediacy in terms of an intuition, however, goes too far in that it suggests
immediate *evidence*, an intellectual grasp of a primordial fact. Because it is a *pure*
immediacy, however, a bare intellectual intuition cannot found a relational system
(DT 15–16). Regarding Fichte's other starting point—that is, the assertion of the
primacy of freedom based on self-interest—Miller again has significant sympathies
but unavoidable differences. Miller's *interest* in making a case for freedom, for the
possibility of action against scientistic versions of objectivity, has already been
noted. On this point, and at others where he is holding out against behaviorism,
Miller's outlook appears distinctly dogmatic and his first principles seem to be
products of willful assertion. Yet even if principled, this dogmatic approach does
not fit well with actualism more broadly considered. It is a constant refrain of
Miller's that philosophy must be without assumptions (DT 11–37). So even if one
must, in a sense, *decide* to "save the activity," any such attempt cannot rely on the
mere assertion of the priority of activity to passivity, freedom to determinism.

What remains after this comparison? Foremost there is the sense that gain-
ing clarity about action is very difficult. The most obvious routes to the unconditioned lead to a snarl of unavoidable structural difficulties. Recognizing this,
Tyman recommends a "compact" presentation of action that aims at evocation

but not demonstration. A compact description is, Tyman writes, characterized by "simplicity, irreducibility, unavailability to discursive thought" (1993, p. 45). Yet Tyman's compact presentation of action verges on the mysterious—that is, action, because it cannot be cognized like an object, is the mystery lying at the bottom of all cognition (1993, pp. 92–93).[5] Action is certainly elusive. Miller states that action is neither a concept nor a datum (TO 403). When it is in force, action makes itself invisible by leading one to things but not to itself (MS 45). Mistaking *elusiveness* for *mystery*, however, confuses the issue and does not do justice to the actualist position. Tyman is on firmer ground when he links this sense of compactness with a dialectical elucidation of action (1996, p. 165). In dialectic both the form of Miller's thought and the very constitutional process are revealed. Because of its dynamic and articulate aspects, dialectic coincides with the actualist approach to the questions of knowledge and being. "In this matter of the 'Actual,'" Miller writes, "we have to do with composition rather than demonstration" (MP 25:27). By examining form as an activity of composition or constitution, one proceeds by addressing order as a *function* of action rather than considering action as an object (DT 177).

Philosophy is, as Miller states, dialectical disclosure that proceeds without an a priori (SC 7).[6] It is neither a deduction nor a dogmatic assertion. Dialectic reveals symbolic order because it insists on the mutual implication of act, concept, and object. While determining structural elements, Miller's dialectic avoids the abstraction of supposing that the elements of the process are self-subsistent; distinctions remain relevant, for action is found in the very distinctions that it generates and relies on. Here it is also shown how contemplation needs activity in order to reveal the very entities and forms of order it seeks to understand. As Miller notes in various places, there are no nouns without verbs (e.g., MS 10, 81).

§2.2 DIALECTIC AND DEFINITION

The revelation of the constitutional significance of action is achieved by showing that action is necessary for understanding the related difficulties of epistemology and ontology. The arrangement of *The Definition of the Thing* highlights and exploits this mutual implication. In brief: The problems of both being and knowledge are clarified by means of an exposition of the process of definition. Any understanding of definition as a *process*, however, must refer to action. This makes action a key to all other problems. Miller's dialectical bent of thought modifies any claim of priority by making it clear that thinking of action in the absence of some articulation of one's conception of knowledge or being is as nonsensical as attempting the converse.

The methodology instanced here and throughout Miller's work is best described as a "very arduous analysis of the finite point of view" (FI 268). The emphasis is on *structure* and its constitutive dialectical relations. This form of analysis is guided by an implicit reliance on the sort of transcendental questioning initiated by Kant and followed on by Royce: Finite experience is examined in terms of the conditions for the possibility of experience as such.[7] More exactly, the finite point of view in investigated so as to discern the conditions of its possibility. Yet, resuming a discussion suspended in section 2.1, the affirmation of the transcendental character of these investigations is not tantamount to embracing *transcendental deduction* or *systematic philosophy* as those terms were understood by the German idealists. All one can do is sharpen, or clarify, the immediate (NL 17–18). The immediate, active present is not liable to fundamental reduction; its key terms are not liable to demonstration. It is an analysis that makes action and structure its "object" and yet is fully cognizant of the paradox implied in doing so.

   The Definition of the Thing will be examined in two stages. The first stage, undertaken in this section, addresses the role of dialectic in chapters 2 and 4 of Miller's book. The second phase, undertaken in section 2.3, develops the connection between dialectic and action by illustrating the primacy of action in relation to the structures made manifest in the perennial problems of being and knowledge.

Miller states that chapter 2, "Definition," is the key to the entirety of *The Definition of the Thing* (DT 7). By casting the matter most generically and most acutely in ontological terms, this chapter does the real work for the conception of philosophy he is developing:

> This essay is concerned with one of these universal aspects, namely, the fact as such. Now it appears that such a study, besides using the method of definition, has definition as its *subject matter*. While this may at first seem an absurdity it is far from that and in truth represents the vindication of this entire conception of philosophy. For were the subject matter other than the method, and assumptive of method, we should be torn away from this pinnacle and projected once more into the field of science where matter and form are distinct, and where the form moves about among the matter bringing order into it. But this type of thinking is not what we have called philosophic. Special facts we abjure. The study of definition by the process of definition is the study of the universal fact. We wish to know what it is that makes this so-and-so, and that so-and-so, *cases of* so-and-so. What is the common factor of "thisness"; when does one have a "this"? (DT 40–41)

Placing the ontological question prior to the epistemological question puts into play the methodological imperative against privileging cognition. Answering the question *When does one have a* this? provides the terms by which the epistemo-logical question will subsequently be addressed. Proceeding in the opposite manner, and beginning with the question of knowledge, would necessitate that certain assumptions be made—for example, about the status of subjects and objects, at the very least.

What, then, makes a *this* a *this?* What are the necessary conditions for mak-ing such a statement as *This is it?* The uncomplicated answer is that it is *distin-guishability* that makes such a statement possible. Quite simply: A person cannot speak of a *this* if there are no grounds for discerning its difference from other things or that *this* implies a different meaning from any *that.* This is an epistemo-logical, or meaning-based, form of distinguishability (DT 43-44).[8]

This is simple enough. Beginning with *distinction* has significant and per-haps unexpected consequences, however. Distinction is a matter of relations and supposes already-existing relations; distinction is simply not a property of a thing itself but of a thing in relation to a field of other things. Thus Miller immediately disqualifies the most obvious answer to the next question in order: So what is it that distinguishes one thing from another? One thing is not distinguished from another merely on the basis of essential properties it possesses yet are not pos-sessed by other things. Such a thing would be an example of the realist's thing-in-itself, an experientially inaccessible entity that Miller describes to as a "static definition" (DT 42).

Miller denies that static definitions—that is, definitions without relations—are possible. Looking toward the history of investigation and the larger history of meanings provides ample evidence that there has never been such a static defini-tion. There has never been such a thing that was always just *this,* a finite and fixed list of properties, resisting emendation or expansion. In seeking a broad *philo-sophical* basis for rejecting static definitions, however, one must also examine "the requirement that there be a concept or object at all" (DT 44). Miller presents the terms of that requirement in a dense argument that alludes to mathematical con-ceptions of series.[9] Stated in summary: Static definitions must be rejected because "any object or concept constantly acquires new relations as a condition of its sep-arate existence and distinctness, i.e., as a condition of its being an object or con-cept at all" (DT 43). *Relations have constitutional status;* the thing is *genealogical* rather than substantial.

The relations in question are predicate relations. And it would appear that only a very rudimentary idea is affirmed here: A thing is the thing it is by virtue of the qualities predicable of it. Put otherwise: A particular thing is what it is because of the relations it has with universal types such as *rational* and *animal.* This recognition alone would not disqualify static definitions. For even if defin-

ition is a matter of relations—that is, individual thing taking universal predicate—
these relations themselves could be unchanging and the thing static if not completely independent. (The bedrock demand of the realist is that the object of
knowledge cannot change, let alone come to be, through our knowledge of it.)
Acknowledging that *thisness* depends on predicate relations reveals an overlooked
dynamic quality (genealogical and indeed historical) to predicate relations. The
object is not just composed of relations but is constantly constituted by new relations. As Miller states, the recognition of the role of predicate relations initiates
a process in which there is "a demand for more and more predicates, a 'Baccha-
nalian revel' with gathering momentum" (DT 43).

If predicate relations are the condition of distinguishability, each thing must
be related in such a way that marks it off from other things. Distinction is not possessed but achieved: Unable to fall back on an essential core of unrelated self-
identity, the demand for distinction generates further predication, further relations,
as fine differences are told in the effort to maintain meaning. In the case of any particular thing, failing to keep up with the process of distinction would mark the end
of its distinguishability as that particular thing. Such a failure would render it synonymous with another, once-dissimilar thing. Indeed the whole series of traits that
distinguish any particular thing is dependent on the ongoing development of its
predicates. Furthermore failing to maintain distinguishability by developing certain
individual characteristics does not threaten just those specific characteristics but the
whole series. Any failure at maintaining distinction represents a step back into a
world with fewer things and less meaning. The collapse of many such distinctions
would signify that a person had significantly less control of his world because the
very factors of control—that is, distinctions—were lost in a resurgence of uniformity.
The maintenance of meaning is a genetic process (MP 29:17). The implication of
this conception of definition is that "this series of differentia is infinite or has no
final member" (DT 43–44).

Examples of processes of definition described in terms of developing terms of
control are abundant. The most obvious general instance is the taxonomic structure
of genus, phylum, and species known to the most casual student of biology. At the
level of kingdom one has determinant categories upholding the broadest of distinctions. The control provided by the categories distinguished at the level of kingdom
is of great assistance; these categories stand as the outline of a biological world. Yet
these categories are only blunt tools of organization. In having a world one has, at
the same time, very little in detail: wolves mix with humans (kingdom *animalia*, phylum *cherdata*), pine trees with ginkgo trees (kingdom *plantae*, phylum *tracheaphyta*).
Details, and thus more sophisticated means of control, are developed as one moves
from phylum to order, then family, and finally species. Specific categories that determine increasingly specific traits are established, eventually rendering a world full

of an almost overwhelming amount of detail. The world becomes more populous as, at the level of order, the wolf parts company with the human (*carnivora* from *primates*), and the pine is distinguished from the ginkgo (*coniferales* from *ginkgoales*). The control made possible by this welter of detail does not, however, become overwhelming because of the broad primary categories at the level of kingdom and phylum. These most general of categories ensure that the differences generated by the production of refined categories remain related and thus significant. Thus moving down the taxonomic structure one develops an increasing amount of control and a more complex context for action. Control, by contrast, is lost when one regresses a step in the development of this structure. When human beings are not thought of as *homo sapiens* but simply as animals—that is, muscular and mobile creatures like wolves—a loss of definition and, thus, control is precipitated.

What the thing is, then, is a definition or a capacity for being distinguished. What distinguishes a thing is a definite but open-ended series of predicates. And what maintains the distinctness, the *thisness* of any thing is a relentless process of specification via predication. These are the constitutional conditions of there being any object at all.[10] In these terms the *this* is a "*relative* permanence" and not an independent or substantial entity (DT 44, 50).

The basic character of these subject–predicate, particular–universal relations is *dialectical*. Harkening back to Hegel's "Introduction" to his *Phenomenology of Spirit*, Miller remarks on the status of the universal and particular predicates:

> [I]t does not follow that the universal can be defined or understood apart from its embodiments, though not associated with any one exclusively. It will be shown in the discussion of the paradox of inductive definition . . . that the universal is always corrected by its embodiments and that it is incomprehensible save through the mediation of all its exemplifications. Although the particular must thus seek a detailed specificity from which the universal remains aloof, it would be a mistake to regard it as having more properties than the universal, for the same reasons that show the error of the belief that there are more integers, odd *and* even, than there are either odd *or* even. On the basis of the extent of qualifications, it is false that the particular has a richer connotation than the universal. (DT 45–46)

The relationship between the particular and universal is dynamic. Neither element is richer than or prior to the other (see Tyman, 1996, pp. 1–21). It is not the case that the subject is prior and thus merely suffers incidental relations. It also is also not possible that universal predicates are self-sufficient and, through some act of cosmogony, generate individuals in their likeness. Rather subject and predicate, particular and universal, mutually imply and clarify one another.

There is an alliance between the universal and particular. Each can only exist in an *opposing* relationship. (They are, as Vincent Colapietro expresses it, "allied antagonists"—at once sharply differentiated and intimately connected [1990, p. 73].) Such allied antagonisms exemplify what Miller means by *dialectic*. Moreover these alliances are not temporary or merely stages in the development of a greater unity. The dialectical process of action is the condition of, the very engine by which meaning-as-distinguishability is generated. Action maintains relations by being "the state of affairs that enforces the distinction" (MS 186; cf. Johnstone, 1990, p. 66).

The dialectical form of predicate relations is illustrated by the paradox of inductive definition. The process of clarifying what a thing is does not just rely on the addition of predicates. It also implies *revision*. "Every addition," Miller notes, "by narrowing the meaning of the just preceding term, alters the meaning of the latter, an alteration which is carried down to the beginning" (DT 47). (For example, the distinction of *carnivora* at the level of order revises the status of those traits held in common by wolves and humans at the more general level of the kingdom *animalia*; wolf and human are carnivores and their particular forms of animality are distinguished as such.) The process of a developing, experientially founded, inductive definition is paradoxical because it holds together two seemingly contrary elements—that is, constancy and revision, stability and change. It involves the peculiar situation where, for example, one knows what *dog* is, has a definition of it, and yet inquires into its actual examples in such a way that this initial definition must be expanded or revised. Engaging in the common activity of inductive definition a person affirms something quite remarkable: While sitting on the front porch and keeping an eye out for passing dogs, she *both* knows and does not know what *dog* is.

The paradox of inductive definition could simply be avoided if we could establish *fixed* definitions. Fixed definitions can be maintained in two ways. The initial definition can be rigorously maintained and these other beasts excluded from the class of *dog*. Equally excluded from all other classes because none will accommodate them under a revised definition, these beasts must wander nameless and classless around town. The other option is making each individual its own class. This assures the fitness and stability of each definition by making it utterly specific. Both of these "solutions" to the problem of inductive definition are equally absurd. In one case the symbol (i.e., the name embodying the definition) is separated from the concrete signification of the term (i.e., those doglike things wandering around town).[11] In the other case the symbol is so closely linked to the particular that it is, in fact, absolutely particular and thus useless as a symbol—that is, it becomes a sign. These absurd conclusions underline the difficulty of maintaining a static definition.

Therefore, to attempt to separate meanings and the concrete facts, stabilizing the former in terms of symbols, is to lose the very meanings that it is the purpose of the theory to hold fast from the engulfing modifications of a changing world. Thus we again conclude that change cannot be avoided, and that the paradoxical situation growing out of a revision of meanings (or the logical growth of things) is not to be solved by attempting to nail down a central core of meaning. (DT 48–49)

Miller finds the paradox of inductive definition illustrative of the dialectical process transpiring between particular and universal. How can a person avoid the situation where nameless beasts are wandering around town and she is left sitting on the porch with a useless definition of *dog*? Or how does she avoid finding herself in the worse situation of having a pluriverse of absolute entities named dog_1, dog_2, dog_3, and so on? The answer is that these undefined beasts must be capable of adapting into dogs and, further, one's definition of *dog* must be capable of adapting by accommodating these beasts. *World and symbol change.* The change in each element occurs in the dialectic of an interpretative relationship. Neither element is strictly generative of the other—inductive generalization without guiding universals is just as impossible as the creation of individuals *ex nihilo* out of universals.

Miller remarks that change is an "inalienable" element of identity (DT 50). What *is* the sort of identity in question? As stated above, Miller is clarifying a *relative permanence*—that is, a form of distinguishability that need not resist but rather incorporates change and thus *relative discontinuity* or history (PC 91). The constancy here, the definition, is not "a group of properties, but the *distinguishability of a process*" (DT 50). It is akin to an ongoing performance, narrative, or "peculiar evolutionary story" (DT 51). Ontology is necessarily linked with an ongoing process of modifying relations and the permanent state of incompleteness that it entails (MS 125). "Final, completed, and independent content is impossible by definition," Miller states. "Content, as limited, necessarily invites restriction, and hence the order of contingency. Consequently, absolutes shade off into mysticism. They become indefinable in any terms through which meaning is won, i.e., through the categories" (FI 264).

This hard-won ontological insight proves its worth in its ready application in the area of epistemology. In chapter 4 of *The Definition of the Thing* Miller develops this dialectical ontology by sorting through the layers of assumptions implicated with the problem of knowledge. Most epistemology begins with an assumption wholly opposite that of actualism: Things and relations are wholly distinct, and neither has any essential relation to the other (DT 83–85). Things, especially subjects and objects, are real. Relations themselves are left entirely undetermined and their existence dubious. Defining a relationship would assume that things are necessarily implicated in relations. Yet this presupposes the solution to the problem of knowledge. Because one cannot identify *relationship* without recourse to the things related—there is no *relation-in-itself*—one must then forsake altogether talking about relations. (The converse fact, that one cannot define a thing in even the most generic sense without relations, is of course equally true; this is a fact overlooked by atomistic assumptions [DT 84–88].) This conclusion, as Miller notes, "sets the stage for an unlimited debate" (DT 85). How can relations be forged by reason when things have already been granted existence as unrelated? Epistemology-centered philosophy thus nullifies its own problematic by allowing itself unwarranted ontological assumptions; the epistemological question becomes chiefly a technical matter but not an actual question.

There is a second, perhaps more serious difficulty: These dyadic assumptions threaten one's very grasp on things. The assumptions underlying the dyadic presentation do not just frustrate discursive knowledge but also the possibility of the immediate apprehension of things. A static and unrelated thing is not even discernible; it is tantamount to John Locke's "I know not what." Absent relations, where does one get a hold on a thing? "The changeless object is either unlike all others and so cannot be identified, or if like others and yet changeless, its conception is contradictory," Miller writes. "Hence a given property would have ambiguous definition" (DT 100). The revelation of this absurdity strikes not only at the principles of the positivist but also against the assumptions of the rationalist and absolute idealist. The simple and pure idea gained via intuition cannot generate a system because it lacks definition and cannot support further elaboration. Miller writes in a reflection on the simple and complex:

> The complex appears to be relational. . . . The simple, then, appears to be the unenvironed, the unrelated. Where there is relation there is complexity. The unenvironed is the unbounded, the undefined, i.e., the unlimited. Where the simple is taken to be short of everything, it is *particularity without limit*. It is "this" not "that," yet not defined through differences, for then its meaning would entail complexity, and relation within an order permitting difference. The simple is the *absolutely limited*. . . .
>
> In general, the simple will never occur as the resultant of any procedure for discovering the "simple," i.e., the *absolutely limited*. It will readily be seen that the particular, or partial, viewed as absolutely limited is indistinguishable from the absolutely *unlimited*. Nothing "ultimate" is a constituent part of anything at all. The absolutely limited has no implications, whether for another alleged simple, or for a relative whole, or for an absolute whole. Any implication is a demand for the relationship that identifies an assumption. What needs no identification within an order can generate no implications. (MP 6:12)

There is neither a reason nor a means for moving forward from an intuition. (Miller and Royce both describe intuitionism and mysticism as philosophies of passivity [DT 188].) The culminating idea of the idealist is also dismissed because the completion of the process of definition would be the obliteration of definition and thus meaning (DT 111); what cannot maintain its distinctness via the ongoing refinement of its definition becomes no-thing. The point made in section 2.1 is echoed: Beginning with the dyad and not the dialectical triad, in which action is the third element, creates an unproductive and hopeless problem of knowledge.

Actualism avoids the fruitless paradoxes of the dyadic approach to the problem of knowledge by proposing a "doctrine of relativism" that denies there is any absolute fact (DT 110). If there are no isolated and undefinable entities at play in one's system—that is, so long as one's experience is not riddled with what is literally nonsense (see AH 262)—then relations must be pervasive and constitutive. Nothing stands alone. Change itself is ontological since it is an inalienable factor in definition. So too is permanence for without it change would not make sense and definition would be fruitlessly vague. What a thing is, then, is a result of the interplay of opposed forces: *Actualist ontology is dialectical ontology*, and action, not cognition, is the moving principle of the process.

§2.3 DIALECTIC AND ACTION

Miller insists that epistemological and ontological problems are only fully clarified when the role of action is considered. In this move one sees Miller following Hegel's lead in going from the *Phenomenology of Spirit* (where the union of subject and object is described logically) to the "Introduction" to his *Philosophy of History* (where the union of the universal and individual is described in existential terms). Miller's comment on epistemological starting places is to the point:

> But why, then, is one not able to deduce all facts given one fact? The answer is that this is entirely possible. But those who ask the question do not and cannot supply that fact. There is no fact save in the making; no final and absolute discovery can be made. To ask the question begs the question. To demand of a doctrine of relativism what it expressly denies is *überhaupt* possible is hardly just. But relativism does not regard this impotence as accidental or unfortunate; rather it is the source of its power and the magazine of its energy. The fact does not reside outside the swirl of contingency. (DT 110)

The simple fact, the thing, is coextensive with action and found via the medium of action. There is no need to *get to* such an object as if it was something other than those very things one comes across in the course of daily affairs. The first fact is an active, and never a speculative, one. It arises in an actual dialectical situation, a *there*, where a person lives, acts, and engages with objects (MS 89). On these grounds, Miller is allied with the pragmatist who "recognizes no absolute object, telling the story of objects only in connection with acts and their discoveries" (MP 14:7). While Miller argues that the ontological implications of action far exceed those recognized by pragmatists such as John Dewey and William James (MP 21:1), there is no contention on the matter of the importance of active experience to the status of and knowledge about objects.

A close examination of definition shows how activity underlies even those experiences commonly considered to be passive. Miller writes:

> It is rather odd, when one stops to consider it, that common sense persists in crediting a tree with color in spite of the alleged subjective status of quality. . . . That the real tree, the cognitive tree, is green because one has been looking (that is to say, acting) was not proposed nor that various qualities are discriminated only as one has done something. Looking is a verb. It is not a common noun. (MS 10)

Action, as Colapietro notes, must be understood as pluralistic and communal: "The world of so-called common sense is more accurately designated as the world of shared action" (2003, p. 12). *Action* is thus a term of first importance when considering the constitution of our common-sense world. Action does more than maintain and rely on distinguishability. It generates distinctions. In unpacking this description it is useful to begin with a paired question-and-answer provided by Miller in the second chapter of *The Definition of the Thing*: "Why is revision necessary? For the same reason, now often mentioned, that makes constancy necessary, namely, the preservation of distinguishability" (DT 53). Given an understanding of the dialectical process of definition (see §2.2), Miller's response is not perplexing. The significant question now is the one following it: Why preserve distinguishability?

It was stated earlier that distinguishability is the very condition of meaning and that without distinctions meaning itself would disappear. In achieving new distinctions the meaning of a person's world is increased whereas in the collapse of existing distinctions the meaning of his world is diminished. Such a response, although correct, is too general. It lacks an existential edge. For what, exactly, is the value of meaning itself? Can the general task of maintaining a rich and burgeoning store of meanings have practical efficacy? Even if a case could be made for maintaining *meaning in general*, it is questionable whether anyone can begin by thinking about meaning in such an abstract fashion. It is difficult and uncommon to make an assessment as to whether meaning is increasing or diminishing on a global scale.

Meaning—its expansion, maintenance, or loss—is largely a local affair and it is from a local vantage point that estimations of this sort are made. As Ortega y Gasset, who Miller finds to be an occasional source of inspiration, succinctly put the matter: "Life is haste and has urgent need to know what it is up against" (1961, p. 182). The need to maintain meaning is more urgent than the speculative concern about meaning in general; the challenge is more particular and proximate.

The process of revision in which particular objects and their organizing symbols are clarified in light of one another is what Miller calls the exercise of "local control." *Local-control* is a phrase that came relatively late to Miller's philosophical vocabulary. Yet in *The Definition of the Thing* one can already see intimations of this concept, which Tyman refers to as Miller's "core ontological concept" (1993, p. 18). Regarding the process of revision Miller writes:

> This revision must always be limited in scope or in its regressive application. For the demand for a revision arose, as we saw, from the definition of some relatively remote predicate or property which could not be preserved unless a later predicate was rejected. It is only on this basis that question is possible. No question about the whole of fact can be asked, for every question requires a point of departure. Yet each special fact can be doubted. No matter how deeply the knife of the logical surgeon cuts, its edge is always in some bit of fact. The law of contradiction saves "things" by asking the questions which revise. But any revision is limited by the questioner himself. (DT 54)

While questions and problems can have general and even universal significance—as do necessary problems—they arise from personal, existential challenges. Questions are not free-floating. So when Miller states that revision proceeds by maintaining or producing "relevant" distinctions (DT 52), *relevance* cannot be taken abstractly. Relevance is discerned from the perspective of persons expending their energies in practical questions geared toward maintaining local-control, organizing experience, fulfilling purposes, and acting with confidence (and perhaps self-control) in an environment. The need for achieving these things, for exercising local-control, is fervent and insatiable. Relevant distinctions are not drawn or effaced by a detached spectator; they are urgently enforced or painfully lost in a struggle for maintaining local-control. The perpetually incomplete condition of local-control, like the systematic incompletion of the process of definition, describes of the very structure of meaning (MS 169-70). Indeed the terms *definition* and *local-control* describe the same process.

When Miller addresses revision in terms of the application of the law of contradiction (as in the quotation above), the dispassionate aspect of this process should not conceal what is at stake in maintaining distinctions.[12] In his mature thinking the locus of control that was represented in the law of contradiction is

replaced by "the body," "functioning immediacies," and "functioning objects"
that embody action and are vehicles of local-control (MS 120, 142–43). The
oblique description of the actual offered in *The Definition of the Thing* is sharpened
by an existential vocabulary. *Egoism*, suggesting as it does the active and willful person, now centers the discussion. Addressing this *ego*,[13] this person, Miller writes:

> Intimations of this self-reliance appear in Emerson, who far surpasses Hegel
> in his grasp of the ontological status of the actual. In the end Hegel did not
> make good on his claim that he had found an energy internal to the spec-
> tacle. His control was not local control. The local is the *same* as control.
> *Geist* is not a local control. But I am local control when I "tell" a tale, or tell
> time, or make a mistake. Egoism, the sense of local control, is no force in
> Hegel. The baffling problems of egoism are a consequence of an imposed
> order, whatever the manner of that imposition, by whatever force. But ego-
> ism is no problem when the local is the same as the enactment of order in
> function, in the functioning object, whether yardstick, grammar, logic, or
> dialectic. (TO 402)

If Kant's philosophy is guilty of being "bloodless," as Miller himself attests, so too
is Hegel's or any philosophy addressing the questions of being and knowledge
from a situation other than that of the active person. If separated from the
immediate demands implied by local-control, structure and definition are lifeless
and at best mechanical. Actualism, on the contrary, binds together structure and
willful personhood.

The process of definition by which things become what they are is begun by
something as intimate and earthy as a bodily gesture. The distinctions brought
forth by the gesture are furthered by symbolic artifacts and functional tools that,
in different ways, reveal a world of things. They are all actions or extensions of
action—that is, active principles in the process of definition, in the coming to be
and maintenance of things. This line of thought deserves significant elaboration
(see §§2.5 and 3.1). Yet painting this rough existential portrait of local-control
assists in coming to some conclusions about the ontological role of action and the
authority of persons. For what this presentation of local-control suggests is that
action both generates and relies on distinctions.[14] That there are distinctions, that
there are things, only makes sense in light of some course of action. It is equally
true that action requires these distinctions just as any traveler must have the barest
rudiments of a map so as to have a conception of direction and thus be headed
anywhere in particular. The more distinctions available, the more detailed the
map, then the more directed and precise the route of the traveler.

Without supposing that one must tell a creation story—that is, marking out
an *absolute* beginning where the first action wrought difference and called forth

the first thing—Miller shows how action is the constitutive factor in the process of definition. Action is ontological; it is at the bottom of form, structure, and order. Action is also the discovery of all content. There is no reason that because one cannot tell a story of an absolute beginning that the ontological status of action itself should be placed in question. The unavoidable accidental conditions contributing to any given action and surrounding the origin of any possible distinction do not affect this account. Certainly, any particular action is tentative. This is because action occurs in terms of the need for *local-control* and a person can imagine other localities as well as other possibilities within his own locality. Further, when talking about particular things and definite types of form, a person cannot avoid paying attention to the detailed circumstances in which that form arose. The dialectic between form and content, between universality and particularity, is ceaseless. That said, it also must be recognized that there is nothing optional about action itself (PH 32–36). In this sense the act is never reducible to the accidental features of its environment. Rather, the act is absolute insofar as it is an ineluctable and thus constitutional element of structure that determines form and locates content (see CRW). Any particular act, no matter how mired in circumstance, bears this ontological force. That is the crucial and generic claim of Miller's actualist metaphysics.

Just as the problem of knowledge (and especially its skeptical result) reveals the person and the problem of ontology reveals the dialectical process, the problem of action reveals human autonomy manifest in the recognition of the ontological significance of one's actions. "In the end," Miller writes, "authority is in the person who *reveals* an environment" (MS 89). One finds action and authority via the media of objects, institutions, and other persons. Action also reveals itself in the contemplative life in the necessary problems that have occupied speculation. It is there that one sees action happening as function and authority as activity. As Miller states regarding the relation between being and function: "There is no concept of finitude. It needs a vehicle. It needs the actual, the here and now" (MP 22:14). Where the answer to a philosophical question is some entity, however, the issue is indeed solved and the processes addressed are *resolved* into their supposedly isolated constitutive factors. Such answers unfortunately offer little insight and they reveal no power because structure becomes an occult factor. Where the problem is conserved, insight and power are maintained. What also becomes evident is that the objects, orders, and processes that the contemplative life (first as philosophy and then as science) addresses are intimately connected to action. Action is not contrary to contemplation but, in fact, gets it started and maintains it. There is no strict opposition between the action and contemplation.

§2.4   ACTION AS CONSTRUCTIVE

If there were not action, what could be said to be? The preliminary answer to
the question is: *Nothing.* From that negative answer positive conclusions have
been drawn regarding the primacy of action. By adding basic existential
insights, a case has been made for the ontological role of action and the retrieval of the status of the active life as ingredient to the contemplative life.
This last section provides a preliminary account of how action serves a constitutional role by generating form and bringing individual things to light. This
shifts the discussion from being to beings, action to individual acts, form to historically instantiated forms.

Miller claims that environment is a revelation of action and, further, that action
is the source of such objective orders as space and time, as well as constitutive of
the larger region of nature (MS 83-90). How is order produced by practical
activity? The answer is implied in the first-person experience of attaining and
maintaining control in the face of uncertainty. Action wrests order from a situation where a relevant form of organization is either not apparent, only tenu-
ously established, or in need of expansion. In so doing, action establishes
limit—that is, enforcing definitions and limiting itself by providing definite
terms of control instead of a vague and indefinite backdrop (RPR 2). Action
both produces and relies on limited orders.

   That said, and only that said, there would not be too great a difference
between the actualist and pragmatic positions. Distinctions can be drawn—and
there are telling differences of interpretation among the pragmatists themselves—yet the connection between order and action would reduce all disputes
to family squabbles. Miller's sense of action, however, goes beyond pragmatism.
First, there is the generic *ontological* requirement of action that is not given adequate attention by either Dewey or James. Second, there are sharp differences
between Miller and especially Dewey's version of pragmatism regarding the
implications of local-control. For Dewey there are no problems in *general* but
only particular difficulties resulting, if successfully addressed, in terminating satisfactions (see DP 62). The way in which order is rendered in any given locale
has no universal implications, cannot pretend to address "the everywhere." By
contrast, actualism claims that action has universal implications. Fully aware
that "the term utopia connotes the impractical," Miller develops this aspect of
practical, local action:

> There is hazard enough in decidedly restricted programs, and it seems mad-
> ness to entertain counsels of perfection when no perfection is attainable.

Unfortunately such a view is not the whole truth, although it might be pleasant to think it so. It seems that human nature is not so easily tamed. Indeed, to suppose that one could deal with the contemporary world on that basis would be the very essence of utopian illusion. Men do not set limited goals for themselves. In fact, and in principle, there is not such sort of goal. . . . Any particular act can, in fact, be regarded as purposive and as fulfilling only as it becomes the local vehicle of an essentially boundless program. It is our attempt to meet local confusion somewhere, to arrest it for a moment, in order to go on to the next point of challenge. One may counsel limited ambition, but no ambition is absolutely limited, and in the measure that it is strong it can derive its strength only from the desperate urgency of the enterprise into which it fits. Men can move resolutely for particular ends only as larger purposes enforce their local surrogate. Every will attempts the impossible. We are incurably utopian, since we must arm ourselves with boundless resolve in so far as we propose to teach and maintain any goal whatsoever. (PC 20–21)

The scope of action far exceeds what the classical pragmatists imagined. The boundless character of programs of action is not just a function of the fact that there are always more particular problems awaiting one's attention. What must be understood, and what pragmatism has difficulty discerning, are not only the implications but also the conditions of recognizing a problem. When physical response (be it muscular, nervous, or chemical) is mixed with reflective (and not just calculative) thought, the problematic character of our experience is transformed to a degree exceeding any naturalistic model.

The animal has immediate needs and, through training, develops habits facilitating their fulfillment. Yet, as noted in section 2.1, when persons are confronted with urgent, local problems they do not just gain habits but, rather, insight into structure. There are classes of problems that reveal general environmental traits; the creative response to one local problem provides the resources for negotiating an indefinite number of other environments. For example, certain lessons about motion, mass, and fulcrums aid a person in everything from amusing a child balanced on her knee to constructing skyscrapers. Through the extension of distinctions an unbounded field of problematic situations and practical resolutions is also revealed. Similarly addressing a singular confusion in a particular environment one is always relying on a vague backdrop of generalized, action-guiding distinctions. For example, the decision as to when to jaywalk on Fifth Avenue relies on the unnoticed support of the categories of space and time, as well as subsidiary distinctions like acceleration. Local circumstances become vehicles for the application and further development of certain generalized distinctions.

Local-control produces distinctions that become generalized insights into structure. The *order* of the world, as Miller notes, is the extension of local-control (MP 40:1). Distinctions guiding action in general are forms of order Miller calls "categories" or "organization words" (PC 189). The gesture toward Kant is intentional. Kant's insight that the categories are integral to human experience, and thus constitute its very form, guides Miller's investigations. Order is not a property of the thing-in-itself—that is the liberating insight informing actualism. Yet Kant's outlook is deficient insofar as it supposed that the categories "are properties of pure reason, that is, that they are laws of order, but of order without specific focus" (MS 33–34). If the *Critique of Pure Reason* made the categories human, they remained detached from action. Kant took his lead from an ahistorical conception of science. Following on Hegel (but also critically revising him), what Miller proposes is that the categories grow up out of attempts at local-control and are intimately connected to action, criticism, and the revisionary processes of history.

An actualist redescription of Kant's category of space serves as a useful introduction to what James Diefenbeck refers to as "categories on the move" (1990, p. 50). Space, as Kant stated, is the universal distinction belonging to all things insofar as they appear outside of a person. In addition to being constitutional, space (in its Euclidean form) is a priori. "Space is a necessary *a priori* representation, which underlies all outer intuitions . . . ," Kant wrote. "Space is not a discursive or, as we say, general concept of relations of things in general, but a pure intuition" (1787/1965, pp. 68–69). The category of space is necessary; it has no intrinsic connection to any particular locale or any specific struggle for local-control. For Kant it is objective space—that is, uniform and a priori, and not the product of empirical induction.

Kantian space and actualist space appear entirely opposed to one another. That appearance, however, is only partially correct. Kant's category of space certainly differs from Miller's on the matter of the role that local-control plays in its generation—Kant saying local-control has no constitutive role and Miller affirming that location is constitutional. Yet both agree that space must be universal and cannot be the result of empirical induction. Space is not formed bit-by-bit, experience-by-experience, so that one might be surprised to find, over the next hill, a six-dimensional valley. The trick of mediating these contrasting statements is in seeing that what is available in the empirical, local situation is not adequately described by the atomistic metaphysics of David Hume that preoccupied Kant.

There is a utopian element in local-control. In any given locality distinctions are generated in response to structural confusions. These distinctions will carry as far as that structure allows. On the one hand, if one is struggling with a necessary problem (a problem of environment as such) then the distinction establishing control will be of *universal* significance. The problem of distinction answered by the universal category of space is such a necessary problem. On the other hand, the confusions within a person's household economy—for example, unpaid bills, unwashed dishes—are accidental problems. Such problems can at best produce categories capable of some limited form of generalization—for example, pay the bills on the first of every month. The control provided by space—but not necessarily only Euclidean space—responds to the most generic requirements of distinguishability. As Kant stated, "Space is nothing but the form of all appearances of outer sense" (1787/1965, p. 71). Without space no appearance and thus no other distinction (with the possible exception of time) would be possible. Every further distinction assumes the category of space and thus ramifies it in an indefinite number of ways.

The category of space is an aspect of the structure of actuality. "Any problem about reality must be identical with reality," Miller observes in a passage quoted earlier. "The problem must be unconditioned if it is to convey an unconditioned answer" (PC 70). Euclidean geometry, insofar as it provides the form for such a generic sort of distinguishability, is universal and pretends to continuity with actuality. Yet this function does not make it an a priori or intuited reality; Euclidean space is not transcendent and may in fact not be the only form of space that can answer the need for generic distinguishability. Action is primary because it addresses the basic need for distinguishability. Euclidean space is pure form, space itself. It is an example of what Miller calls "action in principle":

> Action in principle is obviously not found in the specific factor of the act, but only in so far as it is an act. Action in principle could not, then, be a "response" or a change among already given objects. Or, action in principle can assume no environment. *Thesis: Action has no "environment."*
>
> The action which has no environment must, therefore, be *identical* with "environment" in principle. It must be the actuality of the environment. It must create environment. . . . Pure action, absolute action, creative action occurs in the discovery and articulation *of the general conditions of specific acts.* These general conditions are the categories. (MP 21:1)[15]

Euclidean space is not the result of an inductive process. It is more akin to an assertion. It is an assertion that says what the environment is and allows relevant facts to find their place within that environment. That environment is implicit in the crudest act of measuring. Over time and continued application, rudimentary forms of measurement work themselves pure and the formal element becomes clearer and clearer; measuring becomes space itself because *space* was implied in the first measurement. In measurement there is a *metaphorical* quality that shows that the act is not a mere response to an existing environment but, rather, offers novel terms of description and thereby proposes a new sort of environment.

The disagreement between Kant and Miller is not then so great as it first appeared. Kant's idealism and Hume's empiricism are synthesized so as to maintain the noninductive origin of categories such as space. The problem with Kant's idealism is that he did not place any emphasis on the *telling* of time and the *making* of measurements. (For Miller, all differences, great and small, are told [MP 25:22; cf. Colapietro, 2003, pp. 77–82].) In general, there is no sense of the exercise of local-control. "In the *Critique of Pure Reason* he has nobody living in Königsberg," Miller remarks. "So he gives us a 'phenomenal' order and a morality which draws upon transcendent realities." The problem, of course, is that such a "universality without actuality leads to an abstract formalism or else to a reality discontinuous with the immediate as articulated" (MP 22:14).

Space is a development of local-control. The yard is not a natural fact and the platinum bar in the Bureau of Standards is not a copy of a transcendent idea. One begins with arms, legs, feet—the whole vital human body. It is the body, understood as the "immediacy of function" (MS 43), that centers the process of local-control and from which every distinction has its origin. In this function *the* body is not *a* body (MS 142); it is the source of distinctions and not an object that is itself distinguished. (Physiology is the study of bodies but not *the* body.) In this capacity the body functions as a symbol and not as a sign. The first efforts at measurement show precisely how the human body as symbol makes distinctions and how that original vagueness not even yet called *space* is metaphorically translated into *feet*, *yards*, and *hands*. The order growing up out of the intimate relationship between the body and environment in turn generates artifacts that codify and extend what were once exclusively bodily distinctions.

Miller's favorite example of such artifactual functioning objects is the yardstick. Like the body, the yardstick is not an object of perception. It is not an object to which order is applied (PC 114–15). (Asking how long a yardstick is is ultimately absurd.) The order of action generated by the body's activity is symbolically represented in the functioning object: "A yardstick . . . is a metaphysical actuality, an incarnate power. Until the word was made flesh, it had no actuality" (MS 153). In the yardstick what was first a bodily distinction is conceptualized and stabilized. Not only that: It is extended. The functioning object is the necessary medium between form as immediate control and form as a category applicable to any and every locale irrespective of all differences: The yardstick discloses the universal form of space (MS 140).

The conclusions that can be drawn from this illustration are readily apparent:

> Like all others Kant had to account in some way for the alleged universal.
> He said it was a priori. We had no hand in discovering it. Where I allow

myself to modify that great man is in saying, as I have been saying, that we do have a hand in it—the hand that picks up the yardstick, the tongue that tells time by the clock, the act that keeps a tally cutting notches in a stick or making a notation on paper, where alone the expression $7 + 5 = 12$ or $a + b = c$ becomes manifest. I have been saying—and it is a saying—that the universal is the form of the actual, generated, enlarged, conflicting as the act maintains itself in a local control. (MS 108–9)

The activity of definition treated formally in sections 2.2 and 2.3 is here revealed to be a bodily process, a function of embodied practicality. Categories are universal orders from which predicates are drawn when maintaining the distinguishability of a thing. Yet there is no description, no predicate that cannot be traced back to an original gesture, action, or word. As Miller states, "If one completes the sentence 'The world is . . . ,' one has declared an activity, not a perception, as immediate and controlling" (MS 81). Because the categories are allied with action these forms of order are also always in flux. Any list of categories must be provisional for the very process that generates and maintains them is open-ended and dynamic. Certain categories such as space and time are certainly fundamental. This status, however, does not attest to their a priori necessity or ahistoricity. (Space and time have, in fact, changed over the course of history.) Their relative necessity points to basic needs and the historical career of local-control. Action is oriented by structure, and action is always generating, maintaining, and revising structure. Properly understood, *the environment* of human action is universal, categorial, and historical (see §3.1).

Emphasizing the generative quality of action strikes what can be called "the romantic note" of idealist philosophy (MP 21:1).[16] It sounds resistance to the pretensions of the scientizing attitude and sets the tone for contemporary attacks on Eleatic metaphysics. Thus Miller consciously situates himself in the Idealist and Romantic traditions. In doing so, of course, Miller also places himself in dubious company. Exaggerations of all sorts have been perpetrated by the romantic tendency of idealist philosophy (many of which are on display in contemporary antimetaphysics). Even more exaggerations have been attributed to it. Whether traveling in philosophic circles or talking with the person on the street, *romantic* is more an epithet than a badge of honor. Precision is necessary regarding the implications of actualism's claims regarding the generative, or constructive, role of action.

In assessing the role of Romanticism in Miller's philosophy, we have to admit that the idea of *causality* is fraught with difficulties. It is also burdened by the history of philosophical and scientific thought. Once causality was a richer concept. Aristotle had four causes and so too did the Scholastic tradition inspired by Thomas Aquinas's retrieval of the Aristotelian system. Over time the sense of causality became more precise and amidst the turn toward modernity a refinement of causality was achieved. The result was an almost exclusive concentration on *efficient* causality (while maintaining the material cause, as almost an afterthought, so that there was stuff to move about). In the motion of Isaac Newton's physical bodies and the psychological physics of impressions and emotions described by the British empiricists, the concepts of *eidos* and *telos* were exiled to the territory of faith or cast into the flames as indefensible ideas.

The implication of these long-standing modern assumptions is that Miller's claims about action are liable to misunderstanding. If the only way to understand causality is as *efficient* causality, then the act is either reduced to triviality or catapulted into the heights of Romantic hubris. The first possible misinterpretation supposes that when action is referred to as *causal* it means nothing more than that it pushes things about in the world. Human actions would then be causal in the same sense as are the wind and rain—they result in evident changes in the environment. If human action is like the wind and the rain, it is explicable completely in terms of encompassing environmental conditions—a history of conditioning, the natural environment, and, ultimately, physics. Talking about an *act*, then, simply indicates that something happened, that there occurred an explicable change in the disposition of things in the environment.[17] Yet if action possesses an integrity that sets it apart from natural events, one is apparently pushed toward making hyperbolic claims regarding the efficacy of action. At this extreme, action is not a link in a long chain of efficient causality. Rather it is the efficient cause of all subsequent efficient causes. Thus the exaggerated talk of *creation* strewn throughout the writings of the Romantics: Caught in the language of efficient causality, Romanticism suggested that each person is an efficient cause of cosmic import, a god of (at least) a private universe.

Actualism rejects the behavioristic implications of the first option. Ontology cannot be addressed without a robust sense of action. The proper response is not, however, found in the absolute opposition of unrestrained Romanticism. There is a third way.

An important early essay of Miller's, "The Paradox of Cause," outlines his general response to the trap of thinking exclusively in terms of efficient causality. There he states that "There is one hope and only one; perhaps we have not understood the character of causal order, perhaps we have the wrong picture of the way that cause operates and of what makes it possible as a maxim of natural unity" (PC 13; see PH 27–31). The clue that causality has been misunderstood lies in the pragmatic fact that thinking solely in terms of efficient causality does not provide much guidance for individuals seeking local-control. The particular efficient causes noted by scientists are often perceptible; they are certainly capable of being charted in detail and are liable to calculation. In themselves, however, these causal events are not wholly reliable. They lack a universal element allowing for certainty, not just about what has occurred but about what will occur in the future. Thus scientists also look to laws and not just to events. At the other extreme, an absolute efficient cause may be proposed as a speculative principle. Yet its absolute standing is not in the least informative as to what will happen in particular; there is no way to deduce particular phenomena from a first cause, despite René Descartes's claims to the contrary.[18] Neither approach to causality provides terms adequate to the requirements of understanding and then acting with confidence in an environment.

This presents the paradox clarified by actualism: "[H]ow can cause be universal in its scope, yet restricted in its actual incidence?" (PC 15). What is required is a *teleological* sense of causality so long barred from philosophical discussions.

Teleology is reintroduced in the concepts of *form*, *order*, and *direction*. Introducing *order* into one's philosophical vocabulary allows for the distinction of particular efficient causes from causality itself. *Cause*, singular, is wholly different from efficient *causes* in the plural. It is not a particular event, an individual act, or a particular thing. It is a guiding principle of order:

> Cause is a dynamic concept because it describes an ideal, the ideal of the intelligibility of nature. For nature is in large part a mystery, and causal coherence is but one of the keys to its progressive solution. If we attempt to make this rule of process a character of a supposedly finished world, we can no longer define the rule.
>
> Consequently we are in a position to reconcile the paradox of cause. Cause must be in principle universally valid, and at the same time applicable only to finite and specific actuality. It must express the character of the whole of nature, but it must view that whole only as the ideal completion of a relative point of view through which actual and specific facts win a detailed and particularized causal ordering. It is a principle regulating the forward sweep of thought from a center to its periphery. Every specific event or object, blind and incomprehensible when isolated, demands a search for those conditions through which it may be controlled and even identified. (PC 16)

Perceiving events, noting their connections, and predicting their future consequences all presuppose causality as a principle of order. Causality is a form of appearances, a universal predicate (MP 9:6). As both Hume and Kant agreed, the law of causality cannot be constructed out of incidents. If it is to be anything, causality must be the category allowing for the definition of incidents as incidents in the first place. "And so," Miller notes, "it seems that, far from being inconsistent with teleology, cause presumes it" (PC 17). Empiricism cannot get started without metaphysics.

The form provided by causality as order is entirely lacking in detail or a specific goal. The form is only descriptive of a process. Causality in its teleological sense avoids the paradox of cause because it is both universal in scope and yet restricted in incidence. Miller remarks: "It is correct to say that [the world] is governed by a law of process, ideal in direction, infinite in potentiality, but always finite in status and in point of view" (PC 18). Such order guides understanding and action in all cases. Yet it is only in these actual cases that order reveals itself.

This sense of teleology also helps clarify the function of the categories originally articulated by the body. If the process of definition—beginning with the bodily gesture and eventually spreading outward via functioning objects—is ontological in its import, it is now clear that this is made possible by formal and not efficient causality. Thus, for example, when Ralph Waldo Emerson stated that the eye "makes the horizon"[19] the best actualist interpretation of that statement is not that the eye literally brings the horizon into existence out of nothing. The creation in question is formal—that is, it is a matter of order and definition. The activity of the eye, *seeing,* symbolically defines the horizon and makes it available to consciousness and action (MP 17:15). Something preexists this seeing. But that something is not the *horizon.* Prior to seeing, that something also does not imply anything regarding action or thought. What function generates, are the forms by which the world is revealed and further grasped in practical endeavors of control. Measurement becomes space. Keeping rhythm becomes time. Hearing becomes volume and pitch. Function is the generation of environment as an articulate condition of action (TO 406).

Action generates categories that allow for definition, control, and criticism. Taken together these categories and forms constitute what can be called the "region" of nature (MP 22:14):

> The totalities of action are found where through action we establish overall aspects of nature, i.e. universals. This type of action occurs in the use of symbols. It is in the control of symbols that we control an objective reality. These symbols include those of math, logic, and natural science. Act, too, is often said to be universal, and it is in the sense that act articulates the sentiments of an outlook and is not a local pleasure but a means of expansion and elevation of the mind. (MP 14:7)

Nature is a region of distinction, resistance, and control. It is the result of active metaphoric categories in the form of symbols such as the yardstick, clock, and thermometer. It is the region revealed and articulated by these categories. The realm of these functional and symbolic categories themselves is the midworld. The world and the midworld are the same reality taken from two different perspectives—instantiated form and form itself, respectively. Neither a realm of mere thoughts nor discrete objects, neither a private subjective sphere nor an objective world aloof from human endeavor, the midworld is the realm of action in its many forms—gesture, spoken word, symbol, functioning-object. The midworld is pure action. Yet because actualism is not a version of Platonism, the midworld remains attached to the earth. "Categories are not transcendental, nor are they psychological and accidental . . . ," Miller states. "Thus idealism asserts no Absolute, but rather denies the possibility of any assertion immune from the order of contingency. It is that order which is absolute" (FI 267).

§2.5 CONCLUSION

Actualism's proposal is that the freedom found in the act is the very condition of there being a world of causality, mechanics, and universal orders. The puzzling connections between necessity and contingency, as well as order and originality, bear elaboration in subsequent chapters. Yet it is already evident that the dialectical unity of order and originality supplies a basis for the rapprochement between the contemplative life and the active life. Given the description of action in this chapter, no claim can be made for divorcing the formal and particular, the metaphysical and practical. In action they are unified. Indeed in concrete action these two supposedly distinct ways of being are joined such that, lacking its complement, each is incomplete if not entirely nonsensical. The active life has a metaphysical element insofar as action is intrinsic to the generation and development of formal orders. Yet the contemplative life is also earthy in that it addresses the symbolic embodiments of action and thus exerts reflective control on action. The actual world of experience admits of no clear division between action and contemplation.

In this unity, actualism uncovers a profound sense of authority. By contrast, the strict separation of the active from the contemplative life results in a lack of control, an occlusion of power, and a loss of authority. If the coexistence and interdependence of order and contingency is a dilemma—as the history of philosophy attests—it is in such dilemmas that responsible modes of control are founded.

THREE

Symbol

The subordination of the active life to the contemplative life is premised on the allegedly dubious status of action. Ephemeral and futile, action was displaced by the permanent and the practical in the modes of philosophical contemplation and scientific fabrication. If the active life is to be recuperated, as well as its correlates in human authority and responsibility, these attacks must be addressed. Chapter 2 began the process by showing action to be efficacious in the process of definition. The wonder of perception and subsequent contemplation is premised on action as that which discloses the world. Effective at a formal level, however, the accounts of the former chapter continue to beg the experiential questions as to *how* and *under what conditions* action appears. The present chapter thus explores these questions and, most specifically, what Miller calls "the problem of history"—that is, "How is action disclosed to us?" (PH 67).

The account of action now moves in the direction of the practical, the concrete, and the symbolic. The midworld of symbols has been designated as the embodiment of action. In the midworld, action is revealed as function. In the symbol, *doing* and *thinking* are united in such a way that the midworld becomes the source of not just local-control but also self-control in the mode of reflective and responsible authority.

Section 3.1 will address the disclosure of autonomous action amid the forces of empirical circumstance. This discussion provides an opportunity for elaborating on conclusions, in chapter 2, regarding pure action and form. Sections 3.2 and 3.3 will provide a detailed account of the symbol and the diversity of its modes within the structure of the midworld. To discover action is nothing less than to discover the form of one's world as well as the conditions of its maintenance and revision. The symbol is an object of consciousness and reflection and, as such, a condition of local-control, self-identification, and self-control. These aspects of the midworld are taken up in sections 3.4 and 3.5 where the issues of interpretation and identity are addressed in the context of symbols.

§3.1   SYMBOLIC ENVIRONMENT

In what actions and through what processes is control instanced? An intimate
link has already been established between action and local-control. Action occurs
in a locale, amidst determinate circumstances for which no individual can claim
sole responsibility but with which each person must grapple. The process of definition supposes this situation. This points to a central paradox of actualism—
that is, even as it is instanced in local-control, action also has a fundamental
status. "Let what is considered an act appear as an environed event, and it will
disappear into the circumstances in which it is allegedly found," Miller writes.
"There its autonomy will be nullified" (MS 77).

There are two perspectives at work in actualism. Actualism dismisses
romantic hubris and locates action in the context of local-control. Actualism also
proposes that the act is unique, unenvironed, and radical. This tension is neither
accidental nor unproductive. On the contrary, it highlights the problem of history and what Miller terms "the problem of ethics"—that is, How is an act possible? (MP 12:14). The union of the absolute and finite is constitutive of the
authority exercised in action. If they are truly means of autonomous action, the
categories must be more than products of physical reflex and behavioral conditioning. It is equally true that if one is free with respect to these governing categories they cannot be so absolute that they exist independent of human deeds.
The two perspectives must be joined. The proper relationship is achieved by recognizing that action and its categories are the *absolute* and *revisable* fabric of experience. The key to bringing these two aspects together is the symbol.

Beginning in *medias res* casts into relief the paradoxical circumstance of the
authoritative act. The idea of action beyond or independent of any environment lapses into nonsense; the act is made so much, it becomes so authoritative
that it cannot be located anywhere (MS 89–90; cf. Arendt, 1978, vol. 2, p. 214).
Yet action falls into oblivion when the environment is made absolute; each
action becomes a mere function of a determining state of affairs. One is then
faced with a dilemma.[1]

Miller states that action can be described as either *ontological* or *psychological*
(see §2.1). Ontological action is free, creative, and responsible—that is, the basis of
the active life. Through the generation of teleological categories, it is action that
defines environment. Psychological action is the exact opposite—that is, those
behaviors determined and caused (in the efficient sense) by their circumstances.
Psychology, according to Miller's understanding, encompasses efficient causality
in both its material and practical aspects. Determinism can be either wholly physiological, and thus impulsive, or it can transpire through the media of rational

calculations and hypothetical imperatives (see MP 21:1). Both behaviorism and pragmatism fall under the heading of *psychological*.

This distinction establishes the possibility of autonomy by preventing psychology from consuming ontology. It shuts the door to behaviorism as a complete theory of human action. Any philosophy developing the autonomous character of human agency, and its ethical and political implications, must make this or a quite similar distinction. Unfortunately the distinction itself is problematic. The difficulties engendered by Kant's radical separation of noumenal from phenomenal—for example, in his moral philosophy, the pure will from its motivational factors—suggest that, if enforced absolutely, this separation isolates action from its psychological circumstances. Autonomy and its categories would then exist apart, neither influenced by nor influencing the mundane world over which psychology holds sway.

Nothing is gained, but rather much lost by denying the fact that any given act is mixed with psychological factors. Miller does not attempt such a denial (MP 13:11).[2] Every act is performed by a person with a name, chronology, and daily itinerary reflecting the impinging pressures of circumstance. There is no experience of action-in-itself even if, as in chapter 2, it can be articulated formally. There are only individual acts.

In order to redescribe this tension between the two perspectives, one needs to develop a more complex sense of *environment*. There must be a full recognition of environing conditions and not just a consideration of the material relations presupposed by the behaviorist (DP 90–98). An *environment* in which one simply reacts to stimuli is hardly an environment. It is certainly not a *human* environment. For an environment is a repository of distinctions—that is, a result of control and a source of further control. It is a set of circumstances and distinctions available to conscious thought and thus exceeds any sense of environment based on mere conditioning. Environment, then, is not just a set of impinging forces but also a result of definition. This is Miller's sense of environment—that is, an environment with an actual and historical ontology.

A historical and formal environment need not deny the physical and psychological pressures outlined by behaviorism. Purely psychological explanations, by contrast, seize the whole field and deny any place to the opposition. "So," Miller writes, "there is the dilemma":

> What controls action seems to be impulse and calculation, and these seem to determine an act in its particularity, in its place and time; on the other side history seems more than impulse and calculation, neither fragmentary as an impulse, nor subjectively practical like calculation. History seems more than the vagrancy of nature or the calculations that secure a personal

desire. It seems rather to have a style of its own, a career apart from psychology whether chaotic or intelligent. (MP 13:11)

While Miller accepts the importance of psychology, he also proposes that "all acts with psychology have a disinterested ingredient" (MP 13:11). The suggestion is that psychological and ontological action are dialectically related such that, far from denying the existence of its opposite, each actually presupposes its contrary.

A dialectical account of these two modes of action relies on the development of the distinction between efficient causality and teleology presented in section 2.4. Psychological action concerns efficient causality instanced in either physiological impulses or rational calculations. Miller's claim is that no action is wholly explained by either calculation or transference of motion. Rather "there is, or appears to be, the steadying influence of a situation launching the calculation or even the impulse" (MP 13:11). The shot called in a game of billiards, for instance, supposes gravity. The criminal act comes to fruition only in the context of prevailing ethical principles and legal institutions. Neither gravity nor legality is the efficient cause of the event. The more proximate cause is the stroke of the cue or the drug habit that produced criminal compulsions. Ask the barroom observer or police officer and he will say as much. Yet gravity and law have their respective causal roles. This comes to light when one realizes that the very character of the events described is lost when addressed solely in terms of efficient causality—the game of billiards becomes a comic adventure, the crime cannot even be proposed.

The steadying influence in these situations is properly called teleological—that is, it provides form, organization, and career to particulars.[3] The influence brought to bear by a category such as gravity or law is evidenced in how it shapes the actual environment and guides the disclosure of individual acts. Teleology concerns environing controls and thus purposes in a generic sense. "The teleological occurs in activities that serve no purpose," Miller writes. "These are pure activities. . . . They are the form of all special and purposive activities" (MS 174). (Form, as Stephen Tyman notes, is the ground of action [1993, p. 19].) The paradox is that the observations and even instrumental measurements defining gravity are themselves purposeless in an efficient sense. So too the declaration of a law is purposeless. Each is purposeless precisely because such environment-proposing actions achieve no particular purpose, are uninterested in altering a determinate state of affairs. These actions pertain to the direction of the whole in which determinate states of affairs find their place (MP 9:6). Categories are, finally, psychologically purposeless while being willful or ontologically purposeful (DT 188; see PC 181; cf. Arendt, 1978, p. 150).[4] The two sorts of action are complementary and interdependent.

The relationship between the psychological and ontological is more complex than this sketch of the dialectical relation suggests. Obviously the ontological factors of gravity and law do not burst into the world whole and pure as Athena from the mind of Zeus. There are no actions marked *pure* and others stamped as *psychological*. Beginning in *medias res* one is amid a process of attaining and maintaining local-control. Thus while at this point in history, gravity and law function as seemingly abstract universals guiding local situations, the original appearance and growth of these categories must have been quite different: The universal element arose out of particular essays at local-control laden with psychological factors. The growth of the ontological is provoked by the overabundance of the psychological that, unruly and inarticulate, does not as yet constitute an orderly environment but everywhere impinges in a vaguely threatening manner. Local-control is an attempt at organizing these psychological pressures.

The psychological is an unavoidable point of departure and constant foil for one's essays at control. This dialectical relationship is one in which the human *response* to psychological pressures cannot itself be merely psychological. Human action builds on instinctual behavior. As noted in section 2.4, a person learns more than content, more than the patterns of sense data habitually accompanying danger or pleasure. Buffeted by content, a person responds structurally—organizing classes of cases and fields of possibilities under a single symbol. The act can be no mere response, no reply in kind. "What is free and original is necessarily not to be accounted for through a specific occasion," Miller clarifies. "That occasion will always be there, but only as occasion, never as explanation. Originality quickly shows this by going beyond the occasion that served to propose its necessity" (PH 189).

The break from psychology is basic to action but it is certainly not instantaneous and it is never complete. There is no immediate recognition of the ontological import of an action. The difference can only be found over time, in the historical process. The implication is that "the actual is enacted before it is identified" (TO 406). In one's essays at local-control there is at first only a "lurking association" with the teleological element (MP 28:1). As Miller states, impulse already expresses an unconscious form of will (MP 19:11). The first proposal of a unique measure, a law, or, as Galileo Galilei noted in his *Letters on Sunspots*, the existence of an as-yet-inarticulate force such as "the physical inclination" of bodies to "some motion" (1613/1956, p. 113)—is always almost ignorant of that larger association. The drive is practical and the aims—although implicitly structural and potentially universal—adamantly local. Psychology appears predominant. Yet, unnoticed, what can be called a *metaphorical* transformation has taken place. The psychological backdrop of forces and material pressures has been creatively transposed into terms for which there are no psychological equivalents. Indeed there are no *terms, universals,* or *orders* in pure psychology (PC 113).[5]

The first step in this process is made in the very act of engaging—whether in gesture, fabrication, or speech—one's environment. The continuum of symbolic action begins with this immediacy, this action (MS 119): in seeing the sky becomes *blue,* and distinct from the *green* sea; in measuring the horse stands twenty *hands,* and may not be mounted without assistance by a person who is just four and a half *feet;* the act of constructing *home* is established in walls, roof, and hearth. Examples could be indefinitely multiplied. There is nothing in the world exactly like human language, gesture, or fabrication. Miller often refers to utterance—in all its forms, but most especially language—as magical, poetic, and, indeed, passionate (MS 66–75; RPR).[6] In the act of metaphorical transformation one discovers that the word or gesture is not *about* anything. Rather it is the spontaneous *coming into being of something* (PH 129; PC 177). As Miller remarks, "[A]ll languages, including science, are works of the imagination, i.e., the disclosure of infinities in the ordering of the actual" (PL 807). This is nothing other than the process of definition. All those acts are a fund of articulate action establishing order in what are by now *dead* metaphors and further offering a boundless source for interpretation (see §3.4).

In the very simplest acts of doing and saying a symbolic form of organization appears that has no psychological equivalent but is continuous with the psychological environment insofar as it establishes environment-defining terms. It is the advent of what Miller calls "non-analogous" forms of order (PH 133). It is nothing less than the radical transformation—indeed the birth—of environment.

The transition, the actual break between psychology and ontology does not occur in the act itself. The word, gesture, or fabrication—all examples of utterance—is the condition. The true difference is realized only in a historical moment, in the apprehension of the past as a present factor of control:

> But I affirm further that none of these acts is properly historical [i.e., autonomous] until it has been reflected upon after it has been done. History needs the historian. Not until a later act is directed toward disinterestedness by an earlier one is the earlier act part of history. But this permits the psychological act to enter history in so far as the historian discovers the non-psychological conditions of the psychological act. This seems to me to be a very important part of history. It is enormously useful in disclosing the organizations of will apropos of which the psychological occurs. The absolute must first appear in its unrecognized particular interpretation. It cannot be original. (MP 13:11)

The process by which the ontological or properly historical element of action is disclosed via reflection on past events reveals the "immanence of history," the vision latent in our initial blindness (RMF 29).[7] In reflecting on earlier essays at local-control, consciously employing newly coined organizational terms such as *gravity* and *right*, and then establishing further modes of organization on their basis, these forms of order are lifted out of their psychological circumstance, are brought before consciousness, and become formal.[8] They are not caused, in the efficient sense, by the psychological environment. (The latent order of the spontaneous gesture is enlisted in the service of disciplining the disorderly force of that original act; the spontaneous produces its own organization, and its own nemesis [RMF 26].) It is a decisive moment. The historical action achieves what can be called *symbolic import*—that is, not a function of circumstance but an articulate vehicle for organizing experience. It is a historical achievement.[9]

For persons the psychological environment is not the primary environment of action. There is no naïve, immediate intuition of data (MP 10:3), and no action could even be proposed in response to such "data." Action is organized by formal controls and cannot precede such controls (DP 139).[10] A person's first *response*, if it can be called such, is directed toward those general factors of control, of which gravity, law, and space are examples. Better put, he establishes the capacity for responding in the psychological sense via a teleological category embodied in a symbol. Miller remarks:

> All action occurs apropos of this midworld. It is a control in terms of what has been uttered, a number, word, line, a temple to Athena or to Notre Dame. In cognition, order has no vehicle. That is why it is not found there. So, to be simple, I emphasize yardsticks and clocks. They are verbal, not substantive. You handle a yardstick, you tell a tale, you tell time. But you do not "react" to a yardstick unless someone uses it as a weapon, and then it has lost its status and functioning authority, as a commanding and momentous present. (MS 18)

The midworld of which Miller writes is a realm of symbolic control. The midworld contains no stimuli. Symbols guide action insofar as they demand a "total response," nothing less than the recognition of environment as such (MP 17:23). That recognition is the unavoidable starting place of all determinate action. For action without, or irrespective of, order is *no action at all*.

Ontology is moribund without the provocation of psychology and content is chaos without symbol. Yet the immediate environment of action (and not behavior) is symbolic. That is to say, along with Ernest Cassirer, that the human being is an *animal symbolicum* (1962, p. 26).

Here the *constitutional* becomes equivalent to *responsibility*, an active and thoughtful involvement with one's circumstance (PC 73). A robust concept of action requires just this type of responsibility. Symbols are nothing other than those disinterested factors of control developed via the original metaphorical efficacy of action (see §3.4). Action transpires, then, in terms of *prior acts* and develops in accordance with its *own rules*. Miller's conception of action thus incorporates the qualities that define the active political life but spreads them across a whole range of acts including labor and fabrication (cf. Fell, 1990, p. 27).

§3.2   SIGNS AND SYMBOLS

Miller considered his treatment of the midworld to be his primary accomplishment. Writing in the late 1960s he remarked regarding the midworld: "That is my contribution to philosophy" (PL 13). In this respect Miller, often modest in assessing his achievements, was an accurate judge of his own work.[11] For the midworld is the key to his main philosophical projects. His novel development of ontological and epistemological issues at play in the debate between realists and idealists is achieved via the midworld. The midworld is also a principal resource for clarifying the status of democratic practices and institutions. The midworld is certainly the cornerstone of the actualist project uniting authority and finitude. Thus the midworld is not only crucial in interpreting the political consequences of actualism but is also an important element in the reconciliation of the active and contemplative lives. It is the philosophical means for revealing the authority of finitude, and thus retrieving the active life.

Actualism proposes that there is a *mid-world*, a sphere neither described by the pure intelligence of the knowing subject nor the pure materiality of the known object. Its place is found, to briefly rehearse the matter of section 2.1, in the incapacities of the dyadic model of mind and matter, knower and known. The need is explicitly ontological (DP 160), for the dyadic model of epistemic philosophy is rife with ontological assumptions. "Cognition needed a basis, which it could not supply from its own resources," Miller observes in a comment that could equally apply to sensation. "That basis occurs in the repudiation itself; in an action. The noncognitive basis of cognition is the act." He continues:

> The act, consequently, had to meet two conditions: it had to be noncognitive in status, never come upon by seekers of knowledge, and it had also to be the source and control of all cognition. I had to say that no act will be found among things known, agreeing in this with the view resulting from natural science, from which all verbs have been exorcised. And I had to agree with the psychology of the "stream of consciousness," where there was neither act nor knowledge. After all, is a bit odd to say that one does not

"find" or come upon what one could not possibly come upon on cognitive premises. (MS 11–12; cf. James, 1890)

If these two generally accepted *worlds* are incapable of establishing themselves there is a need for a "third world." That third world is action, utterance, and gesture—*res gestae*—of which the midworld is the embodiment.

The midworld is actual. It constitutes the relationship between intellect and matter.[12] Intellect and matter are among a class of primary distinctions made possible but also required by action. Working in the other direction, generating action from the distinct elements of intellect and matter, fails. Pure cognition or pure matter has no need for action just as it has no need of its opposite. The midworld is best understood as being integral to and generative of *the* world. "This functioning actuality is what I call—lacking a better term—the Mid-World," Miller states. "It is neither subjective nor objective but the basis of that distinction and all other constitutional distinctions" (MP 17:15). The midworld of action is the possibility and actuality of articulate knowledge, emotion, and sensation.

Action in its symbolic form establishes order via the restriction of content (FI 263). Action is always alongside and in relationship with things; the only world of experience is this interchange between action and things—that is, the process of definition (MS 12). The midworld considered *as a whole* encompasses this process. One cannot look for action in and of itself. To do so would be to treat action as a cognitive object, something Miller expressly denies is possible. Given this, one can understand that when he addresses the midworld as an actual symbolic medium, Miller is engaging in abstraction. He does not suppose that one can have action without the region of distinctions it generates—that is, the signs of nature and the world of common sense. He also does not think that action is possible without what can be called its auxiliary semiotic vehicles—that is, functional objects such as tools and machines (see §3.3). As a *philosophical notion*, however, the midworld temporarily isolates that which establishes the environment from the very environment it defines.

What, then, are those objects that are not objects of cognition but control cognition? They are functioning objects. They are utterances, embodiments, which determine what is known. They are actualities, not realities or appearances. . . .

To such functioning objects I gave a name. It was the "midworld." The midworld meets the two conditions [noted above, MS 11–12]: it is not cognitive, and it launches, spurs, and controls all cognition. It is actual. It is not "real." It is not "apparent." *Unenvironed, it projects the environment.* (MS 12–13)

In the concept of *the midworld*, the authority of action is distinguished in a way alien to common experience. The midworld proper is control-in-principle and includes those symbolic vehicles—especially the body and functioning objects—embodying such control (TS 17). It is a distinct aspect of the ongoing process of maintaining local-control. Taken as a whole, that process does not appear as *control-in-principle* alone but always active, embodied *control-in-fact*.

The midworld is a peculiar concept. It is complex and interestingly vague when considered, as above, in light of the pragmatic question of control. It is equally ambiguous when one inquires as to the ontological standing of the midworld and its symbols. At one level the midworld is a philosophical *notion* clarifying epistemological, ethical, and ontological problems via the symbolic element. In this sense it is a metaphysical term, a vehicle for generic articulation and abstract reflection. Yet as a class of embodied symbols the midworld is also a *fact of experience*. Symbolic objects such as yardsticks are picked up, referred to, and employed in making decisions every day. The midworld is a class of mundane things—beginning with the body and including everyday objects, institutions, and practices. Because of this symbols remain obscure, confused with objects or mere artifacts. Their dual status as signs and symbols makes this inevitable—for example, the yardstick is a symbol but is also made of a particular wood, of a particular color and grain, and is stamped with specific marks (all signs).[13] The midworld proper is not a class of objects. A critical distinction of Miller's must be reinforced: Not all objects function as symbolic objects. An atom, for instance, is a symbolic object while a stone in a wall or piece of coal in a mine is not. A yardstick is a functioning object while a blender is not. The symbol is set apart by the way it implies a universal form of organization—for example, an atomic theory of matter and uniform space, respectively. As Miller writes regarding a voucher (a functioning object):

> There is no special "object" or group of objects that act as a voucher, i.e., no "class" of objects. The reason: 1) a voucher is no "object," but determines objects; 2) any object can become a voucher by becoming a determiner of objects. (MP 20:7)

The difference between symbolic objects and other objects is not registered in terms of those distinctions available among physical objects. In physical terms a stone is very different than a blender. Yet no possible difference between them could establish a distinction equal to that existing between them both and the yardstick. The stone and blender are defined objects. The yardstick, by contrast, is not an object defined by action but is *action itself*. "Such functioning artifacts define the environment," Miller states, "but are not objects in a prior environment" (MS 72). If one treats a yardstick or The Declaration of Independence as a thing *in the world* and not as a symbol *projecting a world*—that is, if a symbol is reduced to its significant traits—it becomes elusive. Hidden under its signifying capacity, a symbol is easily mistaken for a piece of wood useful for propping up a window or a bit of scratch paper for a shopping list.

The symbolic object is not an *object* in the ordinary sense of that word. As Vincent Colapietro writes, "What [Miller] calls functioning objects are not foci of attention but loci of control" (1990, p. 79). This is the basic distinction between signs and symbols. Symbols are the embodiment and extension of function and order. The midworld relocates the factors of ontology and authority in objects and institutions. Authority is embodied and accessible to reflection—that is, the self-consciousness that is the signature of autonomy.

The distinction between signs and symbols bears on authority and self-control (DT 186).[14] The distinction is suggested in the course of *The Definition of the Thing* where Miller marks a separation between indicative and expressive signs (DT 71). That distinction is refined and presented as a difference between object signs and expressive signs or symbols. In each case the important difference is that symbols, in contrast to signs, "refer" to something nonparticular (TS 16; DT 171–75). (The very sense of *reference* here is unusual.) Signs, by contrast, are exclusively indicative. Object signs, of which there are two types, point to things in their specificity; they lead one directly to content (see fig. 3.1). They are denotative and their usage is exhausted by reference. Object signs are what Charles S. Peirce referred to as signs of existents, *sinsigns* (1903/1998, p. 291).

Figure 3.1   Signs

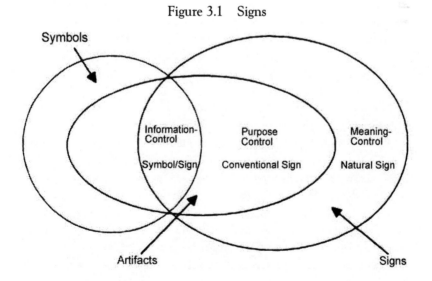

The first type of sign exhibits what Miller refers to as "meaning control" (TS 2–4). These are signs, primarily natural, that establish the meaning of a certain thing by means of various observational, taxonomic, and functional descriptions. If one experiences the signs *cold, rigid, translucent,* and *prone to melting under certain thermal conditions,* then one has a preliminary definition of *ice.* If one has an adequate definition of *fire* then the smoke seen on the horizon will lead to the belief that there is a fire occurring somewhere just out of sight. Meaning-control is synonymous with the defining traits of a thing (MP 17:1).

The second type of object sign exemplifies "purpose control" (TS 7–8). Among such objects are milestones, traffic lights, windsocks, harbor buoys, and direction flags. Although they are also describable in terms of meaning-control (i.e., their physical characteristics), signs of purpose-control are different in that they are properly defined by convention and how they function to provide direction in a more encompassing set of purposes and modes of communication. The examples just noted are conventions of land, sea, and air travel. Unlike meaning-control, the signs of purpose-control do not change with their environment in an indexical fashion. When certain signs of meaning-control shift from *rigid* to *viscous* and *cold* to *cool,* then one understands that the state of the water has changed from frozen to liquid. In the case of purpose-control the signs are stable, and whether and how the signs indicate depends on the care or neglect of persons. (The windsock and direction flags may continue indicating that the wind is right and the runway clear for landing, for example, but the airstrip may have been abandoned for decades and the runway extremely hazardous for landing.) Purpose-control thus can be misleading. What both meaning- and purpose-control have in common is that they indicate states of affairs, natural or conventional (MP 4:10).

In contrast to object signs, expressive signs "refer" to something *nonparticular* (TS 16; DT 171–75). At most they are vague forms of indication. Indeed the word *indication* is an inappropriate way of addressing their function. Expressive signs do not point to objects; they *declare* the terms for the organization of objects (MS 8, 185). Peirce's law-giving signs or *legisigns*—also referred to, in a different mode, as symbols—are close equivalents to what Miller intends (Peirce, 1903/1998, p. 291).

Rather than being the equivalent of an ostensive gesture and statement such as *This is hot!, It is five o'clock,* or *That is a crime,* an expressive sign would be the body feeling the flame, the clock by which the time is told, or the declared law establishing the criminality of the act. This organizing factor is symbolic. Instead of denoting particular objects, symbols establish what Miller refers to as "an indeterminate region" (MS 158–59), an ideal and infinite form of order. Expressive signs are conditions for the possibility of the disclosure of data. Therein lies their priority. In disclosed regions, signs function according to the terms of relation established by symbols such that even the simplest act of ostensive reference is dependent on the organizational function of symbols (MP 14:12). "The sign must declare what order it appeals to" (MS 158), Miller states, but symbols can only appeal to themselves. Symbols are their own rule; they are self-legislating (MP 26:8).

This basic division of object signs from expressive signs requires a further refinement. There is a third type of sign (alluded to above) and a third form of indication (information-control). While saying that expressive signs declare the form of environment in which object signs appear is essentially accurate, this sharp distinction is not adequate to all forms of semiotic activity. If one considers semiotic activity to be either indicative *or* expressive, one would lose some objects highly important to symbolic control—for example, barometers, thermometers, voltmeters. These objects are not just declarative. They are also *indexical* and thus as responsive to environmental changes as are signs of meaning-control. Such objects are a mixture of the symbolic and significant functions.

Signs of information-control (TS 4–7), such as thermometers, indicate states of affairs. They register conditions that the basic functioning of the body (the first symbol) has already disclosed in a rudimentary fashion. What distinguishes information-control from meaning-control is the heightened level of articulation achieved by the artifactual transformation of the bodily articulated signs of meaning-control into a distinct, and more precise, order of signs. Bodily sensations of heat or chill, for example, are transformed into the rising and falling of a column of mercury. The height of a column of mercury becomes temperature proper and, with usage, serves as a control for one's bodily sensations. (For example, a person stands before a thermometer and says, *Oh, it feels hotter than that.* If he is confident in the integrity of the instrument then he seeks out other reasons for the discrepancy between the thermometer reading and his bodily sensations—e.g., perhaps he is too heavily clothed or has a fever.) Objects such as thermometers reflect "the conscious discovery" of object signs that "lifts meaningful perception out of the accidental and casual" (TS 6). They revise a person's primary relationship to the natural environment and, indeed, revise his conception of the original symbol, the body.

Signs of information-control are different in their function from what are referred to here as *pure symbols* (e.g., yardsticks). A thermometer unites symbolic and significant functions. (For this reason it will be referred to, within the sphere of symbols, as an *indexical* symbol.) Via the thermometer one witnesses the dialectic occurring more generally between all symbols and signs. There are neither signs nor states of affairs without symbols. Yet the denotative function of the sign is a necessary element in the structure of the midworld. No form achieves itself; disclosure is a null concept without indication. In their manner, object signs are also constitutional factors. "A sign must appeal to some universe of discourse or to some type of order," Miller states by way of clarification. "But signs themselves have no special order. The order of signs is order in principle, the structure of the necessary" (MS 158). The body and action know nothing about themselves—their possibilities and limitations—until there are data. The symbolic import of one's natural and practical functions is clarified and revised via the data disclosed by symbols. The distinction between symbol and sign is radical, and yet it is a distinction that is only achieved in dialectical interaction.

This clarification of the status of signs provides a good preliminary account of the symbol and its function. Unlike the sign, which is an aspect of a state of affairs, the symbol *formally establishes a world*. A world is a formal, teleological, and systematic organization that is incomprehensible in terms of bare data—that is, no world at all and, by definitional relation, no data either. That is why, even as one recognizes the necessary role played by signs, the symbol is the crux of the midworld. The symbol, by restricting content, establishes specific forms of order. More than that, the symbol "forces attention to its use and its user" (MP 14:13). Miller writes:

> I borrow now from Hegel and from Royce. The easiest approach comes from Royce, I think. It is his doctrine of "signs." I would prefer to use the word "symbol." A symbol is an object. A yardstick, a spoken word. These words are all objects. But they are objects *which nature cannot produce*. They are "expressive." They are objectified thought. They lead to the original of the portrait. (PC 60; see DP 152–62)[15]

The symbol is "the objectified act" (PH 185). The symbol not only projects an orderly environment of distinctions but also refers back to the *action* and the *person* who undertook the action (MP 10:3). The midworld is the implication of authoritative acts, and symbols are the vehicles of human control and will (MP 17:23). Human authority and its modes are clarified in terms of the symbol. An understanding of the midworld makes "man at home in the world" by revealing the stake each person has in the world (PC 117).

§3.3   SYMBOLS AND ARTIFACTS

The symbol projects an indefinite field of control.[16] But a singular symbol, or a singular type of order, only provides a very limited sense of control. The midworld, although a *singular* symbolically organized region, contains a *plurality* of developing orders.[17] This plurality is accounted for by the variety of the types of symbols, the manifold of actual symbols, and the variety of specific signs. Particular orders declared by individual symbols produce further, and indefinite, gradations of order. "This domain is, despite its infinity, constitutionally incomplete," Colapietro writes, "and, despite its incompleteness, totally inclusive" (2003, p. 101).

The midworld and its categories project both an *ideal* and *articulate* infinity (PC 116), and it is described as an ongoing process of *definition* always aiming at an increasingly detailed and nuanced description of the world. The trajectory of the midworld is toward the greatest amount of detail. In a philosophical account of the midworld much of that detail must be foregone. The task of clarifying such orders is immense and must often be left to, amongst others, historians, sociologists, and political scientists who are experts in particular fields and locales of control. What can be achieved here is an outline of the structure of relations constituting the symbolic region of the midworld and the field of action.[18] Those structures and their relations represent the generic means for attaining detailed control in any given locale.

The symbol, "the object which embodies a power which objectifies a will" (MP 17:23), is the master concept of the midworld. Thus the symbolic sphere has been referred to as the midworld *proper* and distinguished from the spheres of signs and artifacts (see fig. 3.2). All signs, as well as artifacts, display the symbolic structure of the midworld. None of the three classes—that is, symbols, artifacts, signs—exhausts another and none completely excludes another either (see fig. 3.5). Here, attention will be focused on the symbolic and artifactual

Figure 3.2 Symbols (Midworld proper)

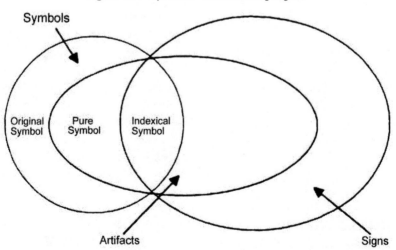

spheres. There are three types of symbols: the original, the pure, and the index-ical (see MP 14:12; MS 154–55). While both pure and indexical symbols share characteristics with artifacts, only indexical symbols share important traits with signs. Unlike pure and indexical symbols, the original symbol is distinct from both the artifactual and significant sphere.

Taking each in turn, one begins with the *original symbol* (see DT 150; cf. Hocking, 1928):

> The original symbol is the body and its organs. Unless one stands off from one's body and alleges a disembodied mode of experience, one cannot quite objectify the body. It is the original instrument and actuality of ex-perience. The body is not a physical body or object, but the condition of all knowledge of bodies. It is not known as body *directly*, but only as part of a region to which it belongs and with which it is continuous. (MS 155)

> The basic functioning object is the body, not a body, but the body. The body is not an object among all other objects. How would one set about finding *the* body? It is an immediacy. It is the immediacy of func-tion. Even the distinction of seeing and hearing depends on action. . . . The body is the functioning center of all declared environment, yet it is not isolated but continuous with air, light, and ground for walking. Func-tioning discovers its environment as it discovers itself. Neither is separa-ble from the other. (MS 43–44)

Just as the body situates a person in history and in a definite locale, the body establishes one in the semiotic process. The body is the original vehicle for the organization of experience. It is a radical actuality (MS 46). It is action and the very possibility of ordered experience.[19] The eye defines the visible and the ear defines the auditory. Through these organs, the most original and natural form of actual utterance is achieved—that is, the metaphorical transformation of bare possibility into order and significance. The eye, for example, establishes the visual world by its very activity. The terms and forms of significance that the eye lends to content are neither extraneous nor accidental; they are the very means for the articulation of experience. As Miller states, "If one completes the sen-tence 'The world is . . .' one has declared an activity, not a perception, as imme-diate and controlling" (MS 81). The body *is* disclosive activity. All other modes of disclosure, and all other vehicles articulating the environment, are dependent on this original and necessary situation (see Fell, 1990, p. 47). By contrast, the yard-stick or clock, while necessary with respect to the form of environment it dis-closes, is not necessary for disclosure as such.

This connection between *originality* and *naturality* should not be mis-understood. The body, although in a sense natural, should not be confused with other natural bodies (see §2.4). For it is the body that declares the very terms of organization that define bodies. The terms of definition provided by the body can be turned back toward itself and describe its own physical aspect. As the origin of those categories, however, *the* body is not reducible to a simple object. It is the functioning center of all environments, including any environment that might come to define the body itself (MS 44). As Miller notes, "Intellectualism nowhere shows its abstraction more plainly than in its attempt to treat the body as *a* body, another object or even as content of consciousness. . . . On this point, it has pretty thoroughly abandoned common sense" (MS 109). Thus Miller refers to the body as the "absolute artifact," and states that it is the source of all artifacts and symbols (MS 46). All ways of defining the body are reflexive and ultimately presuppose the body as symbol (MS 46).

The second type of symbol that Miller distinguishes is "the constitutional symbol" or "pure artifact," the *pure symbol* (MP 14:12; MS 155). The pure symbol is a product of human artifice and so is different from the body. Because of its status as an artifact, there are a great variety of pure symbols and no way to delimit the contents of the class. Miller provides many examples of pure symbols. Words and language are pure symbols. So too are numbers. Coins, yardsticks, and clocks provide more tangible examples.[20] Such things as documents (e.g., the Declaration of Independence), institutions (e.g., congresses and assemblies) and regularized practices or formalities (e.g., *Robert's Rules of Order*), if less obviously symbolic objects, are also examples in that they are "the functioning vehicles of our enduring energies" (MS 86). (Indeed, Miller compares the organizational function of the yardstick to that of the Constitution [DP 157].) What unites this diverse array and makes them all pure symbols is that they exist properly in action and use.

There are, in addition, two subclasses of pure symbols. One subclass includes works of art and monuments which Miller refers to as "imaginative objects" (MP 18:7; cf. Elias, 1990).[21] Regarding works of art, Miller writes:

> There are also artifacts of an individual sort. A work of art is that. What reflective emotion may be is not otherwise to be discovered. Take away art, and one is as impoverished about man as one would be about nature if one destroyed all yardsticks. (MS 189)

> There is art because without art, including the painting-art, there is no way of asserting and proclaiming the relations of non-aesthetic modes of order to the will. The order of man and nature must be not merely understood or even acted out habitually; it must be identified explicitly, and held before us for contemplation. No essential mode of order attains existence until it is so embodied in the symbol. Then, as a mode of order, it enters into will. Art is the reminder of every attained mode of organization to which man is committed, and through which he defines himself. (PC 167)

The monument is like the work of art in being an *individual* symbol. This distinguishes artistic objects from symbols such as yardsticks. The work of art is necessarily unique.[22] Yardsticks, by contrast, lend themselves to, and even require, duplication. Unlike works of art, each of the millions of yardsticks that lay in desk drawers around the world is itself *the* yardstick. No one speaks of having a copy or reproduction of a yardstick. In these respects, there is a distinction between the two symbolic modes.

The larger import of this distinction is most readily understood in terms of universality—the universality of the pure symbol proper and the particularity of the imaginative object. This difference is shown in the forms of disclosure that functioning and imaginative objects make possible. Monuments and works of art embody and reflect orders organizing experience. They *appeal* to symbolic order. Unlike most functioning objects, imaginative objects such as the Washington Monument or Diego Velásquez' "The Ladies in Waiting" *do not apply an order*. What they do is present formal order for conscious apprehension and reflection. Monuments and works of art are also emotional. They show one's "stake" in, and thus attachment to, "the modes of order of which the articulate world is composed" (MP 4:10; see PH 82).[23] They place us before ourselves by highlighting the orders and narratives by which we live (see Bradford, 1997). Notre Dame de Chartres achieves this by symbolizing the mind of Gothic Christendom while the national cathedral in Washington, D.C. (formed by the nave, transept, and monuments of the Mall), attains this effect by symbolizing the American mind. Both declare cultural, social, moral, and political space. In the realm of the arts, one could say that the literature of Toni Morrison and the painting of Winslow Homer perform this symbolic function vis-à-vis American society. Imaginative objects can be both exhortative and critical, highlighting one's commitment to prevailing modes of order even while revealing the overlooked, and possibly vicious, features of these orders (CB 5-6). If society is, as Miller states echoing Josiah Royce, "a community of symbolic power" (MP 14:13), then it is partly through its monuments and works of art that individuals come to terms with the import and fateful consequences of those powers.

In this way philosophical practice and philosophical literature have an imaginative function—that is, an investigation into forms of order and a spur to the sort of self-reflection that is part of autonomy (see DT 11-37; MS 59-65; cf. Strout, 1990).[24]

The second subclass of the pure symbol is the *pluralistic object*, the fetish. The fetish is artifactual—for example, a totem, a ring, an incantation—and is an element of power (DT 189). The fetish is a degenerate symbol, however. "The symbol is power," Miller states, but the "fetish is overpowering" (MP 26:8). The fetish is not a vehicle for maintaining and furthering a person's authority. It is itself an authority, unique and potentially terrifying in its independent power. The fetish is like the imaginative object in its individuality. Unlike a work of art, however, a fetish does not disclose the real but is itself real (MP 19:14). Thus it is *pluralistic*: It does not universalize but rather particularizes authority. (If the totem is damaged, for example, the gods forsake a person's home; no replications will suffice because the power was never her own.) The fetish is neither employed nor is it declared. One is its servant. It is a concealed form of human will, a primal objectification of order and power (MP 21:1; see DT 198). "Primitivism shows experience not in charge of itself," Miller writes, "and so not yet artifactual" (PC 157; see PH 1–2 1950–51, 8–9; MP 24:22).

While the status of the fetish can be elucidated by anthropological considerations, and there is a sense in which the fetish is a specifically *primitive* form of power, all symbolic modes of controlled power can be treated as idols. The power in the fetish is primal, but any relative historical advancement does not spare one from confronting the basic power in the symbol. Indeed any symbol that is not self-critical and expansive becomes, de facto, an idol. This is true whether addressing the fetishes of the Guatemalan Indios or the Dow Jones Industrial Average. The distinction is thus semiotic and not anthropological in its basis.

The third division within the symbolic sphere is that of *indexical symbols*. Indexical symbols are situated at the intersection of symbols, artifacts, and signs; they correspond to what was addressed in section 3.2 as instruments of information-control. These functioning objects have both a symbolic and significant capacity, and thus make room for thermometers and barometers within the larger class of symbols. They bridge the gap between symbol and sign.

The symbolic region has three main divisions—the original, pure, and indexical (see fig. 3.2). Each region has a differing relationship to the other two spheres composing the midworld as a whole. The degree to which each region overlaps—or, in the case of the original symbol, does not overlap—with the other spheres indicates something important about the character of that type of symbol. Yet the distinctions made for schematic purposes should not obscure the basic priority of the symbol. Strictly speaking, the spheres of artifacts and signs remain under the rule of symbols.

Because the symbolic sphere encompasses a major portion of the artifactual sphere, this account already describes much of the region of artifacts (see fig. 3.3). Of the four distinct types of artifacts, three have been accounted for in terms of their role in the symbolic sphere: functioning objects (pure and indexical symbols), imaginative objects (reflective pure symbols), and pluralistic objects (degenerate pure symbols). Stressing the artifactual character of these symbols is critical. The production of symbols marks the transition from nature to history, and thus shows fabrication to be not only a mode of action but also an activity open to philosophical reflection. In the artifact persons express themselves and, further, come to consciously guide their actions by their own expressions (PC 124–25). It is in this vein that the fourth type of artifact, the *functional object*, is to be understood. The functional object also moves toward history and self-consciousness. Even if its ontological implications are not as important as are those of symbolic functioning objects, the functional object is connected with the disclosive function of symbols.

The complexity of the distinction between *functioning* and *functional* objects is owing to the fact that the functioning artifact and the functional artifact have much in common (MS 127–43; MP 28:1). The tool is also a vehicle for discovery and cognition; it reveals qualities of the world and provides access to the world in novel ways. Like a functioning object, it is not a natural object in the world. The difference between these two types of artifacts, however, cannot be overlooked.

The distinction is figuratively represented in how the class of functioning objects is wholly encompassed in the symbolic sphere whereas functional objects are found exclusively amidst signs. Miller states what is at issue in drawing this distinction:

> Just the same, tools require numbers and yardsticks, the nonparticular universal. Functioning objects and functional objects differ as will differs from purpose, the constitutional from the particular, or the structural from the occasional. Hammer, saw, needle are indistinguishable in the order projected by space, all being spatial—substantial, qualified, classified, and so forth. Not so with yardsticks, clocks, words. . . . The disclosures of

Figure 3.3 Artifacts

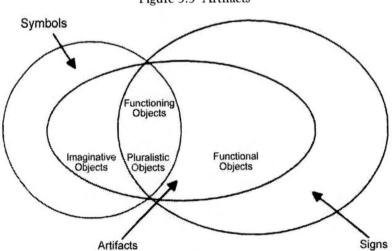

yardsticks and clocks are in terms of a universal; the outcome of hammers is particular. The functioning object yields no "terminating satisfaction"; the functional object accomplishes an end result. (MS 139–40)

The functioning object has an ontological priority because of the universal and structural implications of its use. Putting the matter in other terms, the yardstick "declares" a total environment while the hammer simply "presences" that environment in the specific activity of hammering (MP 28:1; see PC 129). The hammer does not propose the spatial environment but affirms its necessity each time it is extended when striking the head of a nail. In hammering one only admits to an interest in the precise space needed to hammer accurately and effectively. The functional object, then, is defined by its limitation—that is, it is significant not symbolic.

Miller states that "the willful and the purposive are dialectical" (MS 141). The priority of the symbolic functioning objects only occurs in union with functional objects. Via particular purposes carried out with tools and machines, universal forms gain exemplification and continue to grow. "The functioning object is the *formal* constituent of the functional object, which is the content of the actual," Miller writes. "Yardsticks, clocks, words are apropos of purposes, while purposes invoke the universal" (MS 141). If purposes invoke the universal, they also invoke content and those vehicles that clarify content. In that respect, like data, the tool is not incidental but necessary to any point of view (MP 26:11). In its usage, the functional object lets one understand the infinite environment it depends on. Not only that, it can be the starting place for the revision of that very order. So, as Miller writes, "A tool is also an adventure" (MS 139): It is a vehicle for exploration, discovery, and definition (DP 171–72). Indeed, as a concept *tool* is constitutional. One certainly could have an articulate world without a hammer, saw, or printing press. Yet one could not have such a world—that is, any world at all—in the absence of any tool whatsoever (MP 28:1).

Figure 3.4 Equivalencies in the Midworld

Symbol	Artifact	Sign
Original	——	——
Pure	Functioning, Imaginative, & Pluralistic Objects	——
Indexical	Functioning Objects	Information-Control
——	Functional Objects	Purpose-Control
——	——	Meaning-Control

Distinguishing the functional object from the symbolic functioning object not only clarifies the composition of the artifactual sphere but also adds to the definition of the symbolic sphere. As was the case with signs, this distinction does not divide the midworld but, rather, establishes relations among the different spheres and the varying semiotic vehicles operating within them (see fig. 3.4). Functioning objects project form and establish fundamental structures of experience exceeding those basic forms declared by the body. Imaginative and functional objects perform ancillary functions relative to the orders established by functioning objects—imaginative objects remind one of the structures composing a person's world and to which he is so deeply attached; functional objects ramify those structures by invoking them in the context of particular purposes and giving them concrete exemplification. The fourth type of artifact, the degenerate form of symbolism found in the fetish, occults the symbolic power of action rather than revealing it and, thus, shows the employment of symbolic power against itself.

Paying attention to the artifactual sphere as a region also underlines a fundamental distinction in Miller's thought—that is, between *will* and *purpose*. Actualism, like pragmatism, is practically oriented and connects ontology with action. It has already been noted, however, that Miller stresses that his philosophy is not another version of pragmatism. Classical pragmatism is primarily a philosophy of purposes and, thus, of tools. It claims that thought is organized and articulated by the recognition and achievement of short-range ends. Such purposes—for example, driving a nail into a board and building the shelter of a frame house—terminate and produce satisfaction. The pragmatist's leanings are pluralistic and particularistic. That is, the criteria of pragmatism are primarily psychological (PL 743). By placing the tool under the guidance of symbolic orders Miller is claiming that psychology relies on the unnoted influence of universal forms of purpose—that is, will, the utopian element in action (PC 25-26). *These* purposes do not terminate because they are allied with our insatiable need for a moderately orderly world that provides the possibility for meaning and action. Actualism stresses practical needs of a *necessary* sort that are established via symbolic vehicles.

The *midworld* is a field of articulate authority. It is a system of related distinctions and overlapping functions. The conceptual vagueness regarding the status of the thermometer is a perfect example of the complex character of the midworld. At once symbol, artifact, and sign, the thermometer represents different things depending on which of those three aspects one addresses. As a symbol, the thermometer is a formal category, an expression of control-in-principle (i.e., will). As an artifact, the thermometer is an instrument embodying a specific attempt at establishing local-control (i.e., purpose). As a sign, the thermometer tells us something about the world or, even more radically, is an aspect of that very world (i.e., data). In the function of the thermometer one witnesses and comprehends will, practical endeavor, and nature.

These three vocabularies (and spheres) are joined in an orderly unity of trans-latable distinctions. Their basic cohesion is functional, structural, and necessary. Taken as a whole, the midworld is a dialectical interchange between elements of will, purpose, and data. Will, embodied in symbols, is the engine of this process (see fig. 3.5). It is what Miller calls *utterance*, the midworld proper. Without symbols, purposes could not be proposed and data could not be found. But *this priority of symbols is not an independence.* Acts of will do not just accidentally permit or merely abide purposes and data. The will embodied in symbols calls out to data and purposes, and indeed requires them for its own actual achievement. (For example, the body [symbol] can only fully reveal itself if it is implicated with purposes [artifacts] and act-ing with respect to an objective world [signs].) Even as they are ordered according to symbols, then, both artifacts and signs reveal the potentiality and limitation of sym-bols, including the original symbol that is the body and its organs.

§3.4   INTERPRETATION

The midworld is an expression of human authority as well as a vehicle for its extension and elaboration. It is the locus of the active life. Questions remain regarding the constitutional authority of action, however. For while one might imbue action in general with an authoritative and generative force, it is not clear what au-thority is borne by each particular act. The symbolic environment, even as it liberates action from psychological circumstance, can be as inimical to autonomy as the psy-chological environment of the behaviorist. This is a matter of large proportions and an appropriate response will require further development in chapters 4 and 5. The

Figure 3.5 The Midworld

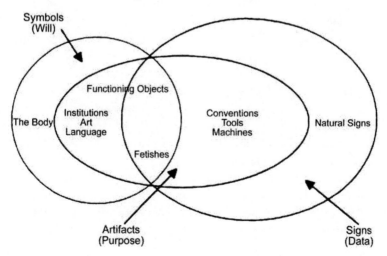

basic actualist rejoinder relies on a consideration of the historical career of action understood as a process of *interpretation*—that is, action that consciously apprehends and amends forms of order and their implications. Interpretation is the structure of all authoritative action; it is also the form of history.

The autonomy of individual actions is found in reconciling discipline and spontaneity (PC 191). The problem of reconciling the two is a version of the dilemma of history that so exercised the Romantic mind. "The new man must feel that he is new, and has not come into the world mortgaged to the opinions and usages of Europe, and Asia, and Egypt," Ralph Waldo Emerson observed in "Literary Ethics" (1838/1983, p. 97). His sense of a proper response to the imposition of the past, its orders, and its authority is proposed in the following sentences:

> If any person has less love of liberty, and less jealousy to guard his integrity, shall he therefore dictate to you and me? Say to such doctors, We are thankful to you, as we are to history, to the pyramids, and the authors; but now our day is come; we have been born out of the eternal silence; and now we will live,—live for ourselves,—and not as pall-bearers of a funeral, but as the upholders and creators of our age. . . . Now that we are here, we will put our own interpretation on things, and our own things for interpretation. Please himself with complaisance who will,—for me, things must take my scale, not I theirs. (1838/1983, p. 97)

The proposals of unchastened Romanticism have been addressed in section 2.4. Yet the concern with liberty and personal integrity evidenced in "Literary Ethics" resonates with Miller's own philosophical interests. There is an obvious difficulty with Emerson's proposal, however. Although one might be "born *out* of the eternal silence" there is no doubt that one is born *into* the noise and tumult of the career of ongoing forms of order. This is the inescapable situation of human being. No one speaks for herself without the need of borrowing terms or relying on the articulate accomplishments of others. This indebtedness is part of the original situation, subsequent only to embodiment. "A rational explanation of our identification with historical processes offers difficulties," Miller observes in a fashion that recalls Martin Heidegger's concept of *throwness*. "We have eased into that intimacy rather than argued our way into it. We find ourselves there" (MP 23:17). The fear of being completely mortgaged to the past cannot cover over the fact that a mortgage of some sort is a condition of one's humanity.

We both desire autonomy and recognize the debt to the past. The specific question is how one reconciles the symbol as discipline—that is, as form, controlling order—with the symbol as spontaneous action and will. How does one find autonomy in history?

Miller himself draws attention to the contrasting moments that compose the difficulty. At times he emphasizes how the person uttering a word or using a yard-stick does not speak for herself but is "possessed" by the order projected by the symbolic and functioning object (MS 114). (For example, the objectivity of science and the justice of law are premised on a situation where the scientist and the judge are not, in fact, speaking for themselves.) At other moments the connection between one's individual actions in the pursuit of local-control and the creation or maintenance of symbolic orders is underlined. Thus the midworld is not only a "great neutrality" (TO 404), but also a region of power, commitment, and identity. The symbol must allow for both of these moments. The symbol is the answer to the question: "What 'order' is consistent with originality?" (PH 7 1951–52, 16). That is to say, the symbol is the basis for processes of interpretation and criticism.

Miller's conception of the symbol relies on Peirce's writings on semiotics as well as latter portions of Royce's *The Problem of Christianity*. Less obvious, but perhaps equally significant, is his positive debt to Suzanne Langer's *Philosophy in a New Key* and his negative debt to Charles Morris's *Foundations of the Theory of Signs*.[25] These resources all form a background for instructive comparison. With this context in mind, two arguments can be made. First, the process of definition, articulated in chapter 2, is recast as a process of critical interpretation based on the symbol. Second, that process of interpretation is developed in terms of the role that metaphor plays therein. On this central issue of authority it might be the concept of *metaphor* that proves most enlightening. Metaphor is basic to the process of interpretation and allows for the originality of historical action as well as for the continuity of ongoing forms of discourse and action.

A metaphysics of finitude begins with the practical activity of searching for, maintaining, and sometimes revising local-control. Action, and not speculation, is the starting place, and action is connected to symbolism. While individual actions seek control, the symbol is control-in-principle; particular achievements in definition always imply a commitment to universal orders embodied in symbols. (As Miller observes, in doing something as simple as asking for the time one has struck an alliance with a universal as well as the functioning object serving as its vehicle [MS 176].) The variety of symbols found in the midworld is actually the plurality of modes of practical activity, definition, and control.

The midworld of symbols is not a static set of embodied actions. Rather, the midworld is the *career* of symbolically embodied action. Each person, as an agent, is situated historically and symbolically between a determinate (if vague) past and an indefinite future. The relation between these two expanses framing one's existence is action: To be human is to be located in a continuum of action understood as a historical, symbolic, and self-conscious process of appropriation and revision. The historicity of the midworld is constituted by two key features. First, particular symbols always bear universal import. Second, these symbols are dialectically related to the locales of their actual application. The dimensions of action, then, include the temporal (past and future) and the metaphysical (universal and particular). There is a dialectic process involving past and future as well as of universal and particular.

With respect to the first point, one can note that the midworld is a *continuum* of action in which symbolically expressed actions apply their orderly form to every possible situation and not just to isolated problems. (The distinction between the functioning object and the tool relies on this difference.) Once the uniform order of measured space is announced, for example, we all become inheritors of its order and thus participate in the career of action implied by this order. Similarly the forms of order generated today will to some degree be binding on generations to come. The historicity of symbols is not, however, simply about inheriting modes of control. Historicity encompasses the possibility, indeed the inevitability, of the *revision* of these controls. This is the second point: The symbol guides action, but its artifactual instantiation, actual application, and the data thereby revealed all affect the symbol as well.

Pure symbols such as maps are good examples of this career of revisionary processes. Early maps of the universe, such as those composed on Copernican principles, were revisable vehicles of symbolic disclosure. One experienced the heavens via these symbolic instruments. The data disclosed in the use of such Copernican maps, however, eventually rendered the maps incomplete and, finally, obsolete. For while the Copernican map disclosed the heavens it did not determine, let alone exhaust, their content. New maps were drawn taking these discoveries into account and the Copernican maps ceased to be instrumental pure symbols and were transformed into, at most, imaginative objects in the form of works of art. Revision can also be prompted by the changes in the artifactual character of the pure symbol. In the field of cartography it is clear that what could be disclosed by a map drawn on parchment is significantly different from what is available utilizing radar. Unlike two-dimensional ink and paper maps, radar is capable of revealing a detailed image of *weather* in its most-sophisticated, meteorological sense. As the artifactual possibilities of maps change so too do the formerly mapped and newly mapable aspects of the world. The world and its various maps are in a dialectical relation in which disclosure (propelled by the symbolic power of the map) and revision (based on the data made available via the symbol, the artifactual composition of the symbol itself, and changing human purposes) are linked (see §2.2).

The process of applying and revising forms of order (i.e., definition) is driven by the insatiable need for local-control—that is, establishing definitions but also maintaining and augmenting them by refining and amplifying their import. Action also has a historical aspect and is grounded in reflection, including self-reflection (MP 17:5). The free act is aware of the symbolic conditions informing action and, thus, addresses the midworld and its developing orders (TS 21; see MP 20:2). As Miller states, "All action occurs apropos of this midworld" (MS 18). The symbolic function of the midworld cannot be separated from its history (cf. Fell, 1990, p. 27).

Spontaneity and discipline are interdependent aspects of the autonomous act. For discipline is implied by spontaneity and subsequent spontaneous acts are guided by the controlling symbol. This is the basic form of history and interpretative processes. Far from a static rule, the discipline lent by the symbol incorporates change into its very character. Miller writes:

> Can one, then, use the expression "the environment"? Not if one means a datum, not if one proposes an object, not if one alleges a fixed and a priori state of affairs. Functioning maintains itself, and does so by proposing infinities, their controlled order, the relation of order to order, of psychology to logic, of physics to history, of clock-time to dated-time, and much else. The environment is the extension of an articulate and controlled immediacy [i.e., the symbol] never fully conscious of itself and of the modes of its maintenance. (MS 85–86, italics added; see PH 113)

The form of discipline established by the symbol makes absolute permanence as impossible as the unintelligible chaos of absolute change (MP 9:6; see AH 262). Earlier discussions regarding the process of definition (see §§2.2 and 2.3) figure significantly in this assessment. Static *symbols* would yield sets of static *definitions*. Yet the process of definition, arising out of the practical need for local-control, is dynamic and ongoing. As Miller wryly observes: "One word leads to another" (MS 114). And the creativity of language is but an example of the originality required by the incompleteness of any authoritative order.

Miller claims that no action or symbol is ever *fully conscious of itself* (see MP 21:6; TO 400). An order is an exercise in control that lacks mastery over its own career. The difficulty here is akin to the structural dilemma of grasping action (see §2.1)—that is, how to focus one's attention on that which, in principle, is the condition of distinction and attention. Disclosure is, as Heidegger stated it in "On the Essence of Truth" (1949/1977), an activity of concealing and revealing. The symbol hides itself from practical consciousness and conceals at least some of its import from reflection. Each essay at local-control gives life to unforeseen consequences, some of which will become the nemesis of the very order that is being applied (PH 140). This is an aspect of what Miller refers to as "the fatality of thought" (PH 1–2, 1950–51, 5; see §4.1).

Important examples of the fateful and incomplete character of symbolic forms of disclosure are readily found in the area of constitutional law. The liberty declared as a truth and fundamental principle in the Declaration of Independence was codified in another symbolic document, the Constitution. What one discovers in the history of the United States is a long struggle with the implications of declaring liberty as a right of "all men." The right of liberty, this symbolic declaration, was not a political and moral order announced once and for all. It provoked an ongoing process of interpretation that required the rewriting of the Constitution via amendment (a revision of the symbol itself). In this case, Miller might rhetorically ask, "But what governs this revision?" He answers his own question as follows: "Merely the necessity of the will, its search for itself, for its clarity in detail, and for its own being as will. . . . History is the progressive clarification of will" (PH 34). The debates surrounding slavery in the mid-nineteenth century, especially those between Lincoln and Douglas, provide important insight into the opaqueness and hidden fate of any given symbol. Subsequent struggles regarding women's suffrage, Jim Crow, and, more recently, the legal standing of immigrants all bear out Miller's point. The import of the symbol necessarily exceeds the circumstances in which it arose. It launches an ideal career, the implications of which can be only glimpsed at the outset, and which require an ongoing process of critical interpretation in order to be realized.

Not only does the symbol—by restricting content—make error possible (MP 17:15), but the *implications* of any given symbol can be misunderstood (MP 5:9). Definition and confusion are equally part of all symbolic processes. Revision via clarification, and even redescription, is always required. As Miller notes, the symbol is never fully conscious of the requisite modes of its maintenance. The first remark regarding the constitution sketched how the symbol is, so to speak, *internally* dynamic. The present concern, however, is with how the symbol is dynamic in relationship to the *external* contexts of its application. The origin of the symbol is local but its extent is ideally universal. Between the context of its origination and these other contexts of its application—be they spatially, temporally, or culturally distinguished—there can be significant variations. These variations may be so great that a symbol that was an effective vehicle of control in one situation cannot achieve such control in another. Thus if the symbol is to remain a viable vehicle for definition it must undergo revision.

A good example in this case is the process by which the Fourth Amendment has undergone revision in the Federal courts in light of developments in technology, policing techniques, and criminal activity. While there is room for debating whether the current tendency toward relaxing search and seizure requirements and waving Miranda rights represent good applications of the Fourth Amendment, there is no doubt that many legal interpreters see these revisions as necessary if the Fourth Amendment is to remain pertinent. If maintaining the integrity of the Amendment means that it must remain unchanged, some interpreters believe, the Amendment's purity will be purchased at the price of its obsolescence, the loss of effective local-control. The symbolic order of the Constitution, then, is pressed to develop in specific ways. "Symbols," Miller states, "are objects which control the exploration of objects" (MS 155). If any given symbol is to remain viable it must then come to terms with the data provided by its own explorations and be revised accordingly.

The symbol is both opaque to itself and a generator of novelty. Miller states that the midworld is not just "the vehicle of all order" but is also the vehicle "of the revision of order." The midworld is "self-revisory" (MS 110).[26] Interpretation holds these two moments—that is, discipline and spontaneity—together in a productive tension. Metaphor is the key to this process.

The metaphoric revision of order is nothing less than the introduction of disciplined novelty into an existing order. Change is not introduced ex nihilo but rather always on the basis of a symbolic continuum. There are no absolute beginnings; each metaphor (e.g., a new radar map) is disciplined by its symbolic environment (e.g., paper maps) as well as the realm of data currently disclosed and the new data sought. Of course not all revision is worthy of being described by the strong term of *metaphor*. Some processes of revision are analogous (e.g., the development of the Fourth Amendment as a principle of privacy is being redescribed subtly); the more regular and orderly a process of revision is, the more likely that it will proceed on an analogous basis. Yet no matter the character of the revision, metaphor is an ingredient to the form of order in question.

The role of metaphor has already been highlighted (see §2.4 as well as §3.1). Metaphor was used to describe original forms of organization—what Miller terms "non-analogical order" (PH 131)—that define environment rather than being defined by an environment. *Metaphor* refers to those assertions of order that are not reducible to their environing conditions and that do not trade on the relevant existing set of symbolic commonplaces. Metaphors announce a new vocabulary for articulating the environment and, if successful, transform that symbolic environment. They are the radical, and lively, element within the larger process of interpretation.

The sense of metaphor that has been hitherto relied on follows developments in the philosophy of language since I. A. Richards's *The Philosophy of Rhetoric* and Max Black's "Metaphor." This contemporary account contrasts with Aristotle's or Thomas Hobbes's conception of the metaphorical function. It was Richards who announced that metaphor is neither the rhetorical enhancement (Aristotle) nor the frivolous perversion (Hobbes) of plain prose. Metaphor is, on the contrary, a fundamental principle of thought (Richards, p. 94). Rather than thinking of the

metaphor in terms of analogy, elliptical simile, or substitution as do the classic
interpretations, Black developed Richards's position by proposing that the sense of
"interestingly complex" metaphors does not depend on already existing relations.
He ventured that "it would be more illuminating in some of these cases to say that
the metaphor creates the similarity than to say that it formulates some similarity an-
tecedently existing" (1981, p. 72). The metaphor forges relations and, as Langer
noted, responds to a symbolic need for organization (1957, p. 132). Such a proposal
clearly shakes up any strictly representationalist conception of language. Since the
work of Richards and Black, metaphor is more commonly understood as an element of real novelty in language—a principle of growth and actual change.

Miller himself writes little about metaphor in specific other than briefly suggesting its role in the formation of language and ordering experience (MS 74–75).
Yet metaphor is an intrinsic part of what Miller means by *utterance* or *action* insofar as it is a disclosive, and not representational or determined, mode of human
activity (Corrington, 1986, pp. 176–77). For utterance, as Miller describes it, is
concerned with poetry, magic, and revelation (MS 69–70, 153)—all traits illuminated by the concept of metaphor. Metaphor reveals itself as a mode of action; it
is an element in the process of interpretation.

Connecting metaphor to symbol hinges on two important claims. First, the
symbol is primarily *action in a metaphorical mode* and the pervasive symbols
ordering one's daily experience are what are called *dead* metaphors. Order is not
just read off of experience, it is applied via gesture, speech, and fabrication. Second, symbols and metaphors are in a dialectical relationship. Metaphorical
actions give birth to symbols but symbolic orders are themselves disciplines giving rise to further metaphorical actions.

A metaphor, like a symbol, is expressive and not denotative. It does not
point to an already-existent state of affairs but, rather, establishes a state of affairs
by providing a unifying insight or organizing structure. "What denotes no particular object is either nonsense or an element of order" (MS 157), Miller states.
Sight does not only point but also organizes. (Indeed, the fact that it can point
is dependent on its organizational capacity.) Units such as *yards, ells,* and *fathoms*
give rise to articulate space. The words *the spiteful sun* do not refer to a state of
affairs in a denotative sense but form a new situation—the bodily experience of
the sun as a sensation of warmth and visible light is further defined in terms of
emotion and will. From the most basic functions of the body to the expressions
of literary prose, one witnesses the metaphorical quality of constitutive activity:

> All objects or meanings are in relation to all others, and so to the physiolog-
> ical organism. But it is a truth about any object that its appearance, i.e., its
> definition, is a function of the animal body which is called mine, as well as

of all other bodies, all of which again, naturally enough, are in relation to the human body and partly understood through that relation. Other objects are important only as related to "the" body, but the reverse also holds and in equal measure. (DT 150)

Every prosaic description of the world relies on a primary organizing factor of symbols and, thinking genealogically, the metaphorical assertions implicit in all actions.

Action introduces a form of nonanalogical order. In terms of our actual, historical experience this is achieved by inserting a new term of organization into already established orders. Just so, visible qualities forming the content of empirical reports rely on vision as a process of composition and organization. Or the bodily sensation of heat or chill is transformed into the more precise and objective measure of degrees Fahrenheit. This transformation suggests Monroe Beardsley's sense of the metaphorical "twist" wherein new modes of organization are paradoxically achieved by not proceeding analogously within what Black called "the system of associated commonplaces." It is the spring of order within the interpretative process.

Metaphors and symbols are expressive. What the metaphor exhibits as a source of novelty, the symbol exploits as a principle of discipline; they are two moments in the continuity of utterance. As Langer noted, metaphor is "the source of generality" because it describes a "course," a systematic consequence, deriving from the use of a certain word (1957, pp. 136–41). Miller puts the matter in these terms:

The free act is the one that proposes systematic consequences. All the talk about freedom fails in so far as action has not been presented as having consequences formally accepted. No free act can occur in a closed environment. There is no systematic consequence until the act is more than subjective. It must occur as a sign of an order. But that order is also sustained by the act. An act that does not sustain and express an order of nature is only a subjective one. It has a closed environment. . . . Action seems to need a future. Where there is no future in an act, or in a supposed act, there are no consequences, and so there is no importance. The importance of an act must, of course, be "formal." (PH 139–40)

Freedom is not found solely in an act that breaks from the system of associated commonplaces. Nonsense does this as well. A free act suggests that the twist rendered in the fabric of common or prosaic interpretation be generalized. A unique gesture, an unexpected word, a fortuitous construction—all have the capacity of becoming models and thus applicable to a wider range of contexts. Its generality does not, in principle, rely on its actual replication but is owing to its *potential* for replication. Quite simply: The order it lends to one situation is transferable; it is touched by universality. Thus the metaphorical act, insofar as it is original and free, not only establishes a moment but also projects its order as a general prospect for an indeterminate future (TO 400).

The symbol is the stable embodiment achieved via the regularized application of the general order proposed by the metaphorical action. The symbol is the objectified act (PH 185); it is the act (or metaphor) become general, its consequences regularized, and its systematic import made effective. At this point the twist, the disruptive nonanalogical quality of the act, fades. The systematic consequences proposed by the new metaphor forge relations with already-prevailing orders and, further, establish a system of analogous relations under its own rule. (Thus the relations of the wholly dissimilar categories of time and space become regularized and space–time itself becomes an orderly system of analogies based in hybrid symbols—for example, miles per-hour [mph] enables one to describe distance in terms of time.) In this vein Miller remarks that the symbol must conform to what it "represents" (CB 2). Just as the metaphor cannot be effective if it is mere nonsense, the symbol cannot be disclosive and establish order unless it conforms to the matter it discloses. This *representation* is not, of course, correspondence. (Such representation is as useless as pure nonsense is unintelligible.) Rather the symbol establishes a system of transposition that provides a new power via the metaphorical twist it creates even as it maintains order and control by means of the systematic application of this twist.

The symbol does not stifle spontaneity. Symbolic order does not result in a different, historical form of determinism. The life of the symbol is in interpretation and revision. And although in terms of one's actual experience the symbol has a certain temporal priority to the metaphor—that is, one is born into functioning symbolic systems—the novelty of the metaphor is coeval with and ingredient to the discipline of the symbol. The relationship is inextricably *dialectical.* "These immediacies like all others require a medium in which they can appear, and this medium is discourse," Miller remarks. "A philosophy of history is an essay in the establishment of discourse as a *category.* In this way there occurs an emphasis on actuality rather than on reality" (MP 7:4). Discourse, which has been referred to here as *utterance* and *interpretation,* is the process uniting discipline and spontaneity. The authoritative and original act does not occur in an abstract present; it is not a catastrophe or a miracle. It occurs in the career of a symbolic order.

Individual authoritative actions, occurring in this continuum, are best understood as acts of *translation*—that is, creative maintenance and even artistic recreation (TR 15). One inherits a symbolic order by virtue of being born with a body and into history. Yet because this order is symbolic, and at bottom functional, one's individual acts have authority. For even as individual actions are guided by symbolic orders, they are, in turn, the very life of those symbols. As Miller states:

> I come back to the continuum of action. . . . No motive is found apart from some mode of the continuum of action with which one is identified. Action of any sort has a historical basis. On such a basis, one acts as scientist, lawyer, economist, or craftsman. It is now time to stop looking for motives and intent in an alleged state of affairs not itself identified in the energies that define and have sustained it.
>
> *The universal is the form of the* ACTUAL. Except as a person is a universalist, his supposed acts become atomistic, discrete, episodic, and not even his own. Do not look for the person, for his acts or his motives, in an alleged region not the projection of his doing. If you want a person's "motives," you will come to his general outlook, to his world. (MS 90)

The personal and the universal order of the symbol are allied. No acts, let alone facts, are possible without symbolic disclosure. Equally there is no symbol without the acts and facts reflecting and maintaining its formal authority. The very process of maintaining a symbol requires the spontaneity that is part of revisionary acts.

The person is *authorized*, and certainly not dominated by the symbolic continuum.

> History is made by those who realize, however faintly, the status of environment as the actuality of themselves. Any environment-maintaining act is historical.
>
> Technically, an "act" that lacks the quality of maintaining its world, however vaguely, reduces to instinct. There the act and the environment merge. A cat is its world. But where there is action, the person is not only his world but the assertion that he is his world. This can be any world at all.
>
> History is the maintenance of the environment. Action is the same thing. The revision of the environment is a phase of its maintenance. (PH 20-21)

Revision is a mode of autonomy achieved via the modification, translation, and even metaphorical transformation of historical categories. Autonomy does not require that deeds be construed as flights of fancy or acts of sheer imagination. Between mere repetition and absolute novelty there is a middle ground. Revision is, as Miller states, "a disciplined qualification of the past" (AH 267). It is a form of "genealogical novelty" in which "the past derives its life from the original vitality of its heirs" (AH 244).

§3.5 *RES PUBLICAE*

In a lecture he presented in 1948 on the topic of democracy, Miller poses this question: "On what conditions, then, can one tell a story of man as the locus of responsible power?" (PC 102). The project to reestablish the active life is precisely the quest for such a story. It would be an account of a situation in which persons are not merely the observers and reporters supposed by the contemplative life. It would be a story highlighting the crucial link that exists between metaphysics and democracy. Unlike so many contemporary efforts to rehabilitate the active life, actualism does not side-step, let alone condemn, metaphysics. Responsibility is premised on not only recognizing the import of action but also grasping the role of the midworld as the embodiment and means of action. The story of personal responsibility must be, in Miller's estimation, a metaphysical story—that is, a story capable of articulation only insofar as metaphysical concepts and forms are allowed standing.

This form of democratic responsibility can now receive a preliminary description. The symbol establishes authority by joining action in its formal sense with action in its particular instantiations. In this dialectic we find the efficacy of word and deed, of interpretation and revision. This authority, embodied in the symbol, is instanced in three crucial modes: *identity*, *legislation*, and *criticism*. These three modes of authority, in turn, provide the basis for a vital sense of democratic responsibility. Encompassing and allowing for these three modes or capacities, symbols are shown to be *res publicae*—common vehicles of action and representation that bear our democratic impulses.

The symbol is the vehicle for the establishment of *identity*, the first mode of authority. The symbol is the means through which differing individual and symbolically constituted identities meet, understand one another, forge larger associations, and claim personal power. For identity is linked to participation in a common actuality. "We understand each other," Miller states, "through the circuit of objects now known or knowable to another and private to none" (TI 1; see DT 150). This is certainly true of the everyday artifacts and tools that surround us—for example, clothing, typewriters, pots and pans. It is also true of the class of common nouns everyone recognizes, such as *trees*, *chairs*, and *rocks*. Yet the common objects essential to identity are symbols such as yardsticks, documents, artworks, and, indeed, the human body. For they do not just reveal what action has defined, they embody action and make further action possible. The connection to these objects is not hypothetical, but, rather, necessary (MP 14:15); they are a person's vehicles for control, articulation, and expression at the levels of self and commumnity.

A person composes, and thus expresses, an identity by virtue of the vehicles that are at his disposal. Being sighted, having tactile capabilities, and being a user of yardsticks are, for example, three requirements (and symbolic modes) of being a person who appreciates sculpture. Some formal codification of law is a requirement for being a law-abiding person. An appreciation of the significance of meters, scales, and balances is necessary for being an engineer. Symbols bespeak what a person is capable of and what controls he recognizes. It is not just a matter of what he is familiar with. While saying *I own a pair of golf shoes* speaks of one's identity, there is far more implied, and far more at stake, when one says, *I am a law-abiding person*. There is a difference between using a tennis racquet and engaging in monetary exchange, for the latter action implies a series of concrete symbols with some systematic organization—for example, the legal and monetary systems and their documents, principles, and institutions. (Even the simple statement of identification, *I am Bill*, implicates one's identity with the symbolic and functional structure of language.) "[W]e purchase finitude only at the price of infinities which reveal the conception of the self with which we are identified" (PC 144), Miller observes. Identity is inextricably bound to orders of symbolic control:

> Nature as object shows no mind. It shows none because it produces no artifacts. Everything there is what it seems to be. As object, nature is the order of appearance. Mind, however, is the order of existence. Nature is "real" rather than illusory because there is order among appearances. Minds exist because they produce appearances which determine and announce the order of all objective appearances. (DT 187)

Identity is achieved through a commitment to particular orders of appearances and to certain limits (PC 85). In turn, one maintains identity via *a commitment to specific symbolic objects* that are the vehicles for articulating these orders. Symbols are "the substance of their thought and the evidence of their reality as persons" (PL 714; see DT 186). Similarly a recognition of and commitment to particular symbolic modes is the only way to meet another person. As Miller likes to say, "I cannot get a hold on a person except as I take him at his word" (MS 110).

Emerson had an insight into the relationship between objects and identity when he wrote of the person: "He is placed in the centre of beings, and a ray of relation passes from every other being to him. And neither can man be understood without these objects, nor these objects without man" (1836/1983, p. 21). There is nothing casual about one's relationship with objects, and especially not the symbolic vehicles of the midworld. They articulate identity and are the exclusive means for exercising personal authority. Because personhood is tied to history, locality, and its objects, Miller is suspicious of those who espouse humanism and, at the same time, see technology as opposed to humanity. Of the proposal that one seek humanity apart from technology, and artifacts Miller asks, "But is not that suicide?" (DP 155; cf. Anderson, 1998). It would be. The symbol is not just "the personal world objectified" (DT 178). It is the personal world achieved.

Symbols represent a second mode of authority in that they are *legislative* actions on the part of persons. Individual acts and symbols are intrinsically and dialectically related. Yet the act retains an ontological primacy, and symbolic artifacts are "residues of acts" (PH 108). The control and authority expressed by symbols are aspects of action undertaken at an individual and collective level. Symbols are vehicles for human control, and the articulate world (insofar as it is disclosed via symbols) is an expression of human authority (MP 14:7). "What I am here suggesting," Miller states, "is that we do not lose a world, but gain one, as we identify our own power with the power of circumstance in its orderly form" (PC 183).

The capacity to legislate is the hallmark of authority unrelated to violence, domination, and vagrant power. Expression that takes the form of law does not seek mastery over another but control over a set of relations (see §5.2). Law is not just control over something external to oneself but also the establishment of modes of self-control. Because of its thrust toward universality, law is as much submitted to as it is expressed.

Legislation resists vagrancy because it is embedded in a process of interpretation. The unique is not the utterly new but is the creative revision of a tradition. The authority announced in legislation comes not from rejecting limits but, rather, creatively maintaining and revising those forms of order that constitute one's world and personhood. Thus the notion of legislation implies *criticism* as a form of interpretation and revision. The paired activities of *interpretation* and *revision*—the terms, one implying the other, can be used interchangeably—are the third mode of authority achieved via the symbol. Criticism is the enactment of the authority made available, in principle, by the symbol. Criticism is "the self-control and self-revision of thought in the modes of necessity [i.e., symbols]" (PC 92). This conscious apprehension of the import of one's symbolic environment allows for what Fell refers to as "a human form of transcendence" (personal correspondence, Joseph Fell to Colapietro, July 19, 1989), a form of transcendence founded on an awareness of the conditions of action and discourse.

Criticism, Miller writes, "is nothing other than the self-maintenance of structure" (PC 68). Symbols are vehicles for criticism because they embody terms of distinction that can be brought to bear on any appropriate situation. They provide the resources for distinguishing right from wrong, good from bad, and lawful from criminal. In appealing to these terms a person brings himself, and his circumstances, under control. This process, of course, is not exclusively the business of a single person. It is social—symbols are *public* resources for mutual control and mutual influence. The legitimate use of a symbol cannot be one-sided. Symbols are one's only means for knowing another and are the means for influencing one another as persons (PC 103; see also DT 186; MS 120). When a person becomes aware of the status and import of the symbol, its connection to action, and the critical authority it makes possible, the symbol is transformed into a mode of self-control on a social scale. By contrast, criticism without identification is merely, on the one hand, a technological application of rules or, on the other hand, simple arbitrariness.

Revision is a form of criticism fundamental to symbolic order. As was made clear in section 3.4, in revision the symbol is reinterpreted either in light of its own fateful consequences or the changing demands of local-control. The implications of this are profound. What the symbol makes possible is not just identification with the terms of control. The symbol places one in *control over the very terms of control*. The symbolic realm of the actual is the "fulcrum of all self-possessed enlargement" (TO 401). Via the midworld persons develop current forms of control through their revision, and sometimes exceed them via their transformation into new modes of control. This social process results in the transformation of a person and her world.

This dynamic process—encompassing identity, legislation, and criticism—establishes an outlook that is open to history.

> All categories represent codes for the restriction of content of finite points of view. Every category describes at once an infinite order, and a finite content which seeks to enlarge itself. Categories are not transcendental, nor are they psychological and accidental. They are the structure of criticism, the dynamic of expanding meanings according to law. Thus, idealism asserts no Absolute, but rather denies the possibility of any assertion immune from the order of contingency. It is that order which is absolute. (FI 267)

The symbolic orders through which one lives and governs oneself are revisable and contingent. They pretend neither to be, nor to copy, a final order. Authority always looks toward the future. Because autonomy is inextricably connected with self-revision, authority thus needs a *historical* future. Only in terms of a historical future—a future allowing for revision and genuine novelty (PH 32)—are learning, criticism, and real growth possible (PC 186). There is no terminus to the process of local-control and self-control.

Symbols are vehicles for identity and community. They are also modes of self-legislation and the possibility for criticism, self-correction, and revision. In sum: Symbols are common—socially achieved, maintained, and revised—forms of authority. They are *res publicae* (see PH 134). As public vehicles, symbols are constituted by the authority of persons and, in turn, are the form of their authority.

Res publicae are the enactment, maintenance, and revision of the public itself. The modern appropriation of the Roman *Res Publica* is on the right track. But there is not just one public instrument, not just one vehicle for common representation and public expression. This model of democratic representation—that is, indirect and always mediated participation—must be expanded; its significance is to be discovered in every facet of life. The legislative process embodied in elections, as well as in the offices and procedures of representative bodies, become figures for a more pervasive dynamic. That is to say, *constitution* and *legislation* become metaphors for the revision of one's conception of society and world.

§3.6 CONCLUSION

The symbol implies participation and interpretation—the stuff of democracy. If one is to come to terms with authority, then it is necessary to be in intercourse with things, objects, and symbols—the practical world where thought and will are exemplified and revised. The concept of *res publicae* expands the scope of our political vocabulary and extends the reach of the active life to fabrication and labor as well as to contemplation. If democracy is the preeminent form of responsible humanism, then surely the midworld is a sound basis for such a humanism (PC 114; MS 119). The midworld is the locale and condition of authoritative action. There action comes out of the shadows and is revealed as basic to ontology, epistemology, and ethics, and is not a mere ghost as the contemplative life has so often assumed.

FOUR

History

Contingency establishes authority. Democratic authority is based in this paradoxical circumstance. The contingent and incomplete appear to threaten authority, everywhere showing its inner frailty and outer limits. Yet, John William Miller asks, "What is in control?" The answer is found by insisting on the functioning unity of the apparently disparate: "We want order, but not too much. We want some disorder, but not too much" (PH 128). The dualism of absolute order and utter contingency is false; the zero-sum contest still raging between the philosophic progeny of Parmenides and Heraclitus continues only on the basis of an ignorance of the implications of the very dyad over which they contend. An actualist account of action and symbolism stresses the mutual implication of order and contingency, unity and diversity. *Local-control* occurs where one's world is articulated in terms of incomplete and developing definitions that allow for the limited but self-possessed authority befitting a democratic outlook.

Only in history and historical experience can this dialectical relation of order and contingency take its proper place.[1] As Miller likes to state, history is the study of things done, *res gestae* (DP 141). In history individual authority is recognized and exerted in willful acts of self-assertion and self-revision. History is the condition for revisable, reflective, and, thus, liberating order. In history one learns about freedom (PH 34), ethical action, and democracy (PC 73–74). The active life can only occur within history.

Section 4.1, will show the links among the constitutional concepts of history, action, and symbol. In the course of further articulating history and its constitutional status new concepts will be introduced to the discussion while revisiting earlier topics. In section 4.2 the symbolic environment will be redescribed in terms of the historical and fateful character of symbolic modes. In section 4.3 action and interpretation will be incorporated into an account of conflict, revision, and reflection. While section 4.1 establishes the conceptual unity of history, action, and symbol, sections 4.2 and 4.3 display that connection via a description of key facets of historical experience. On this basis, sections 4.4 and 4.5 address reflection and its importance for actualizing responsible and autonomous authority. In doing so, a connection is forged between history and philosophy, a connection central to Miller's conception of democratic authority and the reconciliation of the active and contemplative lives.

§4.1 HISTORY AS CONSTITUTIONAL

Following the pattern of the contemplative life, thought has consistently sought to comprehend experience in terms of ahistoric principles (AH 237–69). Whether one refers to the will of an eternal God or to the laws of physics, the result is the same: The variety of experience is reduced to principles that do not themselves incorporate historical temporality into their structure. Thus philosophy, science, and, indeed, practical understanding have all tried to view the world *sub specie aeternitatis*. The upshot of this Eleatic outlook is that persons are always mere observers, their foremost "activity" is that of speculation. Thus Boethius remains an outstanding figure in the history of philosophy for so clearly stating what others have simply assumed: Philosophy is a matter of consolation not action.[2] Establishing a place for action requires that the traditional formulation of the philosophical vocation be revised. The point is no longer seeing things from the position of eternity—that is, whole, stable, and complete. Rather the aim is viewing things *sub specie temporis* (PH 85)—that is, incomplete, variable, and revisable. Affecting this change in one's metaphysics entails that history must be a defining *category*, or necessary aspect, of being. It must also be an unavoidable *region* of experience.[3] Constitutional status is thus accorded to a concept that has long been a metaphysical outcast.

Describing history as a category raises difficulties. It does so not least because the sense of *category*—earlier referred to as "the form of definition and control" (see §2.4)—remains slippery. Furthermore there is the Kantian association that the categorical is a priori and necessary. Would not setting up history as a category break down distinctions of common-sense understanding and make history fundamental to all modes of experience?

Regarding categories, Miller offers two clear statements:

> All categories are factors of life and experience. They are not general properties of the content of experience, but the operational modes of a life, its method of constructing itself. (MP 21:8)

> "Categories" are merely other names for "concepts of universal incidence" (not "classifications"). There are "ideas that run in and out of every word we utter" (Plato). (PH 7 1951–52, 2)

Categories establish the *form of experience*, its systematic and pervasive relations. In this respect the Kantian association puts one on the right track. The emphasis is on terms of distinction with "universal incidence." One's more refined and particular essays at control rely on these basic modes and promote an array of distinctions within the primary categories, and in other related categories as well.[4] Both categories and their dependent distinctions disclose orders of systematic content standing in relation to, and even interpenetrating, one another—for example, the time of days and seasons has its translation in terms of minutes and hours (relation) and these two modes of temporal distinction are themselves ramified when related to categories such as causality and identity (interpenetration).

Immanuel Kant's, as well as Aristotle's, categories remain preeminent examples of what Miller intends. Space and time belong to this list as well because, as mentioned in section 2.5, Miller does not respect Kant's distinction between *categories* of the understanding and *forms* of intuition. (Both Kant's categories and forms function as basic modes of definition.) Moving from the traditional to the actualist sense of the categorical, Miller includes *finitude* and the *symbolic artifact* because both are fundamental to the definition of experience (PH 72). The *accidental* would also be categorical in that it is the unavoidable companion to the lawful and orderly (PC 51–55). The *self*, too, would qualify as a category insofar as it is an existential amplification of the category of identity. Given Miller's emphasis on the practical and active origin of the categories, it is fitting to add *the body* and such fundamental bodily disclosures as the audible, tactile, gustatory, olfactory, and visual. All of these are categories because of their inevitability—the world would become absurd and unthinkable in their absence. As Miller says, they are all "compulsive" (PC 80).

More categories could be added and certainly the relations among those presented here made more systematic. Miller himself did not inherit an interest in the Kantian project of establishing a determinate list of categories, let alone deducing them from pure reason. Indeed Miller suspected that one could not set down a complete list of categories (MP 21:1). When discussing the categorical he concentrates on clarifying two matters, both of which were already addressed in chapter 2. First, the origin of these categories is in those *practical* necessities forced on a *person* in the struggle for local-control. Categories are "operational modes of a life." Thus, while he takes up Kant and Aristotle's distinctions, Miller takes issue with their derivation. Categories are not static, a priori forms applied to content. Second, the role played by the categories in the process of definition is ontological. By providing the basic terms of distinction, these categories disclose being; there is no talking about what any particular thing *is* without reference to the categories and thus no being independent of them.

Categories are universal, necessary, and inseparable from active experience.[5] They are constitutional aspects of experience and thus fundamental to any metaphysical account. Can history be a category in this sense? Miller answers in the affirmative:

> Historicism is the affirmation of the constitutional interdependence of center and environment; this relation includes all the efforts that have been made to define it. It is the view that historical time, i.e., dated time, is constitutional and not derivative from any antecedent account of a timeless situation. Obviously this can be the only basis of a philosophy that proposes to include history as a category. (AH 240)

> We cannot escape history, and we cannot escape the study of history. Nor is there any history at all apart from the thrust of present meanings into their yesterdays. History is a category because it is a necessary condition of the present. In history time is efficacious. (PC 92)

The critical connection that is forged is between history and ontology. In history, time displays ontological efficacy. Better put, in history, being and time are coeval such that each is established in and through the other.

The implication is not the weaker claim, articulated by Kant, that all our experiences, and thus moments of being, are serially ordered according to time. This would give time a merely intellectual status (PH 77; cf. Kant 1798/1965, pp. 74–82). What is in question here is not clock time but dated time. The chronological past is different from the historical past (MP 21:6; see PH 165–67; cf. Croce 1920/1960). Chronology divides experience into manageable units and establishes the basis for orderly relations. We are given the conditions of the interrelations of things in terms of the simultaneous, sequential, and causal. However, all distinctions—for example, minutes, years, and centuries—are premised on a more basic simultaneity (PH 88). A scientist, for example, keeps a clock on the distillation of a particular solid compound because the rate of this process assists in distinguishing it from other compounds similar to it in other more obvious, physical respects. The experiment is undertaken and the result is recorded. The time required for performing the distillation indicates something significant about the compound. Yet the process of distillation can be reversed.[6] For this reason Miller refers to clock time as abstract time—that is, the order of accidental content (MP 14:2). "Science is timeless and repeatable. It deals in the eternal present," Miller writes somewhat overstating his case.[7]

Dated time is quite different: "History is the dimension of time, of an actual past, of time generating new and more complete integration. . . . History is revolution because it is conversion. It is the career of conversion" (MP 21:9; see MP 3:12). Historical time has a directionality and relationality that clock time lacks.[8] What Miller is proposing resembles Martin Heidegger's assertion that being is "stretched along" in time and that human being is in the peculiar situation of being "stretched along as it stretches itself along" (1927/1962, p. 427).[9] The claim common to Miller and Heidegger is that time is not just a mode of distinction (however fundamental) but that being itself is thoroughly temporal. This applies not just to human being—as Heidegger would say, *Dasein*—but to all being distinguished via the process of definition. The process that Miller describes in *The Definition of the Thing* connects ontology and history. An ontology formed around action, local-control, and definition is pregnant with history. When one adds to the temporal process the reflective capacity of human agents, ontology becomes thoroughly historical, for the very *stretch* of time of which Heidegger writes and Miller addresses is founded in reflection.

The thing is *by definition* its past as well as its future; we understand nothing about what is before us without being simultaneously plunged into the past and projected into the future. Identity, that form of enduring change generated in the process of definition, must be genealogical (MP 16:14). History defines the process of definition itself.

The failure to keep history in mind invokes some sort of systematic punishment. Omitting one's history, or indeed one's personal narrative, precipitates a fundamental loss of control over things and oneself. To return to the scientific example, because the temporal order of events does not fundamentally constitute the being of things in many experimental sciences forgetting that order meets with no systematic punishment (see PC 79-85; §4.2). One can just repeat the experiment. In the scientific sphere, however, one *would* encounter systematic punishment if one forgot the history of science (including the rise of molecular theory) and attempted to describe water in terms of the elemental theories of the Presocratics. The systematic character of this punishment encompasses not only the social retribution whereby one would be banned from the institutions embodying current scientific practice.[10] It also implies a more fundamental punishment whereby one would lose the many degrees of control acquired through the long history of science (see PH 16). Briefly stated: One would cease to be modern.[11]

"The chronological past has no shape," Miller states. "It is all events common to all points of view. The historical past has shape. It is not a common past" (PH 165). The irreversibility of history owes partly to its individuality, its concern with an actual sequence of events and their constitutional significance in relation to one another in that sequence. It is time as perceived from the standpoint of finite persons struggling to attain and maintain local-control. This establishes its distinctive shape, in contrast to the neutral grid of chronology. The irreversibility of dated time is also premised on the fact that history is made by self-conscious and willful persons (MP 17:5). The past can only truly be efficacious if it can be reflectively apprehended, seen as constitutive of the present, and thus as a fate awaiting acceptance, revision, or destruction in the future. The dated past "entails its tomorrows" (MP 23:17). A historical past is "more than a thing of time," Miller observes, "it is always the bearer of infinity," of authoritative and fateful interpretations (PH 167).

History is a category of recent origin.[12] Miller is claiming that the *predominant* metaphysical category was actually ignored and for some time systematically excluded by other prevailing categories. This implies the paradox that the *first* category is actually the *most recent*, if not the *last*, category.

Insofar as historical time and, say, causality are both categories each must be described as *necessary, ontological,* and *universal.* If so, what could one mean by saying that there is a difference between the two? Saying that one is more necessary than another seems a bit ridiculous. No one can readily think of a world that is historical and yet not structured by causality, space, or identity. The point of distinguishing them all as categories is precisely to say that a person's world would become absurd if *any single one* was missing.

What is unique about the compulsion of historical time? This question must be addressed from an existential standpoint.

> The sense of time is a primitive idea and appears without benefit of theory. One could hardly plan to have a past, or predict that, in view of long experience, there was every likelihood of finding one in the not too remote future. Time is an immediacy, but one that expands and moves into diversity and relation. The present is no more articulate than its temporal environment, and today without its own yesterdays lacks temporal distinction. (PH 74)

> We grew into our past without prior deliberation, without philosophical sanction, and then found that we had no way of accrediting a dimension of learning that contained all that we had ever done, all that we had ever thought, and all that had given occasion for our specific actuality. (PH 56–57)

While Miller prefers to say that one "grows into" or is "eased into" history, the import of these statements is fundamentally the same as Heidegger's more arresting expression, *throwness.* Actualism begins with a bodily and historically defined locality (see PH 167). All the actualist categories are existential categories—that is, derived from and geared toward activity. Yet historical temporality is both an *existential category* and a *fundamental existential condition*. For this reason, Miller writes, "History . . . is an attitude of piety. It is our reconciliation with the conditions of our endeavors" (PH 149).[13] History is finitude itself—it is fundamental and provides the "occasion for our specific actuality." This actuality is further organized and articulated via all of the available categories.

History has two roles. First, history functions like other categories by providing a basic and universal mode of articulation and, thereby, constituting experience as such: "The world is as much historic as static and physical" (DP 158). (History thus takes its place at the heart of the contemplative life—that is, the list of categories.) Second, history is the occasion for, and is not occasioned by, the other categories. (That is, history must be determinative *of*, not determined *by*, them.) This distinction and these phrasings build on earlier discussions in chapters 2 and 3 with respect to the priority of action and symbol vis-à-vis the psychological environment. Like action and symbol, history must be unconditioned by, but dialectically related to, what it conditions if it is to be a key concept in an actualist metaphysics.[14]

A consideration of history and causality (see §2.5) shows that history meets these conditions. Actualism claims that one cannot properly understand causality if that understanding is not informed by historical temporality. This is the primary lesson of "The Paradox of Cause" (PC 11–18). If the principle of causality employed by scientists and psychologists—that is, its exclusively mechanical interpretation—is not to undermine scientific activity itself, then causality must have a historical inflection. Otherwise all is reduced to a physical model:

> Yet mechanism, while pluming itself on its cold impersonality, and upon its devotion to scientific methods, is nothing more than a crude variety of absolutism. It stands on a platform and snipes at the universe. The mechanist is entitled to his causal postulate, but it is the source of his undoing and not of his justification. To assert cause as a property of an absolutely objective and impersonal region is not a dogmatism; it is nonsense. (PC 18)

The exclusive authority of efficient causality arises when the result achieved via a process is deceptively substituted for the process itself (PC 182). This is an example of the fallacy of composition (MP 30:8). In order to save causality as an organizing principle employed by conscious, rational, and finite beings one must reinterpret it in terms of "a world of which the very essence is the adventurous enlargement of a finite point of view" (PC 16). Such a world is a historical world. A meaningful sense of causality requires a world in which finitude is a basic condition and order is achieved via a process of definition understood in genealogical terms—that is, a world "governed by a law of process, ideal in direction, infinite in potentiality, but always finite in status and point of view" (PC 18). The preeminence of history lies in the fact that it can accommodate physical models of causality and grant them integrity; that is, *science can take place in terms of history*. (Similarly clock time can be accommodated by dated time.) Physical models of causality cannot accommodate history, however. A mechanical "history" is not history at all unless one calls any series of events *history* (a tendency whose own history spans from Aristotle to Richard Rorty).

The priority of history is amplified by considering how action and symbolism fit within a historical ontology. Action lacks a good measure of sense when interpreted on ahistoric terms (see MP 23:4). A robust conception of action implies freedom, novelty, and responsibility. As described in section 2.4, action introduces novel terms of definition and responsibly maintains them. History alone allows for this possibility because it is neither a chain of determined events nor a random succession of events. In historical or diachronic time, moments mark actual changes in the shape and course of those prevailing definitions. The moment is the reference point for future action. The act that occurs in and establishes the moment is both *free* and *fateful*. Such action makes time truly historical—that is, a continuum of growth not reducible to uniformity (PH 7, 1951–52, 5).

Similarly, the symbol can only be understood in terms of historical time. What the symbol most effectively shows is the implication of the past in the organization of the present and the fateful consequences of one's actions today. Whereas an action punctuates time and draws attention to the moment, the symbol spans time and shows actions to be part of the continua of personhood and community. Via the vehicle of the symbol the past is in the present and future (PH 109–10), as well as the present in the past and future. This unity of events is not achieved in the simple connection of chronology. Rather the links are those self-conscious and reflective apprehensions of the origins and implications of one's deeds.

Describing actualist ontology in terms of action and symbol is really just another way of saying that it is a historical ontology.

History is the category of categories. While it is true that no being is possible without all of the other categories that were mentioned previously, history is their uncircumventable origin. Every experience that is mixed with consciousness is historical. Thus calling history a *region* of experience now seems mistaken in that this region is so large as to be almost all-encompassing. Yet there is something rash in outright denying a distinct status to those types of experience largely (but not exclusively) defined as *emotional, sensory,* or *ratiocinative.* Thus the ahistoric categories and their regions must be understood as historical achievements and even necessities in one's ongoing efforts at maintaining local-control (AH 255).

The ahistoric understanding of the world has its own history and is infused with the sort of reflective and revolutionary temporality typifying historical consciousness. The scientific mind exhibits its historicity by paradoxically negating the historical. Science is the career of those attempts at attaining control using ahistoric categories. The form of nature that science articulates is not a fact (although it allows for facts) but an achievement (PC 103). Nature, like history, is an idea: "Nature is the articulate objectification of finitude in its impersonal mode" (AH 248). So while "the self-correction of science reveals it as a truly historical mode of discourse" (MS 122), ahistoricism is paradoxically a mode of the historic as well as a stage in the development of the very idea of history (PH 17; cf. Collingwood, 1946).

History, like nature, is a set of systematic relations. These relations are worthy of being designated a *region* and distinguished from other modes of relations. Miller proposes that while there is *one* world there are *three* main modes for describing that world—physical, historical, and symbolic. Thus *nature, history,* and the *midworld* articulate that same world in three distinct manners. Each perspective, however, is integrated with the other two. By allowing for the regional interpretation of history, one avoids making *history* itself a reductive term. "A discussion of history does well to avoid an alienation from natural science so abrupt that in the end the two interests will confront each other as incommunicable," Miller writes. "At the same time one can hardly avoid differences that at first do seem alienating" (PH 107; cf. Corrington, 1990).

The very genesis of history is tied to nature.

> The idea of history waits upon the idea of nature and rises to authority only when time has been lost in the invariant, and when action has been made unintelligible by universal order. The sense of time is original, but the status of time as a constitutional factor of experience is derivative. (PH 17)

The rise of history cannot negate its conditions of origination. Rather than rendering those ahistoric forms null and void, they must be reinterpreted in terms of historical temporality. Scientific investigation and discussion can continue on their own terms even while being amenable to historical, or philosophic, reflection. The priority of history is revealed in the way that it both integrates the different elements of Miller's actualism. History successfully binds together and maintains the integrity of the midworld and nature.

§4.2   FATE, DEMONRY, NEMESIS

History establishes the conditions of both constraint and freedom. Indeed history allows for autonomy *because* of the constraint that it imposes and, conversely, the constraint that one finds in history is a reflection of one's autonomy. In order to show how this is so, the existential theme so critical to Miller's actualism must be highlighted.

Autonomy is found neither in the tranquility of René Descartes's chamber nor in the isolation of the *I am, I exist* discovered there. The anxiety that led Descartes to retreat to his chamber must be constitutive of, and not just the occasion for, his discovery (see PH 19–20, 1952–53, 22). Any account of freedom must pass through, and give a constitutive role to, such existential threats and crises. Moreover, the conflict and tension of historical experience cannot be approached from the outside as G. W. F. Hegel is often accused of doing when he presented the career of Spirit. Rather those very conflicts and tensions must be considered from the standpoint of finite experience—including the wayward, obscure, and negative that the contemplative life found in history, and sought to avoid.

When describing historical experience and its implications one must begin with this existential fact: Without sanction, and prior to reflection, one finds oneself in history (PH 119).[15] Quoting Abraham Lincoln, Miller likes to recall that "we cannot escape history" (PC 82). The power and priority of history lies in the fact that a person does not reason his way but rather is born into the situation where all that he knows, does, and feels is bound up with a heritage of knowing, doing, and feeling. His most basic actions—beyond simple respiration and reflex—are part of a narrative continuum. His more sophisticated acts and efforts at local-control are indisputably historical insofar as they all occur via the symbolic structures of gestures, language, and artifacts.

This is the tenacity of history: It seizes one in every respect and demands that even in order to ask the question Who am I? one must have recourse to history. The question itself has a history. (Descartes, for example, could not escape relying on Augustine of Hippo when describing the route to and the experience of "pure" subjectivity.) History presents the arresting aspect that it not only holds us from without (as the resistance of circumstance) but also from within, from the side of the person. The truth of this first aspect shows itself by means of the peculiar constitution of a person—for example, the fact that my identity is composed in terms made available by the English language, the culture of capitalism, and democratic political ideals all reflect the efficacy of prevailing historical forces. The second aspect comes to light when one notes that history has an intimate hold on us insofar as the very sense of personhood is an idea. That is to say, *personhood* is a fundamental term of control; like all terms of control, *person-hood* must appeal to the symbolic processes from which the term arose, as well as the history of that process. There is no approach to history that is not already a path through history. "To a larger extent than we are aware," Miller observes, "we live through the past tense" (AH 261).

The basic existential situation is as historical as it is symbolic (see §4.5). What, then, is the character of one's experience? What traits are most prevalent? Previously the connections among history and autonomy, freedom, and respon-sibility have been stressed. History is that region where action in its strong sense is possible and thus the active, political life is possible. However, for Miller, no one can understand history unless she also comes to terms with the sense of *fate*:

> If history embodied no fatality it would become an intellectual oddity, and one would have a look at it or not, as best suited one's temperament or practical aims. It is not unusual to find history weakly recommended as a "cultural" subject or more strongly proposed as a "practical" aid, perhaps in diplomacy. It might be thought that one could talk about history in a detached mood, as if history were a phenomenon to be observed with dis-interested calm. Instead, one finds that one has introduced the idea of fate, or contrasted time with eternity or history with ahistoric modes of ex-perience, or in some other way has introduced disturbing ideas. (PH 81)

> History is the dimension in which we see ourselves, not as others see us, but as we are genetically identified. "There, but for the grace of God, go I" is not enough. One has to say, "There, by the abounding grace of God, I too find myself." There is great aversion even to a generous temper when it takes the form of fellow feeling rather than a secure and tolerant superiority. Nobody can, by the grace of God, feel himself saved from participation in the enormi-ties of the past, any more than he can dissociate his own heart and mind from its glories. But one has to take both or neither. One can't pick and choose, play Antonio but not Shylock, Portia but not Lady Macbeth. (PH 84–85)

As employed by Miller, *fate* is the necessary complement to having a particular identity and locale of action. Fate is, quite simply, finitude understood from a slightly different perspective.

History becomes fate because it is the primal ontological situation. It is the inescapable starting place; there is no ahistoric position from which to assess history. History also signifies something recognized and feared by the Romantic mind: One is born with a heavy and, finally, unpayable debt to the past (Emerson, 1838/1983, p. 97). Speaking of fate recognizes that a person lives in and through inherited categories, means of understanding, and control. One is not only *thrown into* history, as Heidegger would have it, but is continually *cast along* by its forces (IH 27). Fate is not just what is first but what *comes again and again*. It is a process in which the past is future and the future is the necessary return to and revision of the past.

Fate is connected with the midworld and its constitutive symbols (see §2.4). An actualist conception of history is impossible without this symbolic element; "history," as Miller writes, "rides on the midworld" (MS 18). The midworld is a repository of evolving definitions. A definition is a limitation on content. Like definition, "the sense of fate occurs where our own activity, whether thought or will, encounters systematic restriction" (SF 1). The form of fate that interests Miller is found in those ineluctable patterns of thought and will established in definitions. The historical world one inherits on birth, this world shot through with fate, is the disclosive symbolic environment.

Symbolically constituted modes of order ultimately derive from the actions of responsible persons. (Here Miller's sense of fate converges with the Greek idea—egoism is the possibility of tragedy [MP 21:1].)[16] Constraint does not descend on the individual but, rather, is constituted in the dialectical relationship between the universal and individual. Furthermore fate is distinctly formal, and not efficient, in character. Each symbol is a bearer of teleological import (see §2.4), akin to the restriction applied by the law (PH 144–45). Thus the specific calamities of nature are not fateful, for their restriction is not systematic. The idea of nature, however, is fateful. The necessity of fate is not equivalent to determinism (Notes PH 1-2 1950–51, 10). Finally there is also not an a priori pattern to history (RFM 21). The question of action points one toward the symbolic environment as the condition, maintenance, and career of action. It also points one toward history understood as "the story of the consequences of our commitments," of what one has ventured and done (PC 186). Action always refers to itself.

Fate is thus not encountered in facts but in the form that discloses facts (PH 8, 1951, 19). One initially confronts fate in that original vehicle of disclosure, the body. One also meets with fate in such pure symbols as language, institutions, yardsticks, and artworks (see PH 81). Indexical objects such as barometers harbor a fate and even such nonsymbolic artifacts as tools and machines, insofar as they carry out and explore the orders articulated by symbolic objects, bear the tincture of fate (PH 83). The sphere of the midworld, and all of its vehicles, are bearers of fate. Via these vehicles the past is intimately present. Via these vehicles one sees the union of individual deeds and their universal implications.[17]

While the fateful character of historical categories holds the hope for autonomy, it also makes these categories blind and destructive powers *almost* akin to natural forces (AH 264). In history the destructive element must be embraced along with its freeing possibilities (PC 191; cf. Conrad 1900/1981, p. 138). "As we build lives and states upon some view of order," Miller states, "we let loose upon ourselves the consequences of any flaw in that view" (PC 72).[18] It is part of the character of historical actions and actors that they perpetuate unknown determinations over which they have little control. Ignorance builds on ignorance. (Ignorance is ingrained in everyday experience, in common sense.) This is a strong antidote. The viciousness of historical, symbolically embodied definitions is magnified precisely by one's confidence in what has been heretofore underlined as the great virtue of historical consciousness—awareness and, indeed, self-awareness.

Actions and definitions become vicious when one supposes that there is nothing more to be aware of either outside or within their structure. In this manner, reflection, or its appearance, turns against itself. Because history is always a continuum of action, this blindness compounds itself. This viciousness is what Miller terms *demonry*.[19]

Demonry is a failure but it is not an *accident* in the trivial sense of the word. It is not just a possibility, a bit of misfortune, that might befall an action and the symbolically enforced definition it perpetuates. Rather, as Miller writes in "The Ahistoric and the Historic," demonry is an integral part of action and symbol:

> The alliance of the individual and the universal may be observed in grave personal difficulties and conflicts. A man with a universal is likely to allow it to become demonic and fanatical. He will be all for unity and dead set against variety, for cause and against purpose, for the individual and against the state, for virtue and against cakes and ale. If the universal shows us a world there may be deformity and fanaticism in it. (AH 250)

The demonry of any symbol and the universal form that it enforces is nothing other than the tendency to make static that which is in principle a dynamic vehicle of definition operating in a field of other such definitions. Here a sensitivity for the totality of the process of local-control—a process linking terms and even opposite terms in a necessary but always problematic fashion—is displaced by a single term or group of terms (see PH 7, 1951–52, 30). It is the defeat of actualist metaphysics by metaphysics in its more traditional form; the assurance we take in the relatively static becomes passivity and perversion when we seek comfort in the completely static.

Demonry is a situation where, as Hegel would have it, each is drunk, impulsively full with a particular idea. This limitation, even in its blindness, is critical to the dynamism of history. For history moves forward via self-satisfaction, the denial that it too will be taken up, reinterpreted, and changed. This is the danger implicit in the universal and utopian quality of all action: Once announced, a form of order can be applied in every possible case. Demonry is a pervasive, ineluctable, and, indeed, constitutional trait. As Miller says, in history one consorts with evil: "In history we not only consort with error and evil; we actually make them, objectify them, enshrine them in institutions, glorify them with rite and ceremony, and die for them" (PH 176).

Another paradox appears: History lives in the ahistoric and the process of history moves ahead on interpretations that deny the process itself. This is why demonry is not just the perversion of the historical consciousness but is also constitutional to history. "History rides on the vehicles of partial truth," Miller observes, "but their demonry is the sole condition of discovering their force" (PC 90). Demonry constrains and narrows history but it also accelerates it by pushing forward a certain set of characteristics, a particular consequence of past commitments and their symbolic vehicles. It gains power precisely by what it denies, accumulates strength by masking its own weaknesses, and finds completeness by hiding its own partiality.

The conflict, struggle, and resistance of history are constitutive of what Miller means by *fate*. Indeed it is a commonplace that absolutes divide as much as they unite. Seen from the inside, the demonic appropriation of a particular interpretation is the labor of truth. Approached from the outside, however, those proffering such interpretations appear as dogmatists—that is, intolerant, oppressive, and violent. One-sided interpretation will meet with resistance somewhere, at some border between the *civilized* and *barbarian*. (This border may lie within a single person, amid different parts of one society, or between societies.) This is part of the structure of the interpretation itself. "The actual is not only incomplete," Miller remarks, "but . . . it is also *incoherent* in the relations of its modes of universality" (MP 21:1). Every act, symbol, and interpretation is pursued by, indeed generates its own *nemesis*. Part of the fateful character of any symbol is its own negative pair in the dialectic, its would-be destroyer (MP 21:6). As Miller states, "Deed and word call down upon themselves the judgment which their own order invokes" (PC 160; see PH 83). Nemesis is the intimate opposition summoned by the one-sidedness of demonry. Even in its blindness, then, the demonic interpretation has some insight into itself and recognizes its larger implications.

The nemesis of any symbol, of any interpretation touched by demonry, appears in two forms. The first form is in its dialectic pair. Unity becomes demonic in monism where pluralism is denied any real standing. Efficient causality becomes demonic in determinism where teleology is denied. Yet the sense of any single pole of a dyad is bound to its pair. What, for example, is the meaning of unity if plurality is a mere illusion? The import of unity disappears, not surprisingly, along with the contrast.

Every universal has its antagonist, in fact summons it. The self confronts the other self, the subjective the objective, the physical order the moral order, the psychological any order whatsoever, rationalism the empirical, the accidental the necessary, the state the individual, the true the false, the real the illusory, the finite the infinite. From such incoherence and conflict no concluding total order is to be derived. Any universal draws its strength from an opponent, which it must conjure up in order to make good on its own claims to distinctness and authority. Utterance in any universal and composed form simply makes trouble for itself, invites it, and cannot evade it. (MS 187)

The first form of nemesis is thus the manner in which terms of definition invoke and necessarily rely on their opposites. Nemesis is another name for the constitutional role of the dialectic—that is, the confrontation of systematic modes of expression (PH 7, 1951-52, 23). While they are a basic form of organization of experience, dialectical pairs also articulate the lines where composition breaks down and where antagonism breaks out (MS 185).

The second form that nemesis takes is more external to the symbol. Each symbol bears difficulties that lie just out of the sight (MP 21:6; TO 400). The relative blindness that characterizes any act is underlined by the notion of *systematic punishment* (PC 84). The affirmation or denial of a principle may have profound, if unforeseen, implications. If the principle is significant enough, these implications can reverberate throughout the totality of one's active life. Rejecting a functioning object such as the atom or even a tool like the microscope, to offer two examples, would alter one's realm of objectivity. One is left practically and intellectually weakened, prey to the resurgence of unruly content let loose by the slackening of local-control. Nemesis is also revealed in any action whose vague and universal possibilities must wait on the vagaries of history in order to be revealed. This topic was addressed in section 3.4 where examples pertaining to the Constitution of the United States. The history of Constitutional interpretation reveals that document to be an opaque symbol requiring time, and even poignant crises, in order to be better understood. "Action advertises limit. But any self-conscious doer of any act does know that he is limiting the future, restricting it. He knows *some* of the meaning of his act," Miller asserts. Yet the poignant aspect is not the restriction that he foresaw but the restriction that was *overlooked* and, indeed, *could not have been foreseen.* It is then that "[i]ts purposes become very clearly seen, because they are seen as secular and as infinite. An act embodies an unknowable nemesis" (PH 166-67).

Demonry and nemesis are inevitable. Short of attaining an outlook on the world in total, the categories that articulate experience cannot be placed in a comprehensive, pacific order. Working from within these orders, and seeing the world insofar as those very orders allow for its apprehension, one is beholden to those categories and bound to their fateful implications. This is the larger fate of espousing a philosophy of finitude: Insofar as order is achieved via limitation whatever measure of local-control that is achieved is systematically ignorant of at least some aspects of its import. Control is never complete. This is so not because the world is too great in scope or too complex in detail. Rather it is because control, based on limitation, is shot through with viciousness.

§4.3 CONFLICT, REVISION, ACTION

Nemesis forces control to face itself. Similar to how Heidegger interpreted the danger of technology as also a saving force (1962/1977), Miller finds that nemesis is equally an *opportunity* for action and a chance for extending and deepening those categories that establish local-control. The historical past arises from neglect and must ever be discovered anew (AH 242). If demonry is the neglect of history then nemesis is the engine of its constant rediscovery.

The dose of pessimism offered in section 4.2 is thus meant as an antidote and not a poison. It is primarily an antidote against Romantic optimism. It is also an antidote against the optimism of determinists and those who affirm the providential character of history. Both types of optimists see history as a region in which a sort of perfection can be achieved. Both, however, misconceive history. Perhaps more critically, in mistaking history they also misunderstand the constitution of authority. For the discovery of autonomy lies in fate and the resources it provides for the disclosure of the authority of finitude. In order to come to terms with this paradoxical relation of constraint and autonomy, conflict is a key resource (cf. Colapietro, 2003, pp. 38–46).

Demonry and nemesis describe the conflictual play between the universality and finitude of each symbolically embodied definition. Not all universals can accommodate one another in every respect. Whether it is the ancient debate between Thales's *water* and Anaximenes's *air* or the modern antagonism between Isaac Newton's *particles* and Christian Huygen's *waves*, such terms of definition incline toward conflict.[20] This conflictual dynamic has its internal, structural aspect as well. Definition is the systematic limitation of content and *limitation is conflict*. Definition distinguishes phenomena one from another but also sets them against one another. Put another way, the symbol enforces conflict and opposition (MP 4:1).

Because there is no static definition (DT 42), definition is as an ongoing activity. Local-control is an ongoing process in which organization is growing, contracting, or a tense equilibrium of opposite forces. The border between these allied antagonists is a site of continual struggle. The category of *unity* may, for example, make forays into *plurality* diminishing the range of *plurality* and enlarging its own scope. The political definition of the human being as *agent*, to take another example, is besieged by the social and psychological conception of the human as a collection of *behaviors*. Definition is always contested, and as the preeminence of certain terms waxes and wanes. (In the case of fundamental categories, such allied antagonists, one term cannot completely vanquish its opposite because they form a dialectic pair. However, the borders of defined objects can collapse and they can be entirely subsumed by another definition.) The conditions of ontology as well as meaning derive from systematic conflicts and the maintenance of the very dynamism of such conflicts (PH 7, 1951-52, 27). As Miller remarks, thought thrives on these difficulties (PH 1-2, 1950-51, 26).

The vehicles by which local-control is achieved are, of course, the symbolic media of the midworld. Apart from symbols there is neither conflict nor control (MS 188). When one speaks of the struggle between modes of control this must be translated into actual conflicts between symbols. Just as control is not abstract but concrete, so too is conflict. Political control is a struggle regarding which institutions will hold sway. Scientific control is a struggle regarding which instruments will be recognized. Economic control is a struggle regarding which means of valuation and formal practices of exchange will be dominant.

When surveying history, then, one is impressed with the pervasiveness of tension and strife (PH 7, 1951-52, 7). In an important respect *history*, like the midworld, is *a process of conflict*. When history is considered philosophically—that is, when one addresses "pure history" (DP 151)—it is a study of these tensions and the import of these conflicts:

> To be brief and direct on this relationship, I will say that nobody can evade the confusions which lurk in thought precisely where thought is at its most systematic. No articulate world is without these systematic discontinuities.
>
> These conflicts are the fatalities of thought and it is the philosophical task to lend itself to these fatalities in order to understand them, and so to reconcile them. The pathos of our deeper antagonisms lies in this fact, that they are always the signs of what we must respect, namely some essay at a rational world. Philosophy is the reason that seeks to comprehend the loci of the breakdown of reason. (PC 189-91)

History is the story of the ongoing constitution of the actual world. These conflicts represent the precise points where the world is articulated. The conflict is where distinction and order are maintained. Yet the point of conflict is also where distinction is lost or its terms revised and, thus, the world itself undergoes fundamental change. Conflict is the critical axis of definition and ontology.

Similarly these conflicts are the loci at which personhood is constituted and reconstituted. Strife points not only to the structure of the world but to the structure of the person insofar as both presume systematic organization (PC 72). Conflict *is* organization.

In actualism conflict is elevated to the status of a metaphysical concept. In history one is harassed by conflicts; one is subjected by fate. Yet this account must be balanced. Conflicts, difficulties, and problems—they are also means of instruction and resources for control. (What one aims for in her personal life and what we aim for in our common political life is not the dissolution of conflict but the maintenance of conflict in nonviolent modes [see §5.3].) "Conflict does not operate to scatter the self but to establish it, even to organize it," Miller observes. "It seems that conflict is not unrelated to the essays at organization" (MS 187). It is not by chance that Miller heeds Hegel's advice and dwells upon the negative (1807/1977, p. 19). Conflict is the doom of demonry. For when a conflict between interpretations becomes explicit the one-sided interpretation is embattled. It becomes unworkable and change becomes requisite.

Two things of a positive nature occur in this breakdown. First, the conditions are given in which novel action can be undertaken. That is to say, revision, "a disciplined qualification of the past" (AH 267), is the possibility afforded by the failure of any demonic interpretation. Second, conflict awakens reflection. By imposing limitation, "nemesis restores the . . . equilibrium which has been lost through man's obliviousness to his own limitations and his disregard for restraint" (SF 13). In conflict the implicit structure of one's actions—primarily the dialectical alliance between the universal and the individual (AH 249)—is revealed. This revelation establishes the possibility for conscious, willful, and responsible action.

Change is an inherent ontological trait (DT 56). Because of this, historical temporality is the doom of all static absolutes (PC 145). History is about the developmental, transitory, and corruptible (PC 75-76); it makes no room for the static except understood as a *relative* permanence, a continuity *through change*. There is nothing that does not have a genealogy.

Historical change is not captured by the characteristics of nature or chance. Much of the change that occurs in nature—excepting certain biological events such as the sport and physical processes following the principles of thermodynamics—is not only blind but is, in a more profound sense, not even an example of change. The sequence of birth, growth, decay, and death found in biological processes or the formation and dispersion witnessed in physical processes are simply distinct moments of a larger simultaneity maintained by the laws of conservation. Chance, by contrast, undoubtedly creates discontinuity, and thus actual change. Yet chance misses the continuity between events. Under the heading of *chance*, history becomes a random proliferation and, thus, a completely blind process. Historical change implies *genealogical progress* as well as a form of novelty in which the present is heir to the past.

The *revisionary act* is the historical act par excellence (PH 34). Only in terms of revision or interpretation can one make sense of the paradox of orderly discontinuity and history as the understanding of discontinuity (RFM 7). For, unlike the two other forms of change just noted, interpretation binds the dynamic character of history to the ontological processes addressed in chapters 2 and 3:

> Whether one deals with the acts of individuals or of groups, this revision of the basis of action is necessary, for it defines action. Without it, there is no purpose. But what governs this revision? Merely the necessity of the will, its search for itself, for its clarity in detail, and for its own being as will. History is will. It is the career of will. History is the progressive clarification of will. It has no ulterior goal. (PH 34)

Action is always a continuum and never just an individual moment (MS 102), and so revision is *the paradigmatic mode of action*. It is a moment in the order of the symbolic processes. And just as these symbolic processes are aligned with the will, so too is revision. For the willful deed—that is, an ontological and not psychological action—is the act proper. Connecting the more abstract conception of action in chapter 2 with its explicitly historical aspect, one sees that action is the disciplined qualification of the past, the respectful amendment of the heritage of symbolically articulated interpretations provided by history.

Because history is rife with blindness, demonry, and conflict, revisionary action is required (AH 244). For even as "it is only the act which makes history possible," it is equally true that it is "only history which makes the act possible" (DP 148). (The problem of action announced in section 2.1 thus receives its full response in history—that is, action is the answer to the question of history and history is the answer to the question of action [see PL 14; PC 95].) It is only in terms of a mode of order exhibiting systematic conflict that action could have a constitutional role. The continuity of physics effaces the possibility of action because its laws exclude the possibility of their own alteration; all is consequence and physical law is uniformity. The complete discontinuity of chance also rules out action because absolute novelty reduces all to mere accident. (A sort of uniformity also arises when discontinuity is made absolute; on this ground, the positive comparison of Heraclitus and Parmenides is to the point.) In contrast to the laws of physics and the phenomena of chance, *action occurs at the points where order breaks down* at those places where order is fractured and in conflict with itself. History is a "relatively discontinuous" order (PC 91)—that is, a form of "constitutional incompleteness"

(MS 125), *a disorderly order*. It is the process of definition understood as "permanency through change" and the condition of the "relative permanence" of defined identity (DT 101, 50).

Revision is not a change of opinions but a change in outlooks (AH 255). "History is constitutional revision, not addition of new information or the correction of errors from an assumed base," Miller summarizes. "It is wholly and entirely concerned with actions, not with objects, not with purposes. It is the revision of outlook in the enlargement or defeat of artifactual controls" (DP 158). The type of action in question, then, is not pragmatic—that is, strictly psychological action. (Although revision will imply changes at this level as well.) Revision is systematic change at the level of will. Revisionary action goes to the symbolic environment (e.g., the body, functioning objects, imaginative objects) and creatively develops its implications by amending its vehicles. Transforming this symbolic environment is the exercise of freedom (EPE 10).

Revision involves the alteration of the conditions of disclosure, and it implies a *change for both the past and the future* (see §2.2). The degree to which revision affects the future is more obvious: By altering an outlook, as well as its organizing teleological terms, action alters the future. Yet because revision is a form of genetic change it also alters the chain of heredity (see §2.2). In this respect revision is a process of self-discovery in two important respects. First, it reveals the past that constitutes the present identity of the person—that is, the more common sense of genealogy. Second, it shows that the past and the future are equally frontiers of discovery, novelty, and revision.

This last is a significant claim. And there is a danger of exaggeration. Before proceeding, then, it must be stated that revision is limited by its historical character. Change that occurs in terms of continuity must preserve the relation between what had been undertaken and what is now proposed. There must be some deference to what Miller refers to as "the authority of the current enterprise" (PL 884). Change that does not conserve this connection to the current enterprise is not revision or the activity of metaphor but either some form of brute opposition or mere nonsense—that is, alteration without rule. In revising prior interpretations, action carries the past forward into the future and to some degree constrains itself and the future according to the order of the past.

There is good reason for saying that Miller's sense of revision owes much to the Hegelian concept of *Aufhebung*. The past remains present because each interpretation is in an important respect conservative. Further, because one cannot approach history but from the standpoint of a present-day interpreter, the past that remains is always the amended past. "History needs the historian" and the historian's reflective apprehension (PH 38; cf. Croce, 1920/1960). Miller remarks that "the past derives its life from the original vitality of its heirs" (AH 244). One can go further and say that history derives its very sense and import from its heirs. Indeed, the historian does not just recount but also makes history (PL 183).[21] Here the processes of history and definition clearly intersect:

> It might be thought that past events at least are not fluid. The apple Eve ate, the death of Socrates, the shot fired on Sumter seem beyond the reach of alteration. Here it is necessary to beware of conceiving an event as once and for all finished or given. Every event changes, and those changes are the event; no change, no event. But this process, like the logical one of definition, is interminable. It would be a mistake to regard a "meaning" as persisting after being given to the mind tightly tied up in a package; such meanings are no meanings. (DT 103)

History develops with the present even as it establishes the interpretive parameters for that present. Thus Miller proposes that a person can be "liberated" from his historical legacy only insofar as that legacy provided the terms enabling that liberation (PH 62).[22] The change that is introduced is not a process of construction in which novel interpretations are added onto an existing structure; interpretation is not a hodgepodge of additions. It is revisionary in a more radical sense for "every addition, by narrowing the meaning of the just preceding term, alters the meaning of the latter, an alteration which is carried down to the beginning" (DT 47).

Any pretension to complete originality is tempered with a strong sense of genealogy. Yet the moment or crisis *is* where historical action takes place. If ontology is truly historical, and thus developmental, then a significant degree of authority and freedom must be granted to the individual moments composing its larger continuity. "For now as in the past we call that our world which gives status and authority to the immediate," Miller observes. "The record of these endeavors is history" (AH 241). In history, difference, radical change, and revolution are original (PH 25). From the standpoint of symbolic action the moment is defined by the will initiating revision. From the standpoint of history the moment is defined by the conflict providing the possibility of and urgency for such revision.

Conflict is a summons to action. At the moment of conflict one cannot act without taking the bases of action into consideration. Moreover conflict demands originality insofar as conflict shows that past orders cannot proceed without some form of significant qualification. Thus history is continually *made and remade* at the points where forms of organization break down.

> Those are interested in history who must idealize the occasion for action in order to have an occasion for action. Traditional morality seeks to idealize

action without idealizing its occasion. That, in short, is the reason for the breakdown of ethics.

To "idealize the occasion" is only to seize upon it as a focus for expending the energies that sustain the world that produced the occasion. An occasion is seized upon for that promise. Action occurs as one has confidence in its occasions. This is more important than "self-confidence." Moralists try to give one confidence in such occasions by saying that one will win happiness, do good, or please God. History occurs in the breakdown of morality. A very moral person would not, I think, get to the idea of history, because the occasion for action would always be clear to him. And, of course, the makers of history are often viewed as immoral because they cannot abide the moral occasions for action. They can't act morally— that is, in terms of mores. But they propose to act, and in that way differ from the immoralist. (PH 92–93)

It is in terms of conflict that the occasion is given in which a person is not only called on to expend her energies but that the import of that expenditure is evident.[23] The confidence that one has in this occasion is not the confidence of being in complete control of its circumstances. It is also not the confidence that looks forward to a positive outcome. The confidence of which Miller writes recognizes conflict as the occasion for true action and, thus, freedom (PH 139).

The significance of the person is a corollary of the importance of the moment. What is really in question in the moment of conflict are the *actors* who recognize the occasion for action. Personhood, the counterpoint of the synthesizing tendency of history, has two instantiations—the uniqueness of the moment and the individuality of the actors who stand in the moment. Even as continuity is critical to the sense of personhood, the revelation of the person is in the moment of disjunction and change. Historical sensibility and first-person, biographical experience run together. (The moralist emphasizes the moment [MP 4:1].) The phrases *It came about that* or *It then happened* are not historical statements. Speaking historically requires that these impersonal statements be replaced with their egoistic counterparts: *I brought it about that* and *We then undertook to make it happen.* An individual person or a definite community is at the crux of historical events. What Miller refers to as "the heresy of history" is the claim that in history one speaks for himself—that is, the egoistic premise (PH 7, 1951–52, 10; see PC 83). The continuity of history is at one and the same time broken and established by the individuality of deed and person.

§4.4   REFLECTION AND AUTONOMY

The egoism implied by action points to another important aspect of conflict—its connection to reflection and self-consciousness.[24] Historical action must address itself, take itself into account. Freedom comes by the way of a historical form of constraint in the process of definition. The action of persons maintains, expands, or diminishes the terms and scope of constraint. History is thus the field for this spectacle of responsible and conscious self-maintenance (PC 104). It is also the condition of a liberating identification with the orders of definition—"History can show us only ourselves, for it is our deed" (PH 81). Here one finds a reconciliation between action and thought, a rapprochement between the active and contemplative lives. This is not just because thought is guided by action. This reconciliation is also founded on the recognition that action is *a form of thought*. Distinct from behavior, any act that is worthy of the name is reflective and aware of the conditions of its possibility. Action is lawful and, furthermore, capable of interpreting and revising those very laws by which it guides itself.

In conflict is not only the origination of the person but a particular understanding of *personhood*—that is, reflective, responsible, and philosophical. The development of this idea has its starting place in an observation common to the idealist tradition. Both J. G. Fichte and Hegel, taking just two examples, stress that the idea of subjectivity is the outcome of a process. In Fichte's case the engine of this process is *Setzen*—the positing of the not-self in the form of nature (1800/1982, pp. 34–35). For Hegel true subjectivity arises at the same time that one's understanding moves from sense certainty to the concept of truth as correspondence—that is, the veridical relationship of one's idea of the object to the object itself (1807/1977, pp. 104 ff.). In each case, subjectivity is inseparable from the dynamic conditions of its origination.

Working with these understandings as his basis, Miller proposes something similar: Personhood is not a fact but, rather, an *achievement*. In his Afterword to a collection of José Ortega y Gasset's essays, Miller remarks:

> The first personal singular pronoun is no denotation word corresponding to some object of consciousness: it is rather a reflective word, a mark of self-consciousness and therefore an equally ideal environment in terms of which the self articulates its identity. The traditional distinction between appearance and reality is no more than the attempt to establish the personal pronoun, to make it articulate, and, at the same time, to avoid the victimization which threatens any extension of the immediate into its environment. In all pretensions to finitude there lurk the conditions which allow it to be identified. (AH 237–38)

When talking about the person, one addresses not an object but a set of conditions and activities that are, by virtue of their organization, revelatory of personhood. Thus the question of consciousness, let alone of personhood, is not one that the physical sciences can properly address. In opposition to certain psychological approaches, personhood is not equivalent to the notion of a "stream of consciousness" (MS 109). Like Fichte and Hegel, Miller holds that the route by which one clarifies the sense of personhood lies along the way of distinction, opposition, and conflict. The dialectic of opposites is the intrinsic order of history, ontology, and, therefore, biography (PH 7, 1951–52, 22).

In order to put some existential flesh on these bare structural bones, conflict must be connected to the sort of self-understanding ingredient to biography (see DP 126–27; PC 66–68). One might ask: *Who* is the person without troubles, conflicts, and compulsions? Who is the person whose every aim has gone unchallenged and whose every project has met with success? Meeting such questions with a positive response is difficult. Even before making the attempt, it is important to be reminded of the character of the problems that interest Miller. These are not problems of the sort encountered in the details of execution (e.g., a confusion in measurement pertaining to an engineering project) but, rather, questions posed to the enterprise as such (e.g., Why build in the first place?, Who am I such that I build?; see PH 91). They are problems that concern an outlook and not the details of an outlook (see §2.1).

So perhaps it is better to ask: Who is the person who has not reflected on herself, her ideals, and her vocation? Who is the person who has not taken herself into account? The appropriate and, indeed, only possible answer is *no one* (see PC 72). There is no recognition of this "person" who is without problems of an existential sort. Such problems describe the threshold between the unconscious and conscious, between natural and human being. In crossing back and forth over this threshold, consciousness is carried to the furthest limits of the unconscious and, in return, the unconscious is everywhere touching on and a part of consciousness. Where there is pure psychology, however, one *only* meets unconscious stimulus response or drives. At that extreme one does not meet a person.

Conflict is the possibility of biography. The corollary of this assessment is that one must look to history when seeking personhood. Nothing is known, not even about oneself, apart from history (AH 263). (In this regard it is revealing that even those figures in the history of philosophy who labored most in establishing the independence and ahistoricity of subjectivity themselves came to this discovery in terms of history and biography.) Without history—that is, a reflective and irreversible mode of temporality—the whole idea of knowing oneself or another becomes ludicrous. As Miller likes to say, "History *re*-minds us" (MS 19).

If psychology is the misunderstanding of ontology and chronicle the miscon-
strual of history, memory is the misapprehension of reflection. There is, of
course, some basis for this misapprehension. Memory is at the root of reflection.
Miller recognizes that memory is "the most elementary mode of the influence of
the past" (PH 100). By means of recollection, objects, details, and events of the
past come into the present and are once subject to apprehension. In this manner
the gap between the present and past is brought to light as a principle of com-
prehension and order. When a child seeks out a toy she had abandoned earlier,
for example, and rediscovers it in the place where it was originally set down, the
growth of a whole new form of organization is incited. This discovery ramifies
other categories of organization and develops capacity for local-control.

Memory is neither the only revelation of time, nor is it the only form of
time. Miller makes this point by observing that memory is a *psychological* concept
and thus inadequate to the larger idea he is developing:

> The past that appears to the humanist is not exhausted in memory, but
> involves always this process of redefinition of the person and his world. Mem-
> ory is a psychological, not a historical concept. It is a formal ingredient in the
> recognition of an object, without which no object can attain outline or clar-
> ity. An object is now what one has found it out to be. We do not merely
> "find" objects, we "find them out" and so discriminate among them, and in
> this process of discrimination the object attains its definition and meaning.
> But the focus of attention in the learning process is the object itself, not one's
> reasoning processes or even one's psychological operations. (PH 96)

Memory is oriented to data. Data are disclosed in light of purposes and rediscov-
ered in memory in terms of some present purpose that bears on an earlier undertaking (PH 74–75). When recalling the location of a mislaid object one often asks,
"What was I doing five minutes ago?" What is remembered, then, are defined
things—for example, physical objects, events, even one's own feelings and ideas. In
being remembered, however, neither the objects nor the processes that brought
them to light are necessarily subject to *reflection*. They are simply liable to recognition and articulation: "Ah yes, *it* did happen that way didn't it?" or "Oh, *that* is the
scarf I lost." Memory represents a personal and individual form of chronology
(PH 99). Like chronology, memory reveals time as a means of division and distinction. Memory is a mode of meaning-control applicable to data or meaning-
control corresponding to rules of use (see §3.2). Such control does not approach
symbolic self-control.

"All consciousness of time entails a degree of self-consciousness. This holds
even for memory which is not the same as history" (MP 17:5). What Miller claims,

of course, is that reflection and the sort of self-control that it implies are only possible in terms of a historical past. If there is such a past, however, there must likewise be a corresponding, historical way of being in the *present*. "In general there are two 'presents,' one for psychology and one for history," Miller states. "The nonpsychology 'present' implies a nonpsychology 'past.' That there is a nonpsychology past is one way of saying that there is history" (PH 91). The psychological present is signified by the discrete moment, framed by other discrete moments past and future, and strung along in a chain of succession described in terms of efficient causality. The historical present, on the other hand, is a figure of time foreshortened, condensed, and immediate. It entails the recognition of an idea, and the career of that idea, in the heart of one's present.

Conflict brings to light the historical present. Conflict throws a person back on himself, initiating a search for sources of control, identification, and authority. In seeking out those resources, the present action must be addressed not as a fleeting moment but as an expression of more encompassing orders. "The present tense of any one person does not include the historical past as either an actual or a possible memory," Miller observes. "Indeed, the past looms only in so far as the present is threatened with some disqualification, so that to understand itself as present it needs to undertake a story of its genesis" (PH 115). It is in patterns of action that one finds these sources of control. Conflict shows these modes of functioning as unstable and in need of some measure of revision. The act of revision is the moment of self-consciousness that expands the present toward both its past and its future, and shows that one's past is one's future and one's future has consequences for one's past.

The matter of conflict and revision is always identity (see PH 128). Thinking back to section 4.3, it is now clear that conflict is as much the opportunity for *self-reflection* as it creates the circumstance in which novel, revisionary action can be undertaken.

> In the revision of outlooks, that is, of the pattern of nature and of human nature, one comes to oneself. These are the essays we make at self-discovery, of the meaning of the self as integral. History and biography (madness) are the loci of such discoveries. Something was known before Freud. But both are the processes of freedom, and both are secular, temporal, and scientific. Both grow out of experience. (DP 126)

Revision displays the intrinsic connection between the order guiding action and the person undertaking action—that is, the egoistic premise.

What is the nature of the ego revealed in revisionary processes? Its form is not that of a solution but rather an abiding problem. Conflict is premised on the unstable but necessary union of the universal and individual (AH 249). "The historical act shows the difficulty as the very man," Miller notes. "He is the same as the difficulty" (DP 149). Personhood is revealed in, and organized in terms of, those conflicts that threaten personhood. Thus personhood comes into its own not through the elimination of conflict but via the *thoughtful control of these problems* (PH 8, 1951, 23). As Miller remarks, "It is only a philosophy which endows limit with ontological status which can turn conflict to constructive use. The use of conflict is the disclosure of the necessary. To make that disclosure is the labor of history" (PC 90). In that labor is also the stuff of biography and, thus, the discovery of personhood.

The most important question raised by conflict is that of *self-control*. Memory provides one with the conditions of meaning-control and, perhaps, purpose-control. What is at issue in both of these modes of control, however, is the organization of defined objects, the detailed population of a world. While they are preconditions of self-control just as psychology is a precondition to morality, meaning-control and purpose-control cannot be mistaken for self-control.

What is involved in self-control? To what is self-control directed? Posing such questions suggests an intent to avoid the obvious. For what else could be at stake in self-control other than the person? Here, however, actualism does throw the obvious into question. The ambiguity overlooked by common sense is the status of the subject–object distinction. Actualism is a philosophy of action and not objects (be they mental or material). When the issue of self-control is raised, then, one must avoid translating the matter into wholly subjective terms. Attention must be directed to the person insofar as he is amid the midworld. The self in question is the active person, the *animal symbolicum*:

> I agree with attempts such as Skinner's to show that no act, no autonomy, can be observed as a specific phenomenon or event. On the other side, a totality of any sort, if *fait accompli*, has always made difficulty for personal autonomy. I am proposing that the act is itself the immediacy that generates those distinctions. But this act is a pure functioning. . . . It appears in what I call the midworld, neither in a hidden soul nor in perceived objects, but in functioning objects. (DP 142)

Personhood must be considered in terms of those vehicles by means of which an individual attains articulation and control in both the subjective and objective spheres. That is to say, the question of self-control must be addressed in terms of the symbol.

Section 3.5 considered identity in terms of the symbolic function in which the connection between persons and the symbolic environment is understood as "the actuality of themselves" (PH 20–21). As an expression of the will and the embodiment of action, the symbol is the objectification of human energies. It is not, of course, an objectification in the sense of a mere representation—as if symbols were literally portraits of humanity, conscious attempts at depicting a self-understanding (DP 159–60). Rather symbols point toward the agent, the active being and not a passive object of study. In the midworld one finds *the means of understanding* and, thus, active understanding itself. To reiterate a point made earlier, when a person wants insight into another community, another person, or his own personhood the best way of proceeding is to ask: What symbols does one employ?, What are the institutions to which one is committed?, What words does one use? These are the questions that reveal the available terms of control and, thus, afford insight into persons as agents.

An orderly world as well as an orderly personality need not be reflective, however. As Miller states, order can be technological and not philosophical (PH 128). Reflection thus marks a difference in control. Conflict assists a person in examining her modus operandi (PH 1–2, 1950–51, 13). Control hides itself so long as functioning is smooth and unproblematic. Conflict reveals symbolic function because the crisis casts her back to certain authoritative symbolic vehicles—for example, revolution is a question of political institutions, betrayal a question of models of friendship, chaos a question of one's philosophical concepts. Rather than plumbing the depths of the soul, self-control involves going, so to speak, *out of oneself* and *into the midworld of symbols*. Taken literally, of course, this figure of speech misses the point in that one need not go *out* to the midworld for one is already there.

The discovery of history is the discovery of personhood: "History can show us only ourselves, for it is our deed. . . . We cannot escape it, because it is ourselves" (PH 81). This understanding parallels assessments Miller makes elsewhere regarding the relationship between symbol and person: "[W]e purchase finitude only at the price of infinities [i.e., symbols] which reveal the conception of the self with which we are identified" (PC 144); or, more bluntly, symbols "lead directly to the original of the portrait" (PC 60). The similarity in the phrasing is by no means accidental. Symbol and history *both* are media of self-understanding and its pair self-control.

Symbol and history have a common function. Symbol and history are joined in action as the constitutional factor. Action manifests itself in the symbolic career of history as what Miller calls "control in principle." With respect to the symbol, Miller writes:

> The question [of how norms can be more than just "ideal" in the pejorative sense] would be resolved if it were possible to discover a local vehicle of universal meanings. The universal is control in principle. It is control, therefore, over nature in principle, not in particular. *The vehicles of this control in principle*

I have ventured to call "symbols." It is proposed that they occur only as particular objects yet have the force of indicating a quite universal order. It is further proposed that as universals, hence as normative, they show self-control. (TS 17–18, italics added)

Similarly, addressing history, Miller observes:

It is this will that identifies circumstances and gives them systematic importance. The cause of a historical event is therefore (1) the actual existence of a will and (2) its continued assertion, or maintenance, in the face of circumstance. Such is the order, or rationale, of history.

Causes are identified in so far as control occurs. This holds for all causes, for all reasons, and for all understanding. *But history is control in principle.* It is the maintenance of control. There is no cause of control, no control of control, no reason for it, no understanding of it. But this does not imply that a particular case of such pure control has no cause or reason. On the contrary, every case of pure control demands a clear perception of the confusion that it seeks to avoid, and recognizes the actual circumstances that threaten control. . . .

The will defines its own circumstances, but does not abolish them. (PH 29, italics added)

Symbol and history, like action, are unenvironed. That is to say, neither symbol nor history is subject to explanation in that each provides the terms of explanation. In explaining symbols one must have recourse to other symbols. In explaining history one by necessity appeals to other historical forms of order. In providing the normative principles of our experience, then, both symbols and history are not properly subject to causation, control, or explanation; such terms are only appropriate for psychological process and defined objects. As has been observed in different contexts, symbol and history are, again like action, *original* (PH 23–26). Symbol and history are also allied with the will. Symbols are embodiments of will in that they are the result of actions with implications that exceed their peculiar psychological motivations, take on universal significance, and become control-in-principle. History is the career of forms of will.

Historical experience can only be fully clarified in terms of symbolism. The characteristics of fate, nemesis, and revisionary action only make sense when interpreted in light of the midworld. History is a region of inherited understandings, opaque and pervasive forms of order, and genetic ontology. Finitude means finding oneself in the current of history whose career is nothing other than the trajectory of symbols. Historical time is thus a form of transcendence—reaching *across* chronology, connecting the past and present in terms of a governing order—and the symbol is the vehicle for that transcendence. The symbol itself is the *transtemporal* factor, the synthesizing medium.[25] History is the form of symbolism, its basic precondition. In return, the symbol is the *actuality of history*.

So, when he counsels that self-control requires a reflective, historical understanding, Miller recommends two things: (1) that history as symbolically constituted control-in-principle be the subject of one's attention and (2) that these symbolic controls be addressed as historical in the sense of having a genealogy and, thus, as intelligible only in connection with their ongoing development. In order to understand one's present as well as oneself in the present—and thus achieve a degree of autonomy—an appeal must be made to the vehicles that articulate that present. Any search for self-understanding and self-control will lead to a sense of oneself as genetically defined (PH 84–85).

§4.5 HISTORY AND PHILOSOPHY

The connections between the historical form of life that is the active life and the apparently ahistoric way of being that is the contemplative life are found along the lines of personhood, local-control, responsibility, and ontology. The implications suggest the philosophical character of political institutions and the political import of philosophical reflection. Uniting philosophy and history indicates not just the possibility but the actuality of a metaphysics of democracy.

The difficulty of writing a philosophy of history remains, however (see PC 75; cf. Colapietro, 2003, pp. 63–71). Philosophy, so long allied with the search for universal and eternal ideas, hardly admits being joined to the historical world of particularity and flux. The desiderata of the former seem to exclude the actuality described by the latter. Yet, since Giambatista Vico, philosophy and history have sought to address one another and even fuse their respective enterprises. There have been *philosophies of history* (e.g., Kant's or Fichte's; cf. Colapietro, 1990, p. 84) as well as *historicist philosophies* (e.g., Rorty's and Friedrich Nietzsche's). The results of these attempts have not been, however, adequate to the aim of actualism.

In the case of philosophies of history, history is reduced under the rule of philosophy. Philosophies such as Kant's or Fichte are ahistorical interpretations of history in which history becomes the surface phenomenon of a deeper, ahistorical concept. This is particularly evident with Kant for whom history is simply the workings of nature in the lives of human animals. Historical forces may conspire, as he suggested in "Idea of a Universal History from a Cosmopolitan Perspective," to produce reflection. Yet history is not itself subject or ordered according to those powers evidenced in human reason and reflection. History, as

Kant understands it, can only be grasped intellectually; it cannot be participated in as an agent. As a theory of the generation of events, history explains and cancels effective human authority. In the case of historicist philosophies, by contrast, it is philosophy that is reduced under a naturalistic interpretation of experience. History becomes mere change, the production of sheer difference, and philosophy's own search for order becomes the surface phenomenon of that process. As Nietzsche proposed, theories, universals, and ahistoric conceptions are not insights into the truth but, rather, behaviors explicable according to natural drives. Interestingly, both philosophies of history and historicist philosophies reduce, on a practical level, to the same thing. Free and authoritative concrete action becomes a myth.

Each of these two possibilities confirms the contradiction between philosophy and history even as it pretends to resolve those differences. For Miller, the apparent contradictions must be precisely that, *apparent*. The connection between philosophy and history must be understood as a paradox that points toward a new interpretation of both, as well as a means for addressing the issues of autonomy and self-control raised by the biographical question.

Simply stated: What Miller proposes is that philosophy be *historicized* and, similarly, history be *philosophized*. There is perhaps a better way of putting the matter, however. For what philosophy and history hold in common, and what allows for the equation of the two, is a concern with *control-in-principle* or the symbol. Thus one need not say that either philosophy or history determines the other. The key is their relation to the symbol that allows for a nonreductive unity, a dialectical relationship between philosophy and history. Philosophy, in seeking terms of universal incidence as embodied in symbols, turns to history because such terms cannot be considered apart from their genealogies (DP 87). History, in understanding events in their concreteness and considering the fate of symbolically embodied actions, appeals to philosophy for such matters cannot be understood apart from universal forms of control they embody. As Miller states, "It is the function of a philosophy of history to bridge the gulf between essence and existence, and it can do this only in so far as essence becomes historical and existence ideal" (PC 96). Both philosophy and history lead to and explore the actual. Without the actual—that is, action and its symbolic embodiment—philosophy and history remain opposed.

In the essay "History and Case History," Miller articulates his equation of philosophy and history:

Of course I can hardly venture in personal safety to say that without the history of philosophy—or philosophy as history—there would be no history at all. Philosophy is pure history and never tells what is so. Nor does one say what is so in terms of philosophic controls. You say what is so in terms of mathematical and physical controls. . . .

If philosophy were anything other than pure history, its failure to tell anyone what was so would justify the contempt in which it has so often been held. All its words would become nonsense in terms of what is so. In fact, that such is the case has been claimed. "What is it about?" people ask, and there is no answer. But history is not about something else. It is the self-revelatory. There were men not long ago who repeated the old tune about "pseudo-concepts." . . . It is plain that they found the constitutional universal a pseudo-concept because they were pseudo-philosophers. They were not historians. The act, which is the basic historical word, made no appearance in the stream of consciousness or in a postulate set. The success of these men shows the depth of our ahistoric temper. . . .

The pure continuum of history is philosophy, where one never says what is so, but where one develops the ways of telling what is so. . . .

So, I grasp the nettle and say that the very authority of those who tell us what is so is historical and philosophical. The modes of telling what is so are all historically generated. The physicist and psychologist look around on their terms and find no actuality, and so no history and no philosophy. In consequence the special sciences do not even find themselves. They are not self-conscious, not aware that their very terms make no sense and have no authority apart from the process that forced their discovery. Yes, forced. Any imperative rests on its historical origin, on the self-maintaining actuality that clarifies itself in asserting causes, atoms, and the psychological itself.

If we want reverence, anything sacred and so imperative, we must advance now to history—and I cannot avoid it!—to pure history, which is philosophy. There is the common world, the actual one. (DP 149–51)

Both philosophy and history are forms of what Miller refers to in another context as "absolute empiricism" (PH 7, 1951–52, 17). Absolute empiricism does not concern itself with experience as detail, perspective, and affection—that is, what Miller refers to as "what is so." Rather it is interested in *ordered* experience and modes of order themselves. The insight here is that empirical history (interpreted as the accumulation of data) rides on a more fundamental level of pure history. Similarly, the empiricism practiced by natural scientists assumes a more basic form of absolute empiricism. Nothing is merely given; there is no possibility for disclosure without the symbol. Attention must be given not just to the act as event but, rather, *the act as will.* This is the direction in which pure history and absolute empiricism are pointing.

Action and symbolism are the concern of both philosophy and history. The two modes of absolute empiricism address the original and not the defined.

Paradoxically it is for this reason that philosophy and history are deemed useless fields of study. Neither philosophy nor history addresses facts strictly speaking. Neither answers questions. Both examine the symbolic process, the fateful development whereby modes of order are generated, maintained, revised, and perish.

Because of their common focus on the symbolic, philosophy and history are dedicated to the examination of this conflictual and problematic career of symbols. Conflict is the *how* of ontology and not the *what*. Thus the conflicts that interest Miller are not a matter of divergent data—that is, the question of error—but struggles between modes of order, or *constitutional conflicts*. Not amenable to empirical resolution, such conflicts require philosophical and, indeed, genealogical consideration. "Those conflicts are the phenomenology of spirit, the stations of its career, the secular stations of the cross. *It is this story which is both history and philosophy*," Miller writes. "[P]hilosophy is the actuality of those conflicts which establish the grounds upon which arguments occur and by which they are regulated" (PC 73-74, italics added).

History-as-philosophy is primarily dedicated to the *how* of ordered experience, the dynamic of control-in-principle. The *what*, the various regimes of established control-in-fact, is of secondary importance. Thus it is Miller's occasional claim that neither history nor philosophy can privilege any mode of order. Insofar as they address ordered experience as such, no particular set of institutions, practices, or facts can be preserved from the larger process. "The disinterestedness of history is not of the same sort as that of the questioner of facts in some established frame of reference," Miller writes. "In history we judge only that we may be judged; we aspire to be worthy of being overpassed, but not ignored" (PH 85). By contrast, when one resists being exceeded—that is, establishing her institutions and practices as an orthodoxy—she rejects history and verges on the despotic (PC 185). Miller embraces the career of will. The result is an alliance between democracy, history, and philosophy: All are beyond orthodoxy and open to endless creation and re-creation in the form of revision (see PH 173; PC 185; IH 30).[26]

Miller states that without the history of philosophical reflection there would be no history at all. If it was not at bottom the dynamic development of modes of control and thus not amenable to reflection—that is, if it was not philosophical at its root—then history could not be discovered. All that would be left would be the flux of natural events, change without measure or meaning. History and philosophy are complements. (And democracy itself is a complement of the two.) Indeed one can go even so far as to say that they are a necessary pair, mutually constituting one another and forming an irreducible bond.

A return to the semiotic vocabulary of "The Symbol" (see §3.2) completes the description of the relationship between philosophy and history. The primary distinction offered in section 3.2 was between sign and symbol. The object sign (the sign proper) is allied with the world understood as defined. The defined world allows for control primarily in the modes of meaning-control and purpose-control. Each of these forms of control is a mode of reference to natural and artifactual objects in the world, respectively. In the world of signs one traffics in facts, data, and purposes understood in the limited sense proposed by pragmatists. The field of symbols, however, expands the area of control. For while a person engrossed in the world of signs may be a powerful technician, she may have precious little sense of herself. What is missing in the technician is *self-control*. This failing is not remarkable. Self-control is not just difficult to attain but is by definition elusive. Unlike the other forms of control it does not point to things in the world but, rather, leads to those categories that compose the world as such. Control-in-principle, unlike control-in-fact, requires more than just being an active, practically engaged person. (Although this is the first step in any process of control.) In addition to practical activity, there is the requirement of *reflection*. Only then can a person move from being a master of a world to having some modicum of control over herself.

The term *self-control* can be situated within Miller's semiotic vocabulary. Figure 3.1 from section 3.2 can be revised to represent a more developed gradation of types of control (see fig. 4.1); here the vocabulary of control is extended to the symbolic sphere.

The proper objects of philosophy and history are the modes of symbolic-control and, more particularly, self-control. They are the basis of control-in-principle. As Miller states, a philosophy of history validates the *medium* that allows for facts and practical action (PC 96). While philosophy and history in a sense ad-

Figure 4.1   Modes of Control

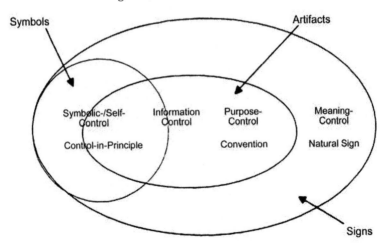

dress the midworld as a whole—that is, symbols, artifacts, and signs—their more precise concern is those symbols that embody will. Actualism is an amalgamation of philosophy and history addressing a conception of control understood in its symbolic sense.[27] It is for this reason that history is "useless" (PL 682), while philosophy is "just talk" (MS 59). Because they are concerned with reflection, they lack direct technical import. Considered in any other fashion, both philosophy and history sink to the level of second-rate science, if not pseudoscience (see Popper, 1992). Far from denying the charge of the "uselessness" of these pursuits, Miller accepts and, indeed, emphasizes it. Philosophy and history are about symbolic control-in-principle or they are nothing at all.

Actualism is a philosophy of criticism. The task is not simply describing, cataloging, and effectively making a system of prevailing modes of control. (Actualism is not a variant of structuralism.) One's concern extends to the life of these symbols or, perhaps better stated, symbolic life itself. Control-in-principle is the means of human life understood as a dynamic, normative, and critical endeavor. Moreover, symbols are not just vehicles for criticizing the world—that is, articulating and examining the region of signs. Each symbol stands in a critical relationship to other symbols and, finally, to itself; symbols are regulative and, indeed, self-regulative. Examining symbols by means of other symbols is the common task of philosophy and history.

> Finally, it seems fair to ask what the history of philosophy is about. Idealism answers that it is the progressive exploration of the structure of criticism, of the possibility of assertion, of the finite point of view. And if that history is more than a collection of variant theories, those theories must be aiming at something. . . . Thus, the history of philosophy is the objectification of the endeavor to reach the conditions of assertion. There will be no bar to new inventions until philosophers focus upon the conditions which make even error possible. (FI 268)[28]

The final goal of such an examination—progressively moving away from data and toward control-in-principle—is "to make the structure of criticism absolute" (PL 302; see PH 181). Here modes of control are addressed directly as control.

Criticism and the question of authority cannot be divorced from the biographical question that initially brought these issues to light. The human form of being comes to light in and through the midworld—that is, Ernest Cassirer's *animal symbolicum*—and individuals also develop a sense of personhood and agency through the activity of criticism (see PH 1–2, 1950–1951, 6). "All categories are factors of life and experience," Miller states in a quotation cited earlier in this chapter. "They are not general properties of the content of experience, but the operational modes of a life, its method of constructing itself" (MP 21:8).

§4.6 CONCLUSION

"We discover our human estate in a world of our own doing," Miller remarks. "It is a region disclosed only by reflection. We cannot escape these reflections" (PH 82). Such reflections are inescapable precisely because they mark the path from the psychological and technical to the philosophical and fully human condition. That path must traverse history. The existential spark igniting the historical attitude is the biographical question:

> So the uneasiness that prompts history is a radical uneasiness. It is based on misgivings over the secular, and also over the transcendent. This seems to be the impasse in which it appears. I think it is a phase of the impasse between skepticism and dogmatism, which itself is felt only as the blockage of energy and not as an impersonal fact or theory. The conflict of those two positions occurs only as the restlessness of an attitude that is both self-seeking and disciplined. As the record of freedom, history is also the idea of self-discipline. Since it is a radical idea, it must occur as an answer to a radical, not speculative, conflict, —that is, as conflict of attitudes understood as volitional and passionate. (PH 94)

What the existential question proposes is the need for an autonomous and finite mode of authority. The options of skepticism or dogmatism do not satisfy one's biographical queries nor conform to the phenomena of personhood. The finite person is a responsible but fragile being, a being occupying a middle ground where control is always in force but never secure. The historical continuum of symbols (i.e., the midworld) is the formal complement to this conception of personhood.

At the close of an essay titled "Idealism and Freedom" Miller states:

> What Kant proposed was the capacity of thought to police itself. He did not carry out that idea. Since then it has grown. Since then the idea of history has been brought into the open. History is the order of the unique. It declares the efficacy of time in the meaning of events. . . . History is the vindication of inwardness, the record of daring and of its transforming victories. The idealism of the future will be a philosophy of history, of action, of a self-generating, lawful finitude. Such are the conditions of a metaphysics of democracy. (PC 74)

This passage, cited before and otherwise referred to numerous times, it is worth revisiting at this juncture. For, to Miller's mind, there is no coming to a proper estimation of politics, let alone a metaphysics of democracy, except via history. His insistence on this point is now understandable. In history the roles of action and reflection within the ontological process—first articulated in *The Definition of the Thing*—come fully to light. These qualities are intrinsic to a sense of democracy that emphasizes responsible egoism and proposes that each person think of himself as a legislator. This responsibility is, in Miller's estimation, unavoidable because in history one's energies are formalized and become the object of critical reflection. There mundane existence—its habits, practices, objects, and institutions—becomes idealized, and the active life and the contemplative life are fused. Democracy can only flourish if the occasion of action is idealized in this way. Otherwise democracy becomes a mode of management, a way of patching up one's unruly communal affairs.

FIVE

Democracy

The expression *a metaphysics of democracy* is inspired by Walt Whitman's *Democratic Vistas*.[1] Miller himself only used the phrase a couple of times in his writing, the most prominent example appearing in the essay "Idealism and Freedom" where he states:

> In politics we are today struggling to secure free institutions. But it is obvious that, to use a phrase of Walt Whitman's, we have no "metaphysics of democracy." Indeed our currently successful doctrines repudiate metaphysics, alleging that democracy is the triumph over such fantasies. (PC 72-73)

As used by Whitman the import of the term *metaphysics* has two aspects. First it shows that *democracy* is worthy of being understood as a metaphysical concept. If the world has changed from undemocratic to democratic, one's metaphysics must change as well. As Whitman attested in 1867, democracy had already become to some extent, and would more completely realize itself as, an *idea* (1867/1982, pp. 935-936). Despite his own differences with the poet,[2] Miller is fundamentally in accord with Whitman on this matter. For Miller, the liberal democratic state is an idea—that is, like nature and history, it is a fundamental mode of control. There is no complete articulation of one's world without this concept and, further, no reflective understanding of oneself lacking its examination (PH 5, 1931, 72-82, 113).

Both Whitman and Miller share a common interest in elevating the mundane. This is the second aspect of referring to metaphysics in conjunction with democracy. Here *metaphysics* is not a technical term but, rather, an expression of value. Insofar as democracy bespeaks the common and workaday, a metaphysics of democracy raises the active life to a level of significance to which it was hitherto excluded. In his *Democratic Vistas* Whitman writes that his aim is imparting to the average person immersed in daily affairs "the breath recuperative of sane and heroic life" (1867/1982, p. 940). There is a need to assure people of the efficacy of their actions. It is a central point of Miller's that common citizens should recognize the authority that they actually command. Only in that way can dignity be accorded to persons. Further, only this recognition legitimates actual democratic practice at the heart of the active life.

Heroism is thus a keynote of a metaphysics of democracy. Like Whitman, Miller specifies Greek heroism as his point of reference (see AH 257, 266-67; cf. Whitman, 1867/1982, p. 668). As understood by the Greeks, the heroic life is a particularly human way of being. Distinct from the eternality of nature and immortality of the gods, human beings exceed mere finitude by acting in a manner worthy of being recorded and remembered; in so acting they find a *mortal* form of *immortality* definitive of the active life. With his use of *res gestae*, Miller captures this classical sense of action. The Latin evokes the past manifestation of action as well as how these achievements demand public recognition. Miller wants to popularize this ancient aristocratic notion in order to transform our idea of public life. That we compose and maintain our world in even the most mundane modes of acting, speaking, and making is crucial to actualism (see PH 83). What occurs in a democracy is that this authority is (at least implicitly) recognized and formalized—citizens are authorized in expressing themselves in and regulating themselves by deeds as they take shape in the form of laws, institutions, and customary practices. Herein lies a heroic and glorious liberty (see PH 121). In this there is also a weighty responsibility. For the degree to which a person attains the heroic life rests on the significance of his deeds and the will to perpetuate the forms of order that they establish.

The foregoing considerations of action, symbolism, and history are integral to this change of mind. By adding the term *democratic* to actualist metaphysics, this chapter undertakes a translation of these basic ideas. This revision is achieved in an elucidation of the problems at the heart of not just Miller's project but the political enterprise as such—joining freedom and authority (PL 143), as well as reconciling spontaneity and discipline (PC 191). Actualism seeks the middle ground between the extremes of monadic and pluralist absolutisms, bringing to light the productive relationship of contraries such as freedom and authority. The concepts of action, symbolism, and history describe the shape of that middle ground. The idea of democracy completes the task by not only offering further terms for the reconciliation of the active and contemplative lives but also by being a *figure for the process of reconciliation itself.*

Section 5.1 is an examination of active, first-person experience that is the basis of Miller's conception of morals and politics. After a discussion of liberal democracy in section 5.2, the procedural commitments of the democratic state are the specific topic of section 5.3. There a detailed examination of the symbolic and formal role of the state is undertaken. Section 5.4, by focusing on the aims of the state, addresses criticism and how the activity of criticism is facilitated by the state. Both sections 5.3 and 5.4 articulate the idea of a *community of power* (DT 189), a community of shared authority that is central to the active life.

§5.1 METAPHYSICS OF MORALS

What is implied by a *metaphysical* clarification of democracy? To Miller's mind, clarifying liberal democracy by esteeming it the best means to certain desired ends is of limited value (cf. Rorty, 1991, p. 33). Hypothetical imperatives cannot establish any necessity for liberal democracy. One would not, however, attain a metaphysical elucidation by simply bringing nonempirical concepts to bear on the matter. Thomas Jefferson's dogmatic invocation of "nature and nature's God" in The Declaration of Independence is not an example of the metaphysical approach Miller has in mind. A metaphysical elucidation implies two things. First, it affirms that liberal democracy has a *necessary* status, and that any account of it is to be rendered in terms of the *structure of human experience.* Second, a metaphysical defense is a mixture of transcendental and dialectical methods—that is, "the very arduous analysis of the finite point of view" (FI 268). Democratic institutions are a conclusion drawn from a consideration of experience as such and how certain key concepts imply one another in the structure of experience. The first glimpse of this integration is found in morality.[3]

The connotations of the phrase, *a metaphysics of morals,* provides more than a clue as to both the object and method of Miller's inquiry. His approach is Kantian and he aims at articulating the conditions for the possibility of morality (see MP 4:1; MP 21:1). Yet, unlike Immanuel Kant's essay at describing morality, Miller claims that an existential orientation is the condition of the metaphysical status of morality (PH 19-20, 1952-53, 37). While the transcendental form of inquiry must be kept in mind, the Kantian starting place for this inquiry is subject to revision. We begin with the egoistic premise at the root of morality (see PH 7, 1951-52, 10; see §§4.3 and 4.4). The object of inquiry is the form of personhood and world.

The *egoistic premise* is the declaration that personhood is the most basic experience, the starting point for philosophizing. This is the "original heresy" of personhood (MP 9:9), as well as what Miller refers to as the "heresy of history." Both of these heresies are connected to a third heresy—"the heresy of liberalism" (MP 21:2; see §5.2). Personhood has a certain priority in the *order* of experience. It is neither the most real nor the only reality. Simply put: It is where one necessarily begins.

In light of these existential commitments the transcendental question should be rephrased as follows: What is logically presumed in establishing the ego? A basic answer to this question is that *sociability* is a condition of personhood

(PH 5, 1931, 70; see §4.4). The conditions of sociability are not merely practical tools. The environment of social, moral, and political relations is the necessary complement of the individual will (EC 6). This claim centers on three aspects of experience: (1) the sense of the efficacy of one's actions; (2) the realization that the present moment is a juncture of decision, action, and consequence; and (3) the recognition of finitude.

As to the first aspect of personhood, it is no surprise that Miller finds the fundamental problem of ethics to be the question of action (PH 19-20, 1952-53, 24). All senses of moral and political autonomy depend on the act. "The interest in morals derives from the prospect of freedom," Miller observes. "We wish above all to be effective, to count for something. We would avoid inconsequence by becoming agents and doers" (MM 1). Another way of phrasing the matter is that a person *is* insofar as she is effective, authoritative, and free. The act is, quite simply, the acting self (MP 14:7).

As to the second key to the experience of personhood, the importance of the moment reveals the irreversible continuum of history. Miller writes:

> It is to history, not to theory, that we must go if the actual is to shine by its own light and not to be obscured in the light which is also the total darkness. Philosophers have been concerned with saving the appearances; if history be a philosophical idea it can only propose to save the moment. This is very hard to do. Ideals are fairly easy to come by and they may even seem reasonable. But a child can scatter them in the fascinated glow of some trivial absorption, thereby bringing humiliating qualms to the observer. The fugitive mind evades the conditions of the lucid moment. It shrinks from the implications of intensity. No doubt it is very difficult to let the moment declare its authority. As a general thing we prefer to regard the moment as subordinate, seeing it from some position which is never itself actual. (AH 265)

The moment is the escape from the eternality and permanence of the Eleatic ideal. It is also a break from mere nature (i.e., "nature" devoid of reflection and authoritative action). The moment establishes the importance of action as the authoritative means of affecting such change. The moment establishes the presence requisite for argument and a sense of responsibility (DP 143).

Historical time is the condition of being a person, an effective and responsible agent. A direct inference from this observation is that morality itself requires the historical moment and its specificity:

> There is nothing to be done about such drifting qualities [attributed to observational experience]; one can only perceive them passively. Morality,

however, fixes the moment. Something must be done now. . . . The moral is established not by doing the good, but by doing something. Even the bad act is an act. It fixes the moment. The moral imperative says only let there be a moment. The moment occurs as an imperative—this is the categorical imperative. (MP 4:1; see PC 89)

Morality requires the discontinuity that the moment provides—that is, an opportunity for choice, decision, and efficacious action. Morality is as dependent on the moment as it is on a strong sense of personhood. There is no coming to the moment without a sense of agency and, thus, no moment in the absence of morality. The specific is, paradoxically, the universal element in morality (PH 19–20, 1952–53, 22).

Regarding the third aspect of personhood, the recognition of finitude shows the moral person to be incarnate, vulnerable, and mortal (PH 19–20, 1952–53, 25–26). Action is also an imposition and comes via constraint (MP 4:1). If, on the one hand, a person were omnipotent then action would always be a possibility but never a requirement. If, on the other hand, he were impotent then action would be impossible. Only the person of limited energies and means can experience the imperative of action.

Action is the announcement of limit, and action can be said to occur only where limit pretends to finality and absoluteness. Action repudiates infinity as the all-embracing locus of energy and order. This is the egoistic core of the moral sense. Morality seeks to enfranchise limitation, and to endow it with originality of being and energy. This is the meaning of freedom. Responsibility occurs in this context of self-controlled limitation. (MM 2; cf. Arendt, 1968, pp. 91–141)

Limitation is transformed: No longer a sign of inadequacy, action is now a badge of autonomy. In action a person commits to forms of limitation such as law, procedure, and instruments (MM 15). In so doing, he reveals himself as authoritative by embracing the conditions of action.

Reflecting on these three points, three general statements can be made regarding personhood. First, other persons are imbedded in an individual's experience and, indeed, are a condition of that experience. As *The Definition of the Thing* demonstrates, any definition, including a definition of the person, implies relations. Second, this outline of personhood already represents a sketch of the phenomenon of morality. Action, the moment, and finitude are all constitutive features of moral experience. Third, because the sense of morality is coeval with personhood, the recognition of other persons is coeval with the discovery of self as agent. The stuff of morality is the stuff of personhood.

The relationship between self and other marks the route from the egoistic premise to morality and, then, to politics. This route has, of course, been well traveled by idealists. (In this respect, the following account is illuminated by comparisons to philosophers well-familiar to Miller such as Bernard Bosanquet, G. W. F. Hegel, William Ernest Hocking, and Josiah Royce.)

The exploration begins with questions. Is morality a necessary idea? Is it integral to one's self and world? Philosophy is not essentially concerned with morality or politics as de facto practices; that is the work of anthropology, sociology, and political science. If morality is philosophical, it is a condition of purposes (i.e., a symbol) and is not simply an instrument for purpose (i.e., a tool). "The practical is never obligatory, but depends upon conditions," Miller notes. "The philosophical is obligatory. Logic is obligatory. Is ethics? That is our problem" (MP 9:9). The key to addressing this problem is estimating whether, as Miller writes just a few lines later, "human nature [is] either neutral to society or hostile to it." That is, can one be a person in the absence of society, its codes, and the elaboration of those codes in sophisticated modes of self- and social discipline known as morality? If so, morality is truly conditional. If not, then the philosophical link is established.

The development of Miller's position involves two steps. First he explicitly rejects the presuppositions of one highly influential reading of the contract theory proposed by the likes of Thomas Hobbes and John Locke (MP 9:9). The proposition that there is a self, endowed with powers and rights, independent of action and social relations makes morality and politics strictly conditional. It is a proposition that Miller dismisses as absurd on the bases established in *The Definition of the Thing*. Second he makes a positive claim for the intrinsic sociability of the person:

> What would make [ethics] philosophical would be the essential social unity of man with man. By essential social unity I mean the indefinability of self in isolation. Or, I mean, the impossibility of the first personal pronoun without the second. By essential I mean that each person knows himself only in social contexts.
>
> The full theory of the essential nature of society would necessarily include a proof that mind is essential to that aspect of our world which we call nature. Mind could not be a product of nature if the laws of mind were to be absolute. . . . Only if the laws of mind are something ultimate, eternal, divine in origin and essence could we take them seriously. Only if they have those qualities could those laws appeal to us as expressing basic truths and not accidental products of an alien process of nature. Obligation, duty, moral necessity requires a world which makes morality possible and necessary.
>
> The general character of concepts necessary to each other is given in the list of mental functions in psychology and in the list of categories used

in physics. Our problem is to find if self and other are also in this way dialectical. We shall also very briefly consider whether self and nature are dialectical. (MP 9:9)

The social world is the condition of personhood. In one respect the person is revealed when confronted by others. In another respect the person discovers herself in the encompassing practices and institutions of society, as well as in those common objects (including natural objects) where she meets herself and mediates her relations with others.

In section 4.4 there was a lengthy discussion of the concept of the person and how its roots are in the experience of conflict. The present question is how that limitation arises and what type of conflict is in question. Within the idealist tradition, the limit that establishes subjectivity has often been described in relation to nature. Both Hegel and J. G. Fichte saw the idea of subjectivity as arising from the opposition of nature understood as a realm of objective fact. Ralph Waldo Emerson, of course, referred to nature as "the NOT ME" and, thus, the revelatory contrast for the self (1836/1983, p. 8). These are important insights, and Miller by no means dismisses the function of nature in establishing personhood. Yet actualism regards the role of nature differently. Nature is not so much to be a force of opposition as a source of *identification* and authority.[4] (This is an idea to which we will return shortly.) Miller also asserts that the supposed brute opposition of nature—that is, the sense in which it is raw data—actually fails to draw a limit to one's consciousness and so fails to define personal identity.

The force of the appeal to nature is considered to derive from the objective and factual character of nature. It is the source of those ideas René Descartes referred to as *adventitious*—that is, foreign ideas that come to one whether she wills it or no. Yet are adventitious ideas clear testimony of an external world? If a person disallows the dogmatic assertion of the external world, then all ideas are to be addressed from the standpoint of a person's experience of them. She must be something of an idealist and approach everything, so to speak, from the inside out. In doing so, it is discovered that, as mere data, nature only describes the *content* of consciousness. As data, nature remains mind-dependent—that is, a part of me and certainly not "the NOT ME."[5] Miller elaborates on this seemingly paradoxically claim:

The distinction between self and its world, between self and not-self cannot occur in solipsism. Solipsism can claim only the content, the data, of experience. . . .

   The not-self is not nature. As a panorama of qualities, data, objects, etc., nature offers no escape from unreflective solipsism. For the solipsist cannot escape from himself via the only material he has. On the contrary, it is the fact that this material is all that he has that establishes his solitude. Yet it is not really even solitude, since there is no self in the picture, *not even his own*.

The not-self can only be another self. Only in this way can self-consciousness be found. Only in that way can nature become opposed to self. Nature is more than one's own idea only because it is *another's idea also*. This is the *impersonality* of nature, namely its *neutrality* to many minds, but not its *indifference* to mind as such. (DP 167–68)

As Descartes, George Berkeley, and others well recognized, having a world is not enough. Data provide no escape from the solipsistic dilemma. The revelatory force must come from another quarter.

What will break in on solipsism is not an item in one's world but, rather, an insight into *the way that world is put together*. The not-self cannot be content. The not-self is a formal issue or it is nothing at all (PH 5, 1931, 94–95). What Miller proposes is that, instead of searching for objects limiting mind, a person should consider *other minds* as the limiting factor (cf. Hocking, 1926, pp. 232–33).

Finitude is established in meeting other persons and understanding how they function to disclose and validate content. In discovering other points of view I realize that the world is other than myself precisely because it is what I hold in *common* with others. I cannot say what I will about nature not precisely because it is forbidden by nature. Rather, I cannot say what I will because the *social composition* of nature—that is, *nature* understood as an intersubjective agreement of sense perception, judgment, and methodology—negates my sheer individuality. Differ as people might about content, they share recognized controls of experience. The opposition between mind and object is a product of a more basic social relation (see DP 167).

Miller is not saying that, among other experiences, the experience of other persons is formative of the sense of finitude. He is arguing that personhood can *only* come about in the social context. The exclusiveness of this claim is grounded in earlier accounts of the person. One will recall Miller's contention as to how persons appear in utterance—that is, one's legislative voice—and nowhere else (see MS 110; see §§2.1 and 3.1). No amount of data, no matter how definitive or unusual, can convince an individual that appearances are not phantasms. Another person, however, is not a datum but has, by definition, an independence of mind, a will, and a power of effective action. In this respect, another of Descartes's puzzlements from his *Meditations* is instructive. What standard could one apply, he asked in the Second Meditation, in discerning whether the figures outside the window are persons or automata? Faced with this question, Descartes realized that sense data alone cannot reveal persons. Similarly Miller estimates that it is not that the data of personhood are elusive. While data are subordinate to the mind and categories that brought them to light, the person cannot be so subordinated. In saying *person* one attests to an independent existence and, simultaneously, to her own finitude.

Individual experience is social experience. "[T]here is no point of view without self-consciousness and, hence, limitation of self," Miller writes. "What limits a self is only a self" (DP 169; see also PH 5, 1931, 77; PH 19-20, 1952-53, 79; cf. Arendt, 1978, vol. 1, p. 187). Thus one does not contract into society as if agreeing to terms of employment. As a matter of the philosophical analysis, one does not arrive at sociability via a deduction. Rather, society, like action, is an immediacy (MP 17:24). There are no degrees to sociability: Either one is a person and is by definition social or one lacks personhood altogether (PH 5, 1931, 92).[6]

This moment of negation in the meeting of another mind is translated into a second positive moment of recognition. Recognition is requisite for personhood (CB 5). Indeed the first and second moments are by no means opposed. The elimination of solipsism, while destroying the fictitious self-possessed ego, relies on recognition and produces self-recognition. If the other person attests to the fact that my world is not *the* world, or the only world, that experience also testifies that the other person recognizes my world. In and through limitation a person comes to be for himself.

Limitation provides a world and extends a person's scope of identification and power. This world is particularly evident in social relations defined not by strife but by cooperation. Taking nature as an example of a systematic region of objects, we see that the negation of the merely subjective self arises from a claim to the *common*. A person does not oppose another as sheer subjectivity; he resists another as a participant, in this case, in the universal order that is nature. He not only recognizes the objectivity of nature but also has an alliance with it. His personhood is forged in this relation, and thus he appears to the other as both particular and universal.

The basic form of recognition just described becomes widespread and diverse in actual relations of concrete sociability. One is always in a social, symbolic, and historical continuum of relations. The person is always in commerce with objects that are bearers of mind and, in that regard, themselves minds in a particular sense (DT 148-155). The amoebas in the petri dish present themselves as biological organisms, a fact of perception and biology. The amoebas also speak to one *in terms of* the conditions of their biological, chemical, and experimental constitution. In recognizing amoebas, one addresses the actuality of other minds. That actuality is present in the most minute thought and sense experience insofar as each is organized by common symbolic controls.

One cannot be an engineer without mathematics, a level, and a plumb line. A scientist has a stake in amoebas, microscopes, and techniques of chemical analysis. A lawyer is attached to the Constitution, a painter to his brushes. One cannot simply say who one is. Rather there is a commitment to a constellation of objects, particularly symbolic objects. They are essential to identity. Thus the paradoxical but basic insight of actualism is that the person is established not by going *within* but by going *out* into the midworld of symbols. These circuits of symbolic objects are vehicles for personhood. They are also one's means of access to other minds (DT 186–89; DP 167).[7] In this vein, symbols have been referred to as *res publicae*— that is, common vehicles of action, communication, and identification (see §3.5). Taken all together, *res publicae* form a "moral universe" in the sense of being an environment generated by and for action (see EC). Without such a social and symbolic cosmos, Miller notes, one becomes lonely and pessimistic (PC 93).[8] More profoundly, in the absence of such a symbolic environment a person loses her identity (MP 12:14).

Is morality requisite for personhood? Clarity on this matter can be gained by asking another simple question: Who is the other person?

What ends solipsism, establishes the objective world, and initiates social relations is a *person*. Escaping solipsism requires that the other not be reduced to a data set or an example of a larger class of beings. In the moment of confrontation where solipsism is destroyed, the other stands before one as unique, free, and authoritative. In short: One is confronted by a will.

This sense of personhood rests on a version of the noumena–phenomena distinction. Actualism clearly cannot push the Kantian point too far (see §§2.1 and 2.4; cf. Tyman, 1993, 45–52). Yet some distinction in modes of being is requisite. Miller follows Kant in insisting that there is a break within the world of appearance:

> A self or subject is a world, and a world is a process of extending experience. . . . A self meeting another self must meet another such world. And it meets that world not as any object in its own world, or of its own. Another self occupies the paradoxical situation of being both an object to another self, and therefore included in it, and radically other than the self which perceives it. . . .
>
> It should be noted that this paradox of self applies not just to the perception of others, but to knowledge of one's own self. (MP 17:24)

Another world confronts and breaks in on my own world. The break precipitated by the other person is not precisely away from appearances or toward an intellectual realm. Rather it introduces what Miller terms *the immediate*—that is, the authority at the root of first-person experience. "The moral situation is itself metaphysical," Miller states. "It is not physical; it is not psychological (of class); it is not logical (hypothetical). It occurs in the acknowledgment of persons" (MP 4:1). The other is a condition of disclosure and an original source of authority.

Personhood—be it in oneself or in another—is thus a fissure in the world of appearance and the routine of practical activity (see Tyman, 1993, pp. 40-41; cf. Arendt, 1978, vol. 2, p. 207).

If the person were simply an appearance, the only laws applicable would be those Kant referred to as "rules of skill" and "counsels of prudence" (Kant, 1797/1996). The person, however, is not a thing. The recognition of personhood in oneself and others implies a moral economy organized around principles of respect and reciprocity. Where Miller's account differs from Kant's is in the description of moral experience itself:

> Where this account differs from Kant's is in the inclusion of nature [i.e., actual, or empirical, relations] in the moral order. The self which one must respect in others is not the abstract locus of self-criticism, but the actual finite person who is encountered in one's own actual programs. The moral will asserts that finitude shall take charge of itself in its concrete egoism, as in becoming a political leader, a general, or a rich man, or a scholar. Yet, I agree with—or follow—Kant in finding a cosmological element in the moral situation. (EC 8)

The dignity of the person and the imperatives following on it are discovered in one's actual relations with others wherein wills conflict and authority is contested. Personhood, dignity, and moral obligation are disclosed in this experience. If one seeks the source of moral obligation outside the moment and in the abstraction of the pure intellect, then one has actually reduced morality to the hypothetical. Reiterating a point made earlier: *the universal feature in moral experience is the specific* (MP 4:1).

While Kant and Miller may disagree as to the character of experience from which moral imperatives are derived, they are very much in agreement as to the quality of the moral cast of mind. The moral person, Miller observes, wants to be universal (PH 19-20, 1952-53, 24). The form of moral action is described by two principles. First, while the moral imperative is always a specific demand, that demand is pronounced in the action of every individual person. Second, the principles of morality are not statements of fact but, rather, concepts organizing and directing experience. While he is emphatic in stating (contra Kant) that freedom is plural in its source, Miller is equally insistent in agreeing that freedom is universal in its ideal (EPE 8-9).

A person's pervasive involvement with others in social intercourse translates into a system of limitations and imperatives regarding conduct. Morality is an intrinsic aspect of one's search for local-control in a social as well as natural environment. It is also a principal aspect of how community is forged in and through actual division (see PC 175). In both of these respects, morality shows its necessity. What tightens the categorical hold of morality, and indeed pulls the knot fast, is the structural relationship between the other person and myself. In recognizing myself as a person, I stand before another person endowed with all of those powers constituting her dignity; I cannot be aroused from my solipsism otherwise. "Moral law," Miller remarks, "seems the consequence of an actual identification with others" (MP 21:13). Intersubjectivity is by definition moral for it is based on the recognition of persons. Morality, in turn, is a necessary condition of personhood (PH 19–20, 1952–53, 103). The relationship is dialectical.

The moral insight is actualized in specific rules of conduct. Miller states that morality needs a medium, a concrete and actual vehicle (PH 79). A medium consonant with the dignity of persons will enforce and embody the mutual obligation and reciprocal respect. The scientific community—with its instruments, methodologies, and refereeing procedures—provides one example of a system of moral vehicles. Legal and medical communities offer other examples. Each of these constellations is an aspect of the whole of moral relations that forms the most encompassing example of what Miller refers to as a "community of power":

> Any vehicle of mind is a "power." The first vehicles of power were charms and fetishes. Words, too, were powers, as in the case of the blessing of Isaac. Another mind is the possessor of such power. Morality is the community of power to which we consent and in which we share. All such power is inherently shared and sharable. This is the whole basis of ethics and morality, as well as of science. (DT 189)

In speaking of a community of power, one recognizes that obligations engendered by the recognition of personhood are not exclusive. They pertain to all persons, including oneself. Autonomy and authority are, paradoxically, only possible insofar as they are recognized as aspects of a *common* existence. Power is not possessed but, rather, shared by others and acted out in common. In this lies the translation of morality into politics.

    While actualism pushes toward the concretization of the conceptual, morality cannot be reduced to mere obedience to rules. Whether the rules are of pure reason or simple custom, the moral sensibility does not fit into such narrow confines. Morality needs the animating activity of reflection. Miller clearly states that "morality seems not to occur until use and morality become separated" in the breakdown of custom (MP 13:6; see PH 93). The question is how precisely to integrate the static (rule governed) and dynamic (reflective) aspects of moral experience.

The traditional distinction between law and morality provides some insight into this difficulty. Whereas law (as the positive code of the state backed by force) is an external constraint on conduct, morality is concerned with what can be called *internal restrictions*. In Kant's language, positive law is *heteronomous*—that is, a conditional proposition wherein either one obeys or invites punishment. Morality is autonomous in that it is self-legislated and the reasons for obedience derived from the reflective process. According to this traditional estimation, morality is an exercise of pure reason implying critical self-consciousness. Tied together with individuality and sociability in the nexus of personhood, morality is defined by reflection and not the compulsive following out of rules.

Moral experience is the desire for control and satisfaction transformed into a discipline of self-control (see NL 7). The transformation of custom into morality is driven by the universal implications of the particular (see PH 19-20, 1952-53, 24). Moral experience establishes a person's finitude; it particularizes. Because what is particularized is not an object but a person, individuality necessarily involves the universal. The person meets another person and she discovers *personhood* as such—that is, authority and its impositions in the form of principles of dignity, oaths of allegiance, and common commitments to methodologies and instruments. Any state of moral affairs is, at minimum, a triadic relation (MP 28:10). The self-conscious thought typifying moral experience does not simply employ organizing principles but recognizes them as conditions of thought itself. For this reason Miller notes that while sheer egoism is amoral, morality is egoism aware of its own conditions (EC 11; see §5.4). The moralist, like the historian and philosopher, seeks to idealize the occasion (see PH 92-93).

Self-control transforms itself from a rude self-possession to a disciplined obedience to the moral law. In this obedience one's autonomy is not lost. This Kantian insight is amplified by Miller's recognition of the human paradox—that is, we are beings who are both controlling and controlled (PC 99). Reflection allows for—indeed demands that—one be simultaneously subject and object. This fact does not attest to a perverse state of affairs—for example, moral schizophrenia or bad faith. Rather this division establishes the human mode of being. Considered on a social and, ultimately, political scale, this dual nature is essential to membership in a community of self-conscious beings.

[I]t may be fairly felt that . . . a man may simply avail himself of such a rich social dependence in order to use society as his oyster. What forbids? Nothing except his own will to power. To have what one wants when one wants it, one must respect the laws through which wants are supplied; and the more complex one's desires, the more dependent one is upon the social agencies of fulfillment. If one wants conversation, shall one go to the beasts or the slaves? If one wants grapefruit for breakfast, it is wise not to disorganize railroad traffic. The man who wants to get what he wants must obey the law—his own law and no one else's. If he wants power, let him look to the conditions which make true power possible. (PL 147)

A person who is purely authoritative is not a member of a community any more than one who is merely subject to the orders of others. (Hegel's lord and servant are thus only members of an incipient community.) In an actual community, however, each wields power only insofar as others may also wield it. Here one finds a "community of power," a community "to which we consent and in which we share. All such power is inherently shared and sharable" (DT 189).

This community of power is a moral universe—that constellation of common objects, practices, and institutions by which a society, guides, organizes, and fosters the growth of experience. For while persons recognize one another in the face-to-face, the most pervasive bonds are those circuits of symbols that form the environment of action.

Thus, the moral universe is the polar complement of will. Penalty is visited upon the will not by an alien force, but by the order that its own assertion invokes. Penalty is the reminder of the price of egoism, namely respect for the nature of things. It is this respect which egoism may forget. Yet, it is only as we are egoists, i.e., moral agents, making claims of control, that the systematic order of persons and things can be discovered. Thus, the moral universe does not repress action, but requires it. It requires egoism. It requires that the self-willed person learn the conditions of his own existence as a person, i.e., as a will rather than as a series of casual desires satisfied in a correspondingly casual environment.

All modes of objective order, including physics, of course, are complements of will. All modes of order are also modes of power. . . . The moral order is not a fact; it is the corollary of our own freedom, i.e., of our egoism. (EC 6–7)

In the moral universe, ego meets and regulates itself. As prior discussions of the ideas of fate and nemesis have made plain, this encounter is never direct and its implications are hardly transparent. Despite that, there is identification in the complementary relationship between the individual and overindividual, the personal and transpersonal. The individual and social are bound together not just in the dialectic of definition but also as a reflective system of expression, recognition, and revision. This is a process of communication. Morality is both a condition and expression of the openness of each mind to its community (MP 4:1). It is what Miller refers to as "the original community"—that is, society formed by and conducive to originality in thought and action (MP 44).

Actualism shows that all concrete practices are amenable to reflection and, thus, responsible control. There is, then, a need for public means in order to exercise control over oneself and others, and thus give concrete shape to the sense of responsibility (see EC 4). Some of these practices that join the active and contemplative lives explicitly include modes of self-consciousness in their very structure. Political association, for example, makes explicit the inchoate community of power—organized around egoism and dignity—present in sociability and morality. The metaphysics of morals is the basis for a metaphysics of democracy.

§5.2 LIBERAL DEMOCRACY

Illuminating finitude, authorizing the person, highlighting the symbolic and historical form of human being—all of these are concerns of actualism. Miller succinctly presents some of the philosophical motivations behind his metaphysics of democracy:

> We are demoralized today because we proclaim liberty but no actuality as local control and as revelation. Nothing is to be revered. There is no eloquent presence. . . . Intellectuals have no verbs; the common man does. I am joining that common man. And if this is a free country, we'd better get ourselves a metaphysic that has respect for the man on Elm Street. As it is, he is treated with patronage and disdain. Nor does he quite know how to stand in his authority because he is there and therefore projects a world in his doing. (MS 191)

Democracy is equally a premise and conclusion of actualism. The democratic impulse toward action and, thus, responsible, plural authority touches actualism in all of its facets. There is no way to pry what Miller means by *liberty*, *presence*, and *authority* apart from his estimation of democratic political association.

Reflecting further on the above quotation, one can discern a common conceptual root to Miller's philosophic and political interests. It is a basic insight of actualism that the ahistoric temper conspires to make personhood dubious and thus obscure the authority of the active life. The political corollary to ahistoric metaphysics is evidenced in the bond between ahistoric modes of thought and forms of social control that tend toward the subjugation of persons and the elimination of the active, political life. A preliminary justification of Miller's privileging of liberal democracy can thus be phrased in terms of *personhood*. The criticism of ahistoric metaphysics implies and further supports an effective conception of human agency.

The state is not a mere modus operandi, a tool, or technique. Miller proposes that the state is a necessary idea—that is, an indispensable condition of one's self and world (PH 5, 1931, 72–82, 113). In that respect, a person cannot philosophize without paying heed to political association. Miller goes even further and claims that there is *only one true form* of political association. To his mind, the democratic state is *the* state, the very paradigm of political association (PH 5, 1931, 82).

These are strong and controversial claims. What is of immediate interest is that liberal democracy fits actualist thinking. Democracy is integral to the whole of Miller's thought, both in terms of his philosophical insights and his methodology. Thus, because it is a metaphysical idea, democratic political association must be addressed primarily as structure. The close study of de facto democracies is left to political science, sociology, and psychology. The general aim of the metaphysics of democracy is to bring to light the terms defining political association and show how they are integral to the very forms of personhood, community, and world.

The state is not primarily a source of fellowship, a means for facilitating the procurement of material goods, or an arrangement to maintain security. Politics is neither a function of the herd nor an attenuated state of war. In Miller's estimation, the state is an opportunity for self-expression and self-control via law making (PH 5, 1931, 95-99)—that is, the establishment of the conditions of one's own endeavors (see NL 15-17).[9] The fullest expression of legislation is found in government "of the people, by the people, for the people." Abraham Lincoln's words describe what one now recognizes as a democratic republic founded on universal suffrage and representation. It is a government whose sanction is that it recognizes and enfranchises the agency of each person. This is the "heresy of liberalism"— that is, the assertion that the people are responsible for the laws (MP 21:2).

Miller is well aware that the term *freedom* is vague and prone to a variety of (often conflicting) interpretations. For instance, the idea of unbounded liberty— that is, that found in certain types of anarchism, as well as in some interpretations of liberalism itself (PL 894; e.g., Locke and Hobbes)—misconstrues the matter of politics by supposing a strict opposition between freedom and constraint. *Control* is a neutral term describing all forms and processes ordering experience. Obviously, some modes of control are oppressive and destructive of agency (e.g., tyranny, censorship). Others, however, augment agency (e.g., law, method). Miller asserts that political association is concerned with the *control* of human nature *in the pursuit of freedom* (PC 98-105).

If political association is a matter of control conducive to freedom, the subsequent question is: What is being controlled? or What is the concept of *person* undergirding democracy? A brief answer would be that democracy controls *citizens*, persons capable of and committed to engaging in the legislative process.

A fair sketch of the actualist conception of personhood was provided in section 5.1. In "Idealism and Freedom" Miller underlines the ethical and political importance of idealism by reference to Kant's idea of autonomy (PC 66–67). The capacity of thought to police and have authority over itself is critical to the dignity of persons. This epistemologically based assertion provides a model for a larger idea of governance wherein personhood is bound to the capacity to announce laws and, subsequently, be free in obedience to laws of one's own making. Yet because political association is a mode of control suited to *persons*, the form of control established in the democratic state will always be uncertain and incomplete. If the reduction of control to technique is inadequate even regarding the data of nature,[10] it completely misses the mark when it comes to political association. "It is command, power, and control which are difficult to define in the context of report" (PC 101), Miller notes of the state. For the "object" of political control is not an object at all. "It" is a reflective agent. Politics shows itself to be a peculiar science. It is an attempt to "know," "manage," and "control" what is essentially beyond modes of meaning-control and purpose-control.

Politics is a form of order that is necessarily reciprocal and never absolute or complete. In a community of power no individual person or ruling body can simply have power *over* other persons without also establishing power *for* them. Miller echoes this in "Idealism and Freedom" when he states that the political question is oriented around the "the problem of winning power for each man" (PC 74). A community of power is established and maintained in terms of "conditions in which men can influence others insofar as those others are in charge of themselves" (PC 103). It is a community that, because of the fundamental assertion of plurality, cannot collapse into the simple mutuality of sociability (cf. Arendt, 1959, p. 158). It is also a community in which authority is always contested and the terms of reciprocity constantly challenged.

Democracy lies between totalitarianism and chaos. It is an integration of mutually defining opposites—for example, an articulate whole, a plural system, a free order. The legislative process and democracy are defined by the problem of control:

> The problem of power in a democracy involves the control of men over each other. Yet, one may distrust all such power. . . . It is, of course, true that power corrupts. Nothing else can. Impotence can do no harm, nor, or course, any good. Politics is a science of the power of men over themselves and over others. Its meaning vanishes when human nature lacks self-assertion and the passionate egoism that is the spring of all control.
>
> Whatever view of man deprives him of power over himself and others [e.g., naturalism or theology] solves the political problem by abolishing it. When men are viewed as objects, command becomes simply a mistaken idea, for it violates the condition on which human nature is presumably discovered, namely, as fact and uniformity. Man becomes lost in

his "nature," and so far from being in a position to rule others, he cannot even rule himself. (PC 101-02)

Democratic order is inherently problematic. "This difficulty involves an old ambiguity," Miller observes. "To preserve the problem it is necessary to make this distinction [between persons as objects to be organized and as sources of value], while to keep the distinction is to abandon the essay at strictly objective defini- tion of human nature" (PC 99). The person is both controlling and controlled. This is not a technical problem but an indissoluble difficulty.

The state unifies persons in their differences. Political association is an "expression of conflict" embodied in legislative procedures and the order of law (PL 120-21). Procedure and law ameliorate the risks of unremitting and violent conflict by providing means for proposing ideas, offering criticism, as well as expressing grievances and exacting redress. Each essay at an answer or definitive conclusion will involve some contest over the results and the appropriate proce- dures for securing those results. Liberal democracy is a venue for conflict (PC 41). This is not, however, a deficiency. War is unacceptable within the state. Yet domestic tranquillity—*pace* Kant and Fichte—strays toward domination. The strict contrast of peace and war is misleading:

> We want peace, but a tolerable peace, a peace that is peace because it includes the value of person and the procedures of law which give the word peace its prestige and ideal authority. Peace does not mean the absence of war, it seems, but such a society which recognizes personal wills and accommodates their differences without abolishing them. (MP 13:10; cf. Colapietro, 1989)

Liberal democracy provides a framework for the advent of such a tolerable peace. Its institutions and practices do not stifle conflict but, rather, recognize and adjudicate conflict on a case-by-case basis. The result, as one finds in the midworld and its historical continuum, is a dynamic process whose order generates disorder (while preventing chaos) and contributes to strife (while resisting violence).

The democratic form of order is embodied in the symbol. The state (*res publica*), like other symbols (*res publicae*), is a nonexclusive vehicle of representation and revision. In "Freedom as a Characteristic of Man in a Democratic Society," Miller notes three corollaries of the democratic form of control:

> These general properties of the democratic man entail many corollaries. As a first consequence may be mentioned the maintenance of systematic thought or inquiry, since only order can be revised, and only the pretension to responsible order can create both humility and accessibility.

A second corollary is this: there must be preserved non-political sources of power, as the centers of privacy and as the authority for criticism of political institutions. Government is the form of community but not its substance. . . .

A third corollary can be offered: democratic man seeks responsible power without asserting a fixed goal. This is the quality of risk. Security of any sort, made absolute, is the stifling of freedom. A risky, but creative adventure is man himself. (PC 104–5)

As summations of the form of social order instituted by political association, these three corollaries are further reducible to two basic principles. First, the dynamic, fallible, and revisable character of these modes of order implies the finitude not only of persons but also institutions. Second, while all forms of control have their integrity, they remain expressions of personhood and are ultimately answerable to the demands of personhood.

As to the first principle, the well-known remarks of Jefferson and John Dewey regarding the great similarities between democratic communities and communities of inquiry are notable (PC 103).[11] In order that the community *as a whole* enjoys such an existence, experimentation must not be a private pursuit. Experiment must define public life itself. The task of political association is to establish and maintain the conditions of experimentation on a broad scale (see NL 10–11). Formal legislatures are the most prominent examples of such systematic processes. By means of its regular meetings and open fora, legislative institutions augment the process of creating and criticizing modes of control. And, in so doing, these bodies provide models for other, less formal procedures in other aspects of public as well as private life.

Experimental democratic life places great demands on persons as well as institutions. In the case of persons, the commitment to experimentation demands that they exhibit "humility and accessibility."[12] A person must continually take the conditions of her endeavors into account and submit them to critical processes. The foundation of this process is the provision for free speech and unrestrained communication (MP 12:1). The political commitment to procedure and the accessibility of minds ensures that institutions are vehicles for this experimental process. The fundamental commitment of the state is to the maintenance of the formal procedures of inquiry—the legislative or term-making process. Political association does not have a goal beyond the creative, historical, political process itself, and cannot be committed to any conclusion in advance.[13]

The second basic principle is that *personhood* is a fundamental concept, an irreducible and basic experience. Building on this, Miller concludes that the experimental order of liberal democracy is itself vouchsafed by nonpolitical sources. Political association cannot pretend to be absolute, the source of all value, meaning, or order. For if the state made such a claim—that is, the claim of all totalitarian regimes—then the distinction between form and content, as well as state and person, would be lost. The unique character of the control instituted by the democratic state derives from its concern with the *conditions* of inquiry, how it organizes the prepolitical forces of assertion and criticism. A distinction, however fluid, is then maintained between state and person, and some priority is granted to persons—"the aristocratic note" of Miller's political philosophy (MP 12:8).

Certain basic modes of sociability and self-control—for example, family, economy, art—are not only distinguishable from, but have a certain priority vis-à-vis, political association (see EPE). If some priority were not reserved, Miller contends that the person himself would be reduced to an object prone to the manipulation of political managers (PC 104). The sphere of privacy—encompassing sociability and morality—describes the irreducibility of personhood (PL 118). Privacy can be eliminated only at the risk of emptying political life of its substance (see PL 706, 809). For Miller defines privacy simply as the chance to be an agent. "The defense of privacy, as in the case of private property, has turned mostly on the exclusion of others from the means of one's enjoyment," Miller observes. "When privacy means the chance to be somebody and to be effective, it seems to me to shed the connotation of the unsocial and to turn the corner into a new and affirmative community" (PL 592, 1943). In establishing a right to privacy the liberal state creates its own antagonist (PL 614).

Political association, like nature and history, is an *expression* of the imperatives of thought, action, and local-control. That said, one cannot overlook the manner in which the state is also the *condition* of personhood. The state is the only sufficient response to each person's search for power and authority. This dialectical relationship describes a route between the two dominant traditions of political thought—that is, Anglo-American empiricism and positive law, on the one hand, and Continental idealism and speculative law on the other. Actualism makes a case for *political persons*, not persons or politics in strict isolation from or dominance over the other. Personhood is fully achieved via the political organization of human will in light of universal ideas. Similarly the life of the universal is manifest only in the acts of individual persons. This is the paradox of liberal democracy.

§5.3 UNIVERSALITY AND PROCESS

"The business of the polis (the state)," Miller remarks, "is to establish the social conditions of local control" (MP 21:2). Or, as he puts the matter elsewhere, the liberal state creates the conditions for the assertion of will (MP 11:9). The state establishes the conditions for the most comprehensive expression of what Miller refers to as the *will to power*—that is, the need for local-control and self-control (see PC 32).[14] Political association provides a symbolic vehicle—or a constellation of vehicles—for the exercise of authority.

Because it is a mature expression of will, the state also represents a further translation and refinement of these basic energies. Thus the state facilitates the will by, paradoxically, offering resistance.

> The turn from negation to affirmation is unquestionably very terrible to consider. The forces it lets loose seem mad, arbitrary, and uncontrollable. In any case, they are disturbing, and it is only natural to try to put them down. We are likely to become drunk with sight of power and loose wild tongues that deny the law. But one thing is certain: that assertion must occur, and so it is equally certain that it can be met only by a counterthrust equally strong and even more persistent. An absolute assertion can get only an absolute answer if it is to be controlled. The concrete actuality that gives that answer is the state. For the state is the objectification of the conditions of the will to power. (PC 32)

The state is the most developed form of opposition within the larger process defining a will. Control and personhood are forged in conflict. Political association more thoroughly restricts persons than either the ad hoc limits of simple sociability or the rational barriers of simple morality. The prepolitical person, if he were to be discovered even theoretically, would be all will to power, energy, and expression: he would not, however, be someone recognizable and possessed of the ideas of rights and responsibilities that define personhood. Political association is the necessary foil, or dialectic complement, of the mature will. While not wholly created by or reducible to political association, the person is in an important respect *re-created* or redefined by politics. Miller concedes the impossibility of fully disentangling sociability, morality, and political association.[15] There are only *political persons*.

The symbol, it will be recalled, is a mode of disclosure and organization. It is the condition of content. Symbols order particulars in terms of universal conditions and establish systematic relations of distinction and commonality. As a symbol, the chief role of the democratic state is integrating the individual and universal in a nonreductive union. A general sketch of political order describes a movement whereby the person is *liberated* from being exclusively defined by social groupings. Yet that liberation, or individuation, occurs only in terms of one's *membership* within a political community. There is no liberation from, no personhood independent of, order. The true political question is that of finding a mode of order, or universality, that enlivens individual agency.

As a developmental process, the growth of political order resembles the Hegelian dialectic of the in-itself and the for-itself.[16] Simple forms of sociability submerge the person in the unreflective unity of the group and cut the individual off from a general community. Morality follows on sociability and marks a distinction within this union. Yet simple morality incompletely articulates sociability. The separation introduced by morality is too absolute and the revised form of universal community too notional. The incomplete condition of these two forms of order sets the stage for political association. The state builds on the ideal universality of morality (PL 582) and, recouping the positive elements of sociability, transforms morality into the actual universality found in the forms of public life (PH 5, 1931, 103–4). This schematic genealogy of political association embodies Hegel's in-and-for itself in that it does not simply overcome sociability and morality but, rather, reinterprets and strengthens them. The state establishes the *universal and concrete* value of those exclusive social and notional moral bonds.

Sociability, like morality, is not in itself a hindrance to the growth of personhood. Family, club, business—each contributes to the expansion of one's world. Far from being the enemy of sociability, then, the state is in league with these commotive forces and aims to contribute to them. What the state resists is making particular family loyalties, regional customs, or private economic interests fundamental to the very rationale of large-scale association. The state thus signals the advent of a new way of thinking and acting vis-à-vis the habits of simple sociability.[17] The change in question involves directing consciousness toward symbols and action. The implications of this revolution are wide-ranging and have been articulated at various points, most especially in sections 3.1 and 3.5. From a political perspective, specific attention must be paid to the authority of the state and the way in which symbolic consciousness introduces a movement from particularity to universality, exclusivity to neutrality, and custom to law. This is the key to the criticism and overcoming of the exclusivity of simple sociability; it is also, in good dialectical fashion, the key to maintaining these basic social bonds.

The power of any symbolic order is that the rule it proposes is applicable to every possible situation. Universal orders are equally available and applicable to all. Consider the measurement of distance. There are an indefinite number of measures, many of which are incompatible or unsynthesizable. What is an ell to a light-year? What is a fathom to a day's ride on horseback? Each mode of measurement lacks the capacity to translate into other modes. The yardstick, by contrast, is applicable to and organizes any distance (great or small), landscape (plains or mountains), or region (terrestrial or celestial). It encompasses measures based on simple extension as well as motion. It reduces the peculiarities of physiognomy and transport to a common unit. The yardstick projects the universal and articulates space as such even while maintaining the integrity of every other unit of measure in the sphere of its appropriate usage. Similarly, the state organizes sociability as such. Clans or clubs also organize social relations; they are important expressions of social energies and personhood. Yet, like the various units of measurement, these modes order sociability in ways that are idiosyncratic and sometimes divisive. Where should a Smith stand in the familial hierarchy of the Watson clan? What is a coin club to do about someone ignorant about coin collecting? Moreover, should one's family standing have weight in a coin club or should numismatic knowledge be taken into account when figuring the family hierarchy? Such puzzlements are as peculiar as they are resistant to solution. The state proposes a mode of social order that is applicable to any clan or club—that is, the status and authority of persons simply as persons.

The state does not try to usurp the authority of these associations. Rather it establishes and enforces laws geared toward "hindering the hindrances," the conflicts and blockages that arise between simple modes of association (see PH 5, 1931, 110–12; cf. Kant 1797/1996, p. 25). The state curtails the authority of exclusive organizations and allows individuals to better exploit the resources of association. It does not vie for the same form of authority held in private relations and, thus, does not challenge such authority.

The reorganization of sociability in terms of political association exacts a price, of course. The degree to which the state augments power by limiting the authority of exclusive associations makes demands on each group and person. To the extent that one's will is given universal scope, it must also accommodate the wills of others. The desire, for example, for social acknowledgment, self-expression, and access to marketplaces demands reciprocity on each of these points. In order to be effective, will to power cannot be simply power for oneself. Rather, the political will to power seeks "true power"—that is, equality of opportunity and mutuality of respect facilitating the search for power on the part of each person (see DT 189). The state is in equal measure a vehicle of coercion and liberation. Limited associations are barred political power or cannot make their categories of valuation universal over all associations—that is, the state cannot be instrumentalized for exclusive ends. The paradoxical aspect of this development toward universality is that it secures the very social values that it could be interpreted as threatening. Political association is not simply a restraint on limited social groups but also imposes restraints on the state in its relations with such groups. The state introduces a dialectical play between the universal and individual: The particularity of social relations drives the movement toward neutrality while the state's restriction of the authority of sociability translates into a basis of personal attachment.

The liberal democratic state composes human relations on the basis of procedure (PH 5, 1931, 84). The mere presence of law and procedure is, of course, not sufficiently diagnostic of political association. Order defines all communities; law is simply the unifying form and is a term equally applicable to physical and human events (MP 19:11). A political association is distinctive in that it is a community (a form of order) with a *critical* relation to its own rules. In the context of simple sociability, order does not extend to instituting rules about the making of rules or establishing standing procedures for their criticism and revision. The state, by contrast, establishes procedures for creating, deliberating about, and modifying rules. These processes encompass not just the making and revising of ordinary legislation but also the declaration of and deliberation about the basic rules for the making of rules—that is, constitutional law. The state institutionalizes reflection and makes the mode of social order itself a matter for consideration and criticism, thus establishing the conditions for what Miller refers to as an explicitly functioning will (MP 9:9; see §5.4).

The distinction between ordinary and constitutional law is very important in assessing law as a condition of disclosure. A constitution—be it written or part of an oral tradition—exhibits two things. First, it shows an appreciation for the importance of procedure (PL 155), and the subordination of ordinary legislation to the overriding concern for procedure. A constitution expresses an interest in discerning those terms according to which any person or group at any time can endeavor to establish local-control. Second, the presence of a constitution is a sign of *political* thought. There is no way to compose a constitution without asking such philosophical questions as: What does it mean to act? What is community? What is responsibility? A constitution does not then just establish a universal basis for endeavor but is also an inquiry into that basis.

Miller remarks that one makes a mistake in substituting results for procedures (PC 182). This is as true for politics as it is for metaphysics (the direct object of Miller's remark). When the immediate concerns of agency are brought to the legislature, it is matters of specific local-control that occupy the agenda—for example, taxation, public works, criminal law. This is normal legislative activity. When agency concerns itself with the *conditions* of local-control, attention shifts to the ongoing processes of composing and maintaining a world. A law, like any order, is basically a way in which things come about. Approached from a strictly political or philosophical standpoint the law is no longer simply a practical instrument but a condition of experience—a form of control modifying a prior law that will, in time, itself be revised. This process is certainly punctuated by the satisfactions sought by local-control. Yet these satisfactions do not define the state; the political process, Miller states, "describes no fait accompli, but an endeavor, and a procedure" (PC 41).

Political association is fundamentally procedural. This highlights the symbolic function of the state:

Of itself the state has and can have no program. This seems to me a most important consideration. It is not the business of the state to promote a

religion, an economic order or a form of culture. Of such special values it
knows nothing. Indeed, any attempt at state enforcement of such special
adjustments is false to its essence. For . . . the state is a function or form,
not an entity. It exists only in its functions, just an eye is an eye only when
it acts as an eye. (PL 153–54)

The critical distinction underlined by Miller is that between that which discloses
(symbol) and that which is disclosed (sign). The state is the condition of public
life construed as a region in which persons meet as agents and engage in activities exercising their will. In other modes of association persons are revealed in
particular terms and their agency defined accordingly. For example, in the family a person might be a parent and an agent in fostering the growth of her chil-
dren. At the workplace, she is defined by certain skills and her place within the
hierarchy of workers. In political association, by contrast, she is simply an agent.
And just as the visible world would disappear without the vehicle of its disclosure, so too would the public sphere disappear without the symbolic media of
laws, democratic procedures, and public institutions that constitute the state.
The state is the condition of being a person, a mind (see PH 5, 1931, 113).

Political association should not be confused with or reduced to any of its
individual officers, trappings, or buildings. Impotent unless it is concretely manifested and exercised, the state is not reducible to any of these particular mani-
festations. Here the difference between content and form, signs and symbols,
must be emphasized. Consider how the authoritarian "state" is a tool or fetish
and, thus, a degenerate mode of political association (see PC 37–41). The authoritarian state is a particular set of social relations made systematic and absolute—a patriarchy (absolute monarchy or tyranny) or economic association
(oligarchy) cast as authoritative over all other families and associations. In authoritarian rule an order and purpose at the plural or microlevel (social) usurps
authority by claiming universal or macrosignificance (political). This strict alliance with content distinguishes these arrangements as either instruments or
fetishes. The violence and social disorder that are endemic to authoritarian
regimes are due to their exclusivity, their "procedures" being mere tools to attain
or maintain exclusive ends and their offices as fetishized displays.

Symbols are forms of systematic limitation while signs are restricted content
(see §§3.2 and 3.3). Communication and argument occur *in terms* of symbols.
Signs, by contrast, are the details *about which* one communicates and argues. Content divides. That division, however, is articulated *and* bridged by the symbol. The
middle term is procedure or form. When procedure is not simply disclosive of but
is determined by particularity, however, form is no longer a vehicle for communication, argument, and peaceful conflict. As Miller notes, "static truth abolishes

community" (PC 104). This is what happens in the authoritarian "state." The pure procedure and symbolic control exemplified by political association averts such violence. In moving from simple association to political association the scope of reason is expanded, and common institutions are established as means for ritualized and orderly forms of conflict. These means of expression and opposition are open to all; they define the public sphere.

The neutrality of the state is premised on its commitment to procedure and the assurance that this procedure is not an instrument of some exclusive group. The state "has no program" because it is defined by procedural justice (see PH 5, 1931, 97-103). The lack of a program does not mean that political association the organization of indifference, however. Political association is demanding but, ultimately, only makes *fair* demands.

§5.4   DEMOCRACY AND PHILOSOPHY

Miller asserts that political association cannot be understood in ahistoric terms (see PL 514-15). The historical contour of the liberal democratic state highlights two features. First, the state is a vehicle of *representation*—that is, a means of expression, identification, and reflection. Second, the state enfranchises *criticism* by facilitating the expenditure of energies in the thoughtful consideration of past deeds. Because it unites representation and criticism, the state is fundamental to a developed sense of personhood. Because political association organizes the conscious, dynamic, and revisionary processes that define history, the state also reveals itself as "the vehicle of history" (PL 675-76). In connecting representation and criticism, the institutions and practices of liberal democracy outline the root claim of Miller's metaphysics of democracy—that is, political association is the center of an engaged philosophical life.

In the liberal democratic state the active life and the contemplative life converge. In the state a bond is forged among the workaday activities of government (e.g., representation, legislation, and revision), the historical processes of the midworld, and, finally, philosophy as the form of criticism. In criticism one takes the conditions of action into account. Contemplation becomes not only an adjunct to action but basic to the active life for the object of philosophy is the basis of action in all of its forms.

The advent of the state marks a profound change of mind. It is a break from what Edmund Husserl referred to as the *natural standpoint* (cf. Husserl, 1913/1962). The break involves directing one's attention toward conditions of disclosure (i.e., symbols) and no longer being exclusively concerned with what is disclosed (i.e., signs).[18] This revolution establishes distinctions between form and content, as well as between political association and simple sociability. An increasing consciousness of the factors of control and self-control is developed.

What distinguishes human action from behavior is that it involves the conscious recognition and estimation of the import and conditions of purpose. Actualism does not claim that reflection is solely found in or is even initiated by political association. There is a gradient of reflection. The state embraces and further organizes elements already present in sociability and ramified in morality. Political association is defined by the *degree of reflection* that it embodies and the distinctive mode of control that it makes available to persons.

The state is not only a representative but a critical vehicle. Miller defines the state as an *explicitly functioning will* (MP 9:9). Yet, because criticism itself assumes identification (PL 438; cf. Colapietro, 2003, pp. 226-31), the state's representative function takes priority in any discursive account. Actualism asserts that persons are revealed only in action. Symbols are shared means for action and reflection—that is, *res publicae* (see MS 31; §3.5). In this respect, symbols are crucial in that they establish the terms according to which a personal world can be objectified without being reduced to a mere object (see DT 178). Symbols, as products of such acts of "externalization," are neither neutral nor subject to simple manipulation. Moreover there is an existential bond between fabricator and artifact. The loss of one of these symbolic objects is a loss of an important mode of organizing one's world and defining oneself. True of *res publicae*, this description is equally applicable to the modes of governance found in liberal democracy, *res publica*.

Representation is a broad, quasi-metaphorical term for a range of human activities. *Res publicae* and *res publica* (e.g., the yardstick and the state) differ substantially in terms of the control they institute and the activity they organize. The yardstick is an expression of will insofar as it seeks control over space, spatial objects, and, finally, other wills in their common need for and disputes about the condition of action that is space. The yardstick is not, however, pertinent to all actions. When disputing, say, a mathematical property or a chemical reaction, the yardstick might be but a subsidiary mode of control. In other cases, the form of order established by the yardstick will be moot—for example, when determining the import and proper use of a word. Thus the yardstick is both a universal and limited form of control; it is universal in its field but its field is not itself universal. Political association, on the other hand, is not so circumscribed. The control it institutes it is both more abstract and more universal.

In sum: The state is *an expression of will regarding the very expression of will*. The state is the explicit recognition of the will and the deliberate effort at its control. The yardstick, clock, and balance all instruct the will as to its import, and yet they do so in a vague and indirect fashion; local-control need not always be a form of self-control. Thus the organization of communities of criticism such as the

scientific community is very important. Such communities articulate modes of
control and reflect on their importance in relation to the disclosure of world and
person. All such communities—for example, scientific, medical, linguistic, artistic, political—are expressions and refinements of will, and thus more developed
expressions of control (see PL 174–92). Political association is distinct, however.

In this regard, Miller refers to the state as "a school of the will"[19]:

> The liberal state can do no more than offer an arena for the solution of
> difficulties and of injustice. It is a school of the will, permitting both private
> property and free speech, but perpetually seeking to reconcile particular
> conflicts and local injustice. It allows for relative anarchy and waste. But it
> is the only answer to the bid for power which men must make, and the only
> condition under which they could assert a social or moral will. . . .
>
> When the will knows itself it becomes social, for its freedom can
> escape subjectivity only as it recognizes its limitation in the will of others.
> The objectification of freedom is the liberal state, where by patience and
> labor the free will gives open testimony of its disinterestedness and
> impartiality. (PC 41)

Each school of will other than the state is concerned with a certain manifestation of will. The concern of the state is *order as such*. While the American
Medical Association or the Académie Française are not *mere* instruments, they
are still limited to a specific field and oriented toward definite content. The
state, properly understood, stands beyond all instrumentalities. If a doctor
aims to devise and validate a new surgical procedure and the académicien
guards against *anglicismes*, a citizen simply seeks freedom. Moreover, while
symbols generally disclose and regulate data or signs, the state does not reveal
data. *The state discloses persons.* It is where, as Miller states, "men shall count
only as men" (MP 11:5).

In the same fashion that he pushed the ideas of *nature* and *history*—that is,
to become a whole region of self-conscious activity and a condition of will as
such—Miller is also extending the idea of the state.[20] Like nature and history,
political association is essential to personhood. In the state one comes to terms
with what it means to have and, indeed, to be a will. What it discloses is fundamental, necessary, and philosophical.

Free institutions are means for self-representation and self-direction (PH 178).
Autonomy involves reflecting on, criticizing, and revising prevailing symbolic
forms organizing activity. The morality of any given institution is premised on its
capacity to undergo such critical processes and thus avoid dogmatism. Personhood, morality, representation, and criticism are joined in the political process.

Any adequate conception of the state must define the political process in terms of a dialectical unity of criticism and representation.

The relative priority of representation (provisionally breaking the dialectic unity) is undergirded by Miller's insistence that criticism be accompanied by a strong sense of identification with whatever idea, practice, or institution is being criticized (PL 438). Moral persons are defined by their capacity for identification and, thus, self-limitation (MP 16:9). "Critics will not be heard," Vincent Colapietro writes, "unless they join the discourses to which their critiques are directed" (2003, pp. 213-14; see also pp. 151-74). Similarly criticism cannot be detached from the concept of autonomy. While questions of right and wrong are important, the more basic issue is *how one comes to distinguish* the right from the wrong and the responsibility one has for that very distinction. If the conditions of correction and growth are imposed from without, no level of correctness or improvement can cover over the alienation. One must have a personal stake in the conditions by which one makes judgments.

True criticism, like philosophy, is premised on identification and is never an external attack or a search for victory over another person. Criticism is never utter negation. No matter how radical, criticism is always in an important respect *conservative* and thus an affirmation of the value of the form of order in question or, more generally, the very search for local-control of which that particular order is an example. Accordingly criticism is a form of mutual power; in criticism one moves beyond the search for simple power for oneself and stark opposition to another. In criticism one does not attack the person but, rather, points to the way in which the other person has overlooked some facet or control over the discourse to which she is generally committed. Highlighting the middle terms animating and controlling the conflict among persons, true criticism makes the symbol itself the object of consideration and the ground of contention.

In criticism one struggles with the conditions of disclosure, the structure of one's world.[21] No one is master of them and thus no one can use them to master another. In criticism one may speak and then revise one's thinking without fearing domination by another. It is a free situation. Liberated from the fear of domination, one's engagement with the conditions of one's authority— maintaining and revising, defending as well as challenging—is enlivened. In this respect, criticism is the epitome of the form of conflict that political association aims to promote and of which it is the paradigm—that is, conflict as self-inquiry and not attack, antagonism as affirmation and not sheer rejection. Whether or not there are fora where symbolic controls are considered authoritative is an important indicator of the form of one's community (NS 5-6). Reflecting on his sense of criticism, Miller writes:

I should add that "in some sense" we are indeed critics. I have been proposing in what sense. It is that the individual is identified in the order of his
doing, so that it is in terms of that immediacy that he makes mistakes and en-
tertains structural incoherencies.

I find that common sense holds that view, i.e., the view that the criticism of the act occurs on the basis of what one is now more generally doing.

Unless some enterprise stands now unquestioned, criticism of a particular act has no force. Nor does it carry arrest of attention. In fact such
criticism cannot operate as the occasion for sharpening one's sense of the
more generally engaging present enterprise. (MP 28:13)

Criticism is a vehicle of conversion, revolution, and radical revision. Yet the root
of personhood—the continuum of identity and effort—must be preserved in
some important measure. Wholesale or complete change is what Miller calls
"pseudo-revising" (PL 883). It is structurally impossible and offers no actual possibility of profound change. No effective negation is possible without an affirmation. Indeed the true peril of criticism lies in one's affirmations and
attachments—that is, that any change will have to be integrated with what has
gone before and that one cannot ever start afresh. This dynamic process of criticism is intrinsic to identity. The ability to reflect on and revise those representations is critical to the nature of personhood.

The moral universe is a historical universe. Similarly a moral community is a critical, and finally philosophical, community. The historical and the critical join one
another as dynamic and reflective orders of human action. What role does liberal
democracy play in such a universe, such a community? "Liberalism is the community of criticism" (MP 7:14), Miller asserts. First, liberalism *facilitates criticism* by
establishing the requisite vehicles and orders for responsible communication. Second, liberalism *establishes its very own order as an object of reflection and criticism.*

Communication is at the root of criticism and autonomy. Community is
appropriately defined as "maximal self-expression" (PL 147–48). It is not the
brute antagonist of personal authority. Rather identity can only be established
and grow in terms of communicative processes.

What manner of communication promotes the greatest realization of
authority? Each mode of communication is necessarily a means for exercising
personal authority and revealing shared authority. All are forms of exchange. Each
contributes to the growth of personhood and attests to the existence of shared symbolic means of personal authority. Yet in liberal democracy emphasis is placed on
deliberation. Drawing on Hocking, Miller makes the comparison between the term-
making process that transpires in legislatures and less formal modes of conversa-

tion (PH 5, 1931, 95; cf. Hocking, 1926). Just as legislation is the model for action, deliberation can also be regarded as the paradigm for communication. All acts of communication attest to shared controlling orders of experience and, further, all acts of communication offer the opportunity for assessing those orders. Deliberative communication is paradigmatic because it is a process in which the bases of a given endeavor are highlighted to a maximal degree and then questioned. Deliberative processes address that which is of greatest concern to a person—that is, *his symbolically embodied and historically developing ideas.*[22] Via symbols, minds are available to other minds (see DT 189).

> The functioning object is the meeting place of reason and act, of essence and existence. In the abstract, it mediates between thought and object. In the specific and concrete, it mediates also between mind and mind.
>
> The functioning object is communication. One escapes from subjectivity by finding the evidence of other subjects. The objective is another mind, because only there is one's own subjectivity revealed as one's own approach to the common world. (MS 34)

Deliberation takes into account the forms of one's actuality embodied in the midworld. It does not just utilize the forms of communication but, rather, concentrates one's attention on them. The liberal democratic idea of community is one of constant engagement in the shared conditions of local- and self-control. Deliberative communication is always a process of criticism. The conscious apprehension of the structure of actuality commits one to the genealogical analysis of its orders and their critical development by means of revision.

Liberal democracy is a community of criticism. Communication and its moral import are, of course, by no means under the sole protection of the state; the opportunities for communication and criticism are various and widespread. Much of this communication, while genuine, remains limited—perhaps even limited to technical considerations. Democratic political association, by contrast, avoids more static forms of community based on resemblance and content by explicitly highlighting the symbolic bases of community. A more expansive and political sense of communication requires a common world whose scope exceeds the exclusive worlds established in sociability (CB 4). The state capitalizes on the criticism already at play in simple association and transforms it into reflective and deliberative modes of communication.

The liberal state thus functions as the form and guarantor of an open community—that is, a place where minds can meet and engage in the reflective apprehension and criticism of ideas. The state is also a *model* of deliberative communication itself. In political association criticism is applied not only to the modes of order obtaining in the larger community but also to the very procedures of governance itself. Representative bodies revise the law as well as declare it. Judicial bodies interpret the law even as they apply it. Executives must obey the law even as they enforce it. And the whole apparatus of government (including the voting populace) avails itself of the opportunity to reflect on and revise the very procedures of making and revising the law. Liberal democracy is thus the continual and unlimited activity of criticism involving all levels of order.

Reflection and criticism are the hallmarks of deliberation and have a place in all aspects of life. Each act or statement is given standing, first and foremost, in terms of its openness to reflection and criticism (see FI 264–67). Nothing can be said to lie beyond criticism—not even the state itself. This new conception of the state (res publica) can be read back into the various symbols (res publicae) that articulate one's world and one's self. The relationship between res publicae and res publica is reciprocal.

History and politics are premised on the reflective activity of criticism. Critical processes are themselves premised on the moral or efficacious activity of persons. Thus Miller's description of his own philosophical project in "Idealism and Freedom":

> History is the order of the unique. It declares the efficacy of time in the meaning of events. Physics and logic do not do this. History is the vindication of inwardness, the record of daring and of its transforming victories. The idealism of the future will be a philosophy of history, of action, of self-generating, lawful finitude. Such are the conditions of a metaphysics of democracy. (PC 74)

Actualism is describable as both a *historical idealism* and a *metaphysics of democracy*. The two are interchangeable. There is a confluence of historical and political vocabularies, most especially in the use of terms such as *personhood, action, responsibility, interpretation, legislation, deliberation,* and *reflection.* Historical thinking pushes one in the direction of democratic political association while the practice of liberal democracy shows itself to be the preeminent way of exercising one's historical consciousness.

The basis for this convergence is that both history and politics are dynamic processes. Indeed, with respect to history, Miller states that the very composure, or order, of history is change (MP 14:6). What changes in history, of course, are not bricks and mortar, flesh and bones, or chemical bonds and DNA codes. In history, symbolically embodied ideas change. It is the life of disclosive ideas that defines history and not the "life" of disclosed material objects (PH 5, 1931, 85; see DT 189). It is precisely this sort of actuality that is essential to democratic society—that is, a past that is authoritative as well as an opportunity for revision (PL 431–33). Like history, democracy is the ongoing activity of criticism and revision wherein change is constant and yet also genealogically regulated by the very concepts undergoing revision. Politics is "a matter of fate and history" (PL 713), one's self-regulation and interpretation on the basis of inherited orders. The form, as well as the matter, of history and politics coincide. And it is with this in mind that Miller speaks of the state as the vehicle of history (PL 676).

History and politics also resist reduction. A purely empirical or mechanical reading of actuality results in the dismissal of the possibility of conscious, self-maintaining order. Any attempt to *explain* history or politics is destructive. Action is its own reference point. Translated into the vocabulary of politics, it is the question of freedom or autonomy:

> A free political society will possess and modify its own language, its own literature, religion or science. It will express its discipline in peculiar procedures, in the presidential system or the cabinet system of executive power. It will improvise an educational ladder, different in some respects from that of another equally free society. But these limbs and branches of the growing social organism can not be cut off without killing the roots. Nobody's independence is abstract. Free societies and free individuals are identical with their historical self-revision. Nobody can act in the abstract, but only in terms of the body and mind which is closely and intimately his own. Nobody can obliterate the past and then make plans for what to do next. Indeed, freedom may be regarded as the revision of the intimate past. It is historical, never static or "scientific." It is growth not mechanism. It is spontaneous not devised. It is reflective, never logical. (EPE 10)

It is only by means of establishing a historical consciousness that one can hope to authenticate the present and the first-person authority of persons (see MS 19). Thus Miller claims that freedom can only be actualized in a historical community (PH 7, 1951–52, 7). The political desire for freedom and self-rule is incompatible with any environment other than the historical environment of symbolically embodied actions. Similarly historical consciousness demands political consciousness in that the questions of self-control and social order are unavoidable once action is recognized. History and politics are not just self-defining actualities but mutually implicating processes of criticism.

The assurance derived from the practice of criticism is linked to both democracy and philosophy. Politics is fundamentally philosophical and, thus, political practice is philosophical practice. The *bond* between the political and the historical is of course an ancient one; they are modes of being and order that pertain to the finite,

the variable, and the mortal. Equally ancient, however, is the *division* between the
philosophical and finite. The ahistoric ideal has, for millennia, driven a wedge
between the historical and philosophical as well as between the political and philosophical. Proposing the unity of all three is a significant revision of the tradition.
This revision is the very point of a metaphysics of democracy. The dismantling of
the ahistoric ideal means that the aspersions cast by Plato and his philosophical
descendents on the political life must be corrected by fully reintegrating the finite
orders of history and politics with philosophy.

The most direct way of approaching Miller's case for the unity of politics,
history, and philosophy is to revisit briefly the arguments against the static cosmos. It will be recalled that, for Miller, the claim of finite agency "involves a
secession . . . from any universe regarded as a fait accompli." The ahistoric ideal is
effectively the denial of agency because it considers the universe as a fact. The
claim to have acted breaks up the static cosmos and sets it in motion. It is Miller's
contention that no person can forsake action let alone a conscious claim to her
own agency. If so, then the efficacy of finitude must be introduced into the prevailing ahistoric order and that order revised so as to accommodate agency. As
such, history and politics regain the prominence that they lost, first to Ideas, then
God, and finally science. The will leaves behind the subordinate role that it bore
under these authorities (EPE 3). Yet the reclamation of agency does not result in
the haphazard and chaotic flux suggested by the radical pluralism that William
James proposed when attacking the "block universe" (James, 1943). Rather the
movement is historical and takes the form of a *genealogical* order, an order whose
very character is paradoxically open to accidents, original deeds, and even revolu-
tions. Indeed Miller's argument against the Eleatic ideal is most interesting because it does not merely stand the Eleatics on their heads. Actualism revises
Eleaticism as well as Ionianism. Philosophy maintains itself and continues its
search for universal and necessary orders. Those very universals, ideals, and laws
of the realist's moral cosmos are, however, redescribed in terms of finite activity.

Philosophy need not lead away from the transient and fragile order of historical events. Philosophical thinking is indispensable for articulating these
dynamic orders and engaging in their continuous revision. For philosophy is not
speculation but is, as are politics and history, an activity of identifying and criticizing modes of control. As Miller states, philosophy must be criticism (FI 265–67).
For that reason, philosophy must also be historical and political.

History is allied with revision (PH 178; see §4.3). It is a dynamic process
wherein each order vies for permanence and is outstripped by its predecessors. In
history change comes about via a reflective process wherein conscious acts are
overcome by other conscious deeds. This is the process of criticism and history is
best understood as the realm of valid criticism (Notes PH 7, 1951-52, 8). In

elevating criticism, however, history offers more than an account of the dynamic variety of experience. It also illuminates the search for local- and self-control. As an area of study, history articulates the rise and fall of modes of order in terms of this search. As an account of actuality, history reveals both the import of agency and the fragile character of the modes of control that agency establishes.

Politics, in turn, can be described as the conscious engagement in the historical process. This description is apt because in liberal democratic political association persons undertake to make systematic and explicit the informal and ad hoc process of criticism that constitutes all modes of historical experience. Politics is the reflective engagement in and conscious organization of critical processes. It is for this reason that Miller refers to the state as the vehicle of history. Political association puts into concrete and public practice these insights regarding the historical constitution of being and enfranchises communication, criticism, and revision. Miller writes on the topic of tolerance:

> It is true that the dogmatic state is the enemy of other dogmas; but it is not true that the liberal state is indifferent to dogmas. What the liberal state affirms is intolerance to all dogma, not to some particular dogmas. For the affirmation of liberalism is the unity of men in self-critical association. It is humanism, but a disciplined humanism. It respects other opinion where that opinion confesses its openness to dispute, its possible error, and its subordination to the [illegible] of test available to all. It holds that whosoever holds opinions not open to criticism and not defined by their emergence from the context of criticism has forfeited the right to tolerance. (MP 7:14)

In politics, as in history, no ideal can stand aloof from the process of criticism and no one can pretend to speak from outside that process. To reject criticism constitutes not only a rejection of history but also forsakes the liberty and self-control intrinsic to historical experience.

It is owing to this common commitment to criticism that Miller states that both history and democracy are without an orthodoxy (PH 173). Their basic concern, and fundamental supposition, is the integrity and agency of persons. Their common expression is the activity of criticism.

In "For Idealism," a chain of associations leads from the basic claim that "criticism as assurance is idealism" and finally links up with the statement that idealism "must claim to be philosophy" (FI 265–67). Philosophy is discourse without an a priori (SC 7; see DT 11–37), a discourse that aims not at the truth but at the establishment of the process of criticism (PH 19–20, 1952–53, 60). Philosophy is unique in comparison to other modes of discourse. For, properly considered, philosophy is not interested in statements of fact, claims to truth and falsity. These matters are left to those disciplines concerned with facts, hypotheses, and experimental modes of verification. Philosophy is the constant engagement in self-criticism as well as the criticism of others in one's community. Philosophy is moved not by responsibility to maintain definitions and local-control. (Although it encompasses these concerns.) Rather Miller finds that philosophy is animated by a sense of "responsibility of mind for mind" (MP 13:20).

With respect to history, philosophy is premised on and further reveals the open-ended and dynamic character of the orders constituting human existence. Rejecting the split between the contemplative life and the active life, Miller sees philosophy as committed to the examination of those historical and quasi-transcendent symbolic orders that are the conditions of disclosure of self and world. Because the philosopher is not a neutral observer considering the eternal to the exclusion of the finite, such efforts will result not just in the contemplation of the historical continuum of order but will lead to participation in its maintenance and revision. Philosophy not only affirms historical ontology but, in criticism, contributes to the development of historical orders. The "world as philosophically defined" is thus "the world as incomplete" (MS 191)—not accidentally or provisionally, but necessarily incomplete.

With respect to politics, philosophy is based in an understanding of autonomy. The philosophical life, Miller attests, is attached to the idea of freedom (PH 5, 1931, 108, 155). Such freedom is not a liberty from constraint or need. The freedom with which philosophy is concerned is found in taking responsibility for one's actions and their guiding controls. This is the liberty of actual authority. Thus freedom is instantiated in criticism whereby a person claims authority for her actions—that is, their basis, performance, and consequences. Insofar as philosophy is criticism, political activity needs to look to philosophy when searching for a model. Here political speech joins with philosophical communication, deliberation melds with inquiry.

§5.5 CONCLUSION

Actualism is a philosophy of criticism. It is criticism that cements the various elements in the structure of Miller's thinking precisely because of its capacity to join action and being. Criticism has "ontological status" (FI 264), it both reveals and has an efficacious force relative to the forms of disclosure. In "Idealism and Freedom" Miller writes:

> Idealism after Kant consists in the discovery and exploitation of the non-psychological factors of experience. They are the factors of structure, and consequently of criticism, for criticism is nothing other than the self-maintenance

of structure. It seems tolerable to assume that the denial of structure is all the same as the denial of criticism. It seems equally persuasive that the authority of criticism depends on the necessity of those structures in accordance with which criticism operates. Let it be urged that the modes of criticism lack equivalence with the real, and it follows that authority itself is only appearance, animal faith perhaps, or a convenient code for getting a little order out of a mess of running experience. (PC 68)

In criticism a person attests to, and thus discloses, the structure of experience. Moreover, he affirms the authoritative character of that structure as a condition and guide for conduct. (Every gesture of criticism attests to the authority of that which it aims to revise.) Criticism itself is always apropos some current or proposed action. It is action that casts structure into relief, framing both its strengths and deficiencies. And it is action undertaken in light of such criticism that brings reflective thought to bear on structure. Action informed by criticism may result in the ongoing maintenance of the existing forms of disclosure. It may also affect a revision or perhaps a revolution in those forms. The central issue is that action is not cut off from the structures of disclosure. Action reveals and contributes to the evolution of these orders. History, politics, and philosophy are all of equal ontological import—that is, they are all modes of responsible, reflective, and critical action. In all three the distinction between the active life and the contemplative life is redescribed as an articulate unity. The capacity of each person to participate in the process of criticism redescribes this ancient division and reintroduces the bond between the person and the actual.

Epilogue
The Scholar and the Citizen

In short, we must disintellectualize the real if we are to be faithful to it.
—Ortega y Gasset, "History as a System"

In Miller's estimation, the Eleaticism of Parmenides or the Ionianism of Heraclitus offers few resources for understanding democracy. At their extreme, monism or radical pluralism destroys the bases of authority. These conceptual and practical confusions are related to the split between the active life and the contemplative life wherein action and thought, individuality and universality, as well as history and philosophy are alienated one from another. A *metaphysics of democracy*, by contrast, joins a strong conception of authority with an equally robust estimation of the finite person by integrating reflection and action. In the *responsible agent* the false division between the active and contemplative lives is ameliorated.

Two claims have been basic to the preceding chapters. The first is that the principles, procedures, and institutions of democracy have metaphysical import. They are not just useful means for coping with actuality but, rather, are modes of disclosure and provide terms according to which actuality is articulated. The second claim is that Miller's metaphysics of democracy elevates the finite and thus transforms mundane activity into something of greater, indeed universal, significance. These claims are the keynotes of the heroic character of democratic life. This idea of *heroism* is developed via a consideration of two specific forms of life—the scholar and the citizen. In these two figures of contemporary heroism we find concrete instances of the reconciliation of the active and contemplative lives, as well as bases for reenvisioning democratic practice.

Miller notes that the modern temper does not allow for heroes (MP 19:3). Modern individuals are understood to behave but not to act. There can be no true heroes. Those who pose as or are set up to be "heroes" are no longer admired or emulated but rather explained in terms of motivations and habits. On the topic of heroism, Miller writes:

This man, the individual, has been lost and is not to be derived from physics or the regnant psychology. "A so-and-so" yields no individual, no act, no local control, no midworld, no *vehicle of the unique*. . . . [W]e lack a medium in which the individual could declare himself or be manifest to others. We allow no heroes. "A so-and-so" is never a hero, saint or devil, wise man or fool. There is no moral problem . . . until unique individuals supply a locus. (MP 31:5)

The rarified forms of the contemplative life cannot abide heroes. (It is a peculiarity of the parallel histories of the contemplative life and democracy that the growth of democracy has been coincident with the development and magnification of this distinction.)[1] The result has been the subordination of the active life to the contemplative life to such a degree that the active life has sometimes appeared to be eclipsed entirely. *Personhood, history,* and *politics* have all, to varying degrees, been brought under the rule of theory. One result is that much of what constituted the import and glory of the political life has been removed and politics has been interpreted on psychological and technical models.

Miller counters this trend and insists that democratic practice requires heroism—both the recognition of the heroic actors of the past and of one's own capacity for heroic action (cf. Colapietro, 2003, pp. 79–80). Liberal democracy needs a profound sense of the import and responsibility of agency— what Hannah Arendt termed *natality* (1978, v. 2, p. 217). There must be persons who speak original words and do novel things. Those words and deeds must be legislative; they must have consequences for the disclosure of one's world (see MS 110). And while there may be few grand heroes, "those who live and justify life," the deeds of such persons "call the rest of us back to a new courage" (PC 29). In this vein, Miller describes his approach to philosophy as one of bolstering *morale* (see AH 257, 266–67; MS 185–92). Actualism is interested in establishing assurance or confidence in action and instilling vitality in our democratic practices and institutions. Miller's metaphysics of democracy is as prescriptive as it is descriptive.[2]

In his *Democratic Vistas* Walt Whitman wrote of breathing into the average person "the breath recuperative of sane and heroic life" (1867/1982, p. 940). Miller's interest is in reestablishing the confidence of "the man on Elm Street." Here Miller makes what might seem to be a paradoxical point: It is the ahistoric absolutes in which the Eleatic ideal sought assurance that effectively strike against agency. Assurance must be sought elsewhere.

It must be admitted that, despite his interest in morale, Miller has removed many of the props by which a person might support himself. Thus it is fair to ask: By making historical temporality a fundamental category, has Miller not substantially weakened the status of *truth, right,* and *goodness*—ideals for which a person might exert himself in a heroic fashion? Has he not, along with Richard Rorty, shown that standards and ideals are transient? And does this not render moral confidence impossible and established the necessity of irony? Certainly, as chapter 1 shows in detail, Miller and Rorty share a number of philosophical commitments, perhaps the most important is their common stand against the premises of the contemplative life. Even as Rorty informs one that the world of the realist is "the world well lost" (1982, pp. 3–18), Miller announces that "morality involves a secession from any utopian version of the universe, from any universe regarded as a fait accompli" (MM 2–3).[3] But as we have seen before, Miller finds hope and encouragement (and not the meager cheerfulness of irony) in the revision of the lofty ideas of the contemplative life.

The juxtaposition of heroism and irony highlights the sort of radical opposition that actualism avoids. Miller does not tie morale to Platonism or any other version of moral realism. Yet the failure of the Eleatic ideal does not signal the failure of morale and a descent into nihilism. Rather morality, responsible action, and heroism are all made possible by the historical constitution of reality. History is that relatively disorderly order between a monistic universe and a sheer pluriverse (see PH 128). Such a universe is incomplete as a matter of its very structure. And it is precisely in such an environment—and certainly not despite it—that moral, democratic, and philosophical sensibilities arise: "History does not show men good or bad; it operates by assuming that they are moral—that is, agents," Miller writes. "Good, in history, can mean only the perpetuation of those critical processes that define the moral" (PH 192). Responsibility cannot be eschewed and all ideals are at risk. The absolute comfort derived from the fixed moral cosmos of the Platonists (both pagan and Christian) is not only ahistoric— it breeds complacency. But so too does ironism. Ironism makes a related mistake when it supposes that, in turning away from Platonism, that all standards become equally suspect and action reduces to psychology and behavior. In both cases, action lacks the element of natality—novelty and authority.

Miller thus takes up the Platonic notion of the *moral universe* and renders it amenable to action (see §5.1). Miller's sense of morality is both more spare and more vital than both the Platonic conception and its pessimistic alternative figured in Rorty's pragmatism. Morality is equated not with justice or goodness. It is a matter of the *agency*—that is, a person's capacity for action and responsibility. The type of confidence in question is not derived from the knowledge that one is right or following the truth. The most fundamental form of confidence the moral person needs is the basic understanding that her action is requisite and, moreover, her action can be effective. It is a matter of understanding that the actuality of *right* or *truth* depends on her action. Miller writes:

> Above all, what characterizes the free man is his capacity and determination to make history. It is not the static truth that makes men free. In that guise the truth always enslaves. It is rather in the *revision* of truth that freedom is found. Furthermore, the static truth abolishes community. The revision of truth is the maintenance of community, not, of course, the anthropological, or sociological, community, but the community of free men. One cannot argue or deal with static modes of truth. In history, we see the awful, but responsible, spectacle of man's reinterpretations of himself and nature, and reassessment of our heritage. One can inherit neither truth nor freedom. Every heritage must be understood in its own creative motives and then overpassed in amendment and revision. We cannot escape nature, but neither can we escape history. (PC 103–4)

The need for order gives rise to the need for action and the recognition of responsibility. The emphasis of actualism falls on *res gestae* or public deeds, as well as on the ideals or forms of order these acts establish, maintain, and revise. In a moral universe of such a fragile and incomplete composition the responsibility of action cannot be shirked and cannot be concluded.

Actualism, by revising rarified forms of the contemplative life, does not then undermine morale. Rather it bolsters agency in two distinct ways. First the moral person finds assurance in the fundamental assertion of the import of action (MM 21). This basic confidence derives from the sense of the authority of one's own deeds and their efficacy in those processes by which one maintains and revises prevailing orders. Second action derives assurance from having a reliable—although dynamic and revisable—basis in those objective orders which are part of the historical continuum of the midworld. Every action, including the act of criticism, draws support from the relatively static forms structuring experience. *History* is the condition of each agent's morale as well as the ongoing process of revision.

In sum, the heroic confidence Miller seeks to instill is based not on the fact that one's ideals are beyond criticism but, rather, that they are always amenable to criticism.

Miller remarks that what endures is not any specific form of order but, rather, the activity of *criticism* in which the present seeks to understand and maintain itself (PH 7, 1951–52, 32). This ceaseless questioning is each person's fate and, Miller suggests, each person's vocation (see PC 174–92). It is the epitome of scholarship. Thus confidence must be reconceived in a fashion that suits the existential basis of actualism, growing out of and further contributing to human finitude.

Criticism is an essay at original action in the form of the "disciplined qualification of the past" (AH 267). In criticism one recognizes a continuum of action and sees oneself as an heir of past deeds. Criticism also shows one to be an agent *within* and, indeed, by virtue of this continuum of deeds. Thus the critic in the actualist sense mediates as well as reconciles freedom and constraint, spontaneity and authority, as well as originality and history. Criticism is scholarship understood as *active reflection*. Mere reflection on history and the order of its various symbolically embodied orders (i.e., the contemplative life) does not amount to criticism. Yet undertaking to change these orders without an adequate understanding of history (i.e., a base understanding of the active life) is not criticism either; it is only wayward behavior. In criticism, action and reflection are interrelated. It is the essence of what Miller means when he writes of *history as a form of piety*—"our reconciliation with the conditions of our endeavors" (PH 149; cf. Colapietro, 2003, pp. 143–74).

What the democratic hero seeks above all else is responsibility. Such responsibility demands a commitment to criticism. In the intersubjective exercise of criticism a person affirms his freedom:

> There is just one quality in every man which he must change at least once; he must change his philosophy. Only in the discovery of some fatal threat to himself in the framework of his inheritance can he discover freedom. There alone does he confront a necessary and an absolute problem, one proposed by himself and suffered in himself. Freedom is not, as so many have said, in choice; it is rather in the revision of the basis of choice. (PC 73)

To repudiate critical scholarship is to cease to be free (MP 3:13). In refusing criticism one not only seeks to elude responsibility but also supposes that either that person was never responsible in the first place or one's actions are absolute. In such an attitude one witnesses the descent into uncritical and nonphilosophical attitudes such as dogmatism, mysticism, or skepticism (see PH 171; FI). It is a descent in which personal authority is forsaken. By contrast, the democratic person cannot deny the force of criticism because he recognizes that the condition of personal authority is found in the fact that all assertions are limited and necessarily prone to revision. Each action puts a temporary stop to criticism. Yet, once performed, each action provides material for criticism and thus generates its own antagonists. To act is to make oneself vulnerable to criticism (PH 19–20, 1952–53, 26). The democratic hero accepts this risk and recognizes that it cannot be avoided. The risk is the very condition of his agency and freedom.

The task of scholarly criticism is inexhaustible and continually calls on the person to evaluate, communicate, and revise. The form of questioning involved in criticism is ultimately philosophical in character. What a person is concerned with is how her world hangs together and comes apart. These hinges—so decisive for her sense of self and for an estimation of herself as agent—are the loci of conflicts within and among the prevailing orders of the midworld (see MS 185–92).

Criticism arises from action and further influences action. First and foremost is the practical matter of the continual organization of one's identity that is itself articulated by conflicts and confusions. "The next step," Miller writes, "would be an attempt to move the conflict from the ego into the open and public world" (MS 188). The connection between identity and symbols facilitates this movement and makes scholarship ingredient to public life. Free institutions—and this category encompasses all of the symbolic vehicles (res publicae) of the midworld—are loci of identity, self-assertion, and self-direction in the maintenance of critical activities. These institutions are also evidence of the will to make the personal and particular universal, to render the finite and mortal quasi-transcendental. This is the other side of the heroic—the will not just to rule oneself via criticism but also to exceed oneself in the creation and maintenance of universal and revisable forms of order.

Miller proposes the scholar as the figure of the self-possessed and critical finitude that is the hallmark of his metaphysics of democracy (cf. Anderson, 1994). What I suggest by way of conclusion is that scholarship is also a model for citizenship and, moreover, that scholarship should itself be interpreted as the form of citizenship. Both are heroic enterprises of self-maintenance in the activity of criticism. Both forms of life are available to and indeed required of each person.

The heroism at issue here is not something grand or uncommon. It is a democratic, popular heroism. Its basic requirement is that one accept José Ortega y Gasset's proposition that "man, in a word, has no nature; what he has is history" (1961, p. 217). Miller writes:

> Who, then, is in history? Anyone whose life has shape and who exerts himself to preserve his integrity has joined articulate forces. This need not be on a grand scale. It can mean no more than doing one's job and keeping the home fires burning. A great deal of our work is no better than maintenance. . . . We have a rendezvous with our time and place, and that is as much of destiny as is generally possible. Once in a blue moon one may hear an original word. Such a word is a disciplined qualification of a past. When it happens we mark a date, a moment stands out, a revelation has been made, a present glows, not with a hard gemlike flame, but with the warmth of an assured actuality. It is these actualities which, for their apprehension, impose a task. (AH 267)

Heroism in this sense is the requirement that one take responsibility for oneself and one's world. Miller remarks that philosophy is not esoteric but indigenous (MS 190). Similarly heroism is the common share and calling of all persons.

The primary task of education and scholarship, as Miller notes, is to "idealize the actual" (PC 176). Scholarship seeks to understand the prevailing modes of order that articulate one's self and one's world so as to put a person in the position to take part in history as the fateful career of those orders. Miller thus reinterprets the traditional sense of what it means to be a scholar and turns us away from the image of a solitary and sedentary person perusing tomes in the dim light of the library. We are discouraged from thinking of the scholar as someone who, as G. W. F. Hegel would have it, discerns the form of the world that is in decay and is thus consigned to writing the epitaph of that order (1821/1965, p. 13; cf. Colapietro, 2003, pp. 151–86 passim). Miller wants us to conceive of scholarship in terms of "the excitement and desperation of controlled inquiry." He goes on:

> All men possess some perspective, all live in live in some world, more or less orderly or confused, more or less dark and incoherent, but never wholly formless or inarticulate. But in the scholar the articulate world has become a deliberate quest and an acknowledged need. Such a world cannot be altogether inherited, but must be won afresh by every student, if only that he may the more surely posses it as his own. The scholar must have the courage and the persistence to repossess his heritage and, if possible, to go beyond it. (PC 174)

Scholarship is the means of attaining and maintaining autonomy. It is akin to what Immanuel Kant meant by *enlightenment* (1784/1959). Yet, unlike Kant, Miller understands autonomy to mean immersing oneself in the historical dynamic of the midworld. It is, indeed, a way of immersing oneself in the "destructive element" (PC 191; cf. Conrad, 1900/1981, p. 138)—that is, life itself in all of its orderly disorder. Scholarship is not a way to flee the world but rather is how one dives into the world. It is only by considering and acting in the complexity of the historical world that one can hope to attain any serenity and composure (see PC 184).

The work of the scholar is that of philosophy-as-history (see §4.5)—the discovery and understanding of the loci of systematic conflict that articulate any outlook (PC 188). The point of discovering these points of conflict is not, however, mere understanding. The goal of the scholar is to join the antagonistic forces at play in the various systematic orders. Better stated: The goal is for the scholar to see how he is *already allied* with constraints of these orders and thus already committed to the conflicts within them. As Miller writes elsewhere: "Conflict does not operate to scatter the self but to establish it, even to organize it" (MS 187). Allying oneself with constraint is to consciously attach oneself to those historical orders and problems that constitute one's identity as well as one's world. This is the full meaning of "idealizing the actual."

By means of the ongoing work of scholarship a person establishes a connection to the world as both a condition and extension of his energies (PC 182). Thus there is *identification*. Yet by virtue of identification there also comes the possibility and burden of criticism. For scholarship, like the world itself, is a developing process. What occurs in education is not just an enlargement of the world but also the establishment of the means to change the world via revision of its basic terms. The commitment that we have to the symbolic orders and their historical career is also a demand for criticism. Far from rote learning, scholarship is the ongoing maintenance and exercise of authority in the responsible maintenance and disciplined revision of the historical midworld.

Scholarship displays the same qualities found in democratic citizenship. Both the scholar and the citizen are responsible and autonomous. Both are also called to maintain their autonomy by means of various forms of study by which one comes to understand the conditions of one's endeavors. The goal of those scholarly pursuits is to engage in the reflective maintenance and revision of one's world. Scholarship is the prerequisite of citizenship, and each scholar is a citizen.

The citizen is not a manager of public affairs and not a voter of preferences. The citizen is an *actor* in the full sense of the term. What Miller understands by scholarship is basically an engagement in democratic processes of inquiry and revision unfolding among a plurality of agents. Early in the formation of democratic institutions, the scientific community (a community of scholars) and experimental processes were taken up as models for political processes. The activity of scientific inquiry transpires in a community of criticism understood as a *community of power*. The democratic community of which the citizen is a member is a community of shared authority and the mutual recognition of persons as authoritative. The democratic community, like other communities of power, has specific aims. Yet the encompassing goal and the very form of the community is that of autonomy—a self-directed process wherein each agent is recognized as free, authoritative, and responsible. Each member is enfranchised in the process in and through the demand to engage in process of criticism. This is the true community of persons who responsibly maintain and revise their common world.

In the person of the scholar-as-citizen the ancient antagonism between the active and contemplative lives is reconceived and, finally, reconciled. The autonomy or self-possessed finitude that Miller holds up as an ideal requires the joining of these two modes of life. What is more, actualism shows that this reconciliation is embodied in the scholarly and civic activities in which we participate. As critics we engage in *active reflection*. We cannot escape the demands of criticism any more than we can escape history.

Notes

PREFACE

1. There is no evidence in either the published or unpublished writings of Miller that he was familiar with Arendt's work. The two were contemporaries, however, and both had a strong historical bent to their thought. Their common disinclination to separate thought from action may have led them both to give consideration to this ancient distinction.

2. See especially Joseph P. Fell's "Miller: The Man and His Philosophy" and George P. Brockway's "John William Miller." Further information is available at the Web site of the John William Miller Fellowship Fund (http://www.williams.edu/resources/miller).

INTRODUCTION

1. In his essay "Miller: The Man and His Philosophy" Joseph Fell refers to Miller's thought as a "philosophy of the act" (p. 27; cf. Mead, 1938). *Actualism* will be adopted in order to convey the importance placed on the act. Miller himself never referred to his position as *actualism* and consistently stated that it was a philosophy of history and a development of idealism. The virtue of *historical idealism* in comparison to *actualism* is that it emphasizes Miller's own indebtedness to, and revision of, the idealist tradition. The great liability of historical *idealism*, however, is that it focuses attention on intellect while neglecting both action and the connection between action and intellect.

2. Miller's philosophy has little to do with the concept of *actualism* used in discussions of possible-world theories. That understanding of actualism is described as follows: "Actualism is the philosophical position that everything there is—everything that can be said to exist in any sense—is *actual*. Put another way, actualism denies that there is any kind of being beyond actuality; to be is to be actual. Actualism therefore stands in stark contrast to possibilism, which, as we've seen, takes the things there are to include possible but non-actual objects" (Menzel, 2000).

3. *Nicomachean Ethics*, 1095^b13-95^b20.

4. For Arendt's explorations of the active life in relation to the contemplative life see *The Human Condition, Between Past and Future*, and *The Life of the Mind.*

5. See the work of Arthur Danto and Donald Davidson for contemporary philosophy addressing action.

6. On this count, actualism diverges from the Greek conception of deeds. As Arendt noted, to the Greek mind deeds were distinct from fabrications. In fabrication something is produced that endures, even if for a short time, without the aid of memory. If it were not for memory, deeds would be entirely lost. Fabrication thus was considered to lack the futility, but also the nobility, of deeds. Actualism aims to integrate action and fabrication along the same lines as Arendt when, in "The Concept of History," she nuanced the Greek understanding of these two modes of human being: "Compared with the futility and fragility of human action, the world fabrication erects is of lasting permanence and tremendous solidity. Only insofar as the end product of fabrication is incorporated into the human world, where its use and eventual 'history' can never be fully predicted, does even fabrication start a process whose outcome cannot be entirely foreseen and is therefore beyond the control of its author. This means only that man is never exclusively homo faber, that even the fabricator remains at the same time an acting being, who starts processes wherever he goes and with whatever he does" (1968, p. 60).

7. See the first chapter of Vincent Colapietro's *Fateful Shapes of Human Freedom*, Fell's "Miller: The Man and His Philosopohy," and the first chapter of Stephen Tyman's *Descrying the Ideal* for other accounts of the historical career and cultural context in which Miller's philosophy has its place.

8. See Ortega y Gasset's "History as a System," in *History as a System and Other Essays Toward a Philosophy of History*. Miller's assessment of Ortega is mixed. Impressed with Ortega's appreciation of history and action, Miller is also uncomfortable with what he sees as Ortega's excessive reliance on imagination and fiction. See an unpublished letter of Miller's (MP 17:15) as well as Colapietro's discussion in *Fateful Shapes of Human Freedom* (pp. 16–17).

9. Paradoxically, the ahistoricism of Christianity is built on a single, exemplary historical being—Jesus. As Miller notes in numerous places, Jesus is a man of action and a maker of history; Jesus is the word incarnate (MS 152–53). The peculiarity of Christianity is that it concentrates historicity and action in the life of a single man and excludes the rest of humanity from the active life (Arendt, 1968, p. 66).

10. Quoted in Arendt (1978, vol. 1, p. 198).

11. On the topic of humanism in Miller's philosophy, see chapter 4 of Colapietro's *Fateful Shapes of Human Freedom*.

12. Arendt defined heroism as a form of courage that exhibits "a willingness to act, to speak at all, to insert one's self into the world and to begin a story of one's own" (1959, p. 166).

CHAPTER 1. A METAPHYSICS OF DEMOCRACY?

1. See *Man and the State* (p. 377), for Hocking's use of this term.

2. Although Miller does not formalize this distinction, the term *person* will be used to indicate individuality that constitutes and is constituted by sociability, morality, and political participation (see §5.1). This richer idea of the individual is usefully contrasted with the sheer individual represented in C. B. Macpherson's conception of "possessive individualism." See *The Political Theory of Possessive Individualism: Hobbes to Locke*, as well as the following discussion of Macpherson's description of liberal democracy.

3. The thrust of Macpherson's description of liberal democracy is that, in the West, there is no separating the market from democracy. Macpherson's more contentious claim is that economic relations are *prior* to political relations. Macpherson writes: "So democracy came as a late addition to the competitive market society and the liberal state. The point of recalling this is, of course, to emphasize that democracy came as an adjunct to the competitive liberal society and state. It is not simply that democracy came later. It is also that democracy in these societies was demanded, and was admitted, on competitive liberal grounds. . . . In short, by the time democracy came, in the present liberal-democratic countries, it was no longer opposed [as had been populist conceptions of democracy] to the liberal society and the liberal state. . . . Democracy had been transformed" (1966, pp. 9–10). The import of this historical sense is encapsulated in Macpherson's concept of "possessive individualism." If political and social relations parallel economic relations, then the individual is primarily "an owner of himself" and "society becomes a lot of free equal individuals related to each other as proprietors of their own capacities and of what they have acquired by their exercise" (1962, p. 3).

4. This definition overlaps with one sense of *philosophy* provided by Rawls in "Justice as Fairness" and quoted by Rorty in "The Priority of Democracy to Philosophy": "philosophy as the search for truth about an independent metaphysical and moral order . . ." (1991, p. 180). It seems fair to conclude that when Rorty is speaking of *philosophy* he is addressing *metaphysical philosophy* and not the more literary style of philosophizing that he himself recommends.

5. Miller's reading of Plato is more complex than the pejorative label *Platonism* suggests. While at times the servant of "Father Parmenides," Plato was often the champion of local immediacies and historical questions of value. This is particularly so due to the importance of Socrates in Plato's thought and writing. See "The Owl" (TO 399) and "For Idealism" (FI 268) for examples of Miller's favorable estimation.

6. Metaphysics is part of the larger project of education that aims to "idealize the actual" (PC 176; see also PH 92–93). Universals are the requisite condi-

tion of autonomy. The fact that such universals are common to our experiences is not, however, a guarantee of autonomy.

7. Judging from the indexes to the four books of his books cited in this introduction, Rorty is inordinately preoccupied with Platonism—a form of realism supposedly "well lost." The very first sentence of the preface to Rorty's *Philosophy and Social Hope* underlines this fact.

8. Miller's sense of the term is quite different from that found in William James's *Radical Empiricism*. One can note that Miller is doing to empiricism what Royce did to pragmatism when, in *The Problem of Christianity*, he wrote of "absolute pragmatism" (p. 279).

9. For Rorty, instrumental reasoning is the *paradigm of public reason*. In the private sphere, to be sure, Rorty is the champion of a poeticized and strongly metaphorical use of reason. Here reason aims to be creative and original. However, in *Contingency, Irony, and Solidarity*, Rorty draws a sharp distinction between the public and the private sphere. This distinction not only serves to keep the private realm free from the moralizing judgments of the majority, but it also functions to keep the public protected from the poetic reason of private citizens.

CHAPTER 2. ACTION

1. The tone is set by Miller's amendment to René Descartes's philosophy: "I rake therefore I am" (PL 515). Miller also proposes a *suffrago* to match Descartes's *cogito*: "I vote, therefore, I am" (PL 515). In the *suffrago*, Miller remarks, "the person appears as agent, and is so recognized by others."

2. Some philosophies see problems as philosophic misunderstandings that must be resolved (e.g., Ludwig Wittgenstein). The problem is a symptom of an illusion, a nuisance that one should dispose of and never revisit. The ideal for such philosophizing is the problem-free life. The pragmatic tradition, by contrast, recognizes the important role played by problems. Yet pragmatists often relegate problems to the level of psychology, to naturalistic descriptions of frustration and satisfaction (e.g., John Dewey). Richard Rorty's pragmatism, criticized in the Introduction, is an admixture of these two approaches.

3. The paradox here is that the individual person and her capacity to act is threatened by those very controls—that is, nature, scientific procedure and instrumentation, epistemology—required for the discovery and elaboration of personal power (MS 121). There are evident similarities between the process entailed by what Miller calls "the ideal of knowledge" and what Max Horkheimer and Theodor Adorno referred to as "the dialectic of Enlightenment."

4. Vincent Colapietro writes, "[M]uch discourse about discourse has been nothing less than an assault upon the status of discourse. . . . For all attempts to

make discourse something derivative, to derive it from a state of affairs in which both speech and speaker are absent . . . amount to refusals to grant discourse any actual and authoritative status" (1990, p. 75; cf. Colapietro, 2003, pp. 127–30).

5. Despite some of his own reminders (1993, pp. 92, 129), Tyman overemphasizes the "mysterious" quality of action. This overemphasis is accountable, in part, to his taking Miller's own turns of phrase too literally. In opposing himself to the cognitive temper, particularly in its positivistic forms, Miller sometimes says precisely what Tyman himself says—that is, action is a mystery. Such statements are inspired by Miller's disagreement with positivism. Most of these statements are more accurately paraphrased as follows: "If we accept the cognitive assumptions of positivism then action must be mysterious; better that action is mysterious than there be no action at all." But the better route is avoiding the cognitive register altogether. As Miller states in *The Midworld:* "The act is not a cognitive mystery; it is not cognitive at all" (MS 113).

6. While Hannah Arendt linked *process* with the contemplative life as a search for an impersonal system (e.g., 1969, p. 65), Miller rehabilitates *process* by centering it on the person and the search for local-control.

7. See Colapietro's discussion of transcendental philosophy in connection with Miller in *Fateful Shapes of Human Freedom* (pp. 32–38).

8. Epistemological distinguishability is different from logical or psychological distinguishability. Logical distinguishability addresses whether a system provides categories that locate a certain thing. Psychological distinguishability is a matter of discerning and differentiating sensory perceptions. See section 3.2 for a discussion of the status of signs (i.e., the bases of distinguishability) and what Miller refers to as "meaning control."

9. See page 43 of *The Definition of the Thing* for Miller's argument in which he cites E. V. Huntingdon's *The Continuum as a Type of Order*. It is a premise of *The Definition of the Thing* that philosophy should not pattern itself after the sciences but, rather, after mathematics. In a remarkable statement, Miller agrees with Bertrand Russell who said that mathematics is a science in which one does not know what one is talking about (DT 25). The import of Miller's attempt to model philosophy on such a conception of mathematics is that, like mathematics, philosophy does not address particular facts, talk about particular things, or sort out why one particular statement is true and another false. Philosophy is concerned with the conditions that make these three activities possible and meaningful.

10. Does this process of predication also rule out an intuitive acquaintance with things? Clearly definition does not rely upon intuition. Yet nondiscursive apprehension is not, at this moment, completely ruled out (DT 44). The possibility of intuition cannot be challenged from within the assumptions of distinction, relation, and meaning that are proper to discursive knowledge. Miller's argument

addressing the possibility of intuition will be presented momentarily when the epistemological discussion of chapter 4 of *The Definition of the Thing*, "Relations and Independence," is considered.

11. Such a situation invites interesting comparisons to the status of dead languages. See Miller's essay "Translation" (MP 4:19).

12. The example that Miller uses on pages 52–53 of *The Definition of the Thing*, that of the inclusion of the predicate *black* into the set of possible predicates for *man*, is arresting. If distinctions allow for the maintenance of control, the more distinctions that a person has at her disposal allow for more control. Any distinction is a factor of control. This could lead to producing what might appear superfluous, even vicious distinctions. An example, of course, is the distinction between the *black* slave and the *white* man long maintained in the United States. What is at issue here is clearly control. Yet, as this example suggests, control is a complex and nefarious process. Indeed Miller recognizes that the processes that he is describing are in themselves neither moral nor immoral (PH 142–46; see also Gary Stahl's essay "Making the Moral World"). Distinguished things or concepts are as likely to be productive moral forces as they are to be demonic (PC 90; see §4.2). Once one steps away from the generic description of definition and control offered by philosophy one must consider more empirical descriptions of control offered by the social sciences and history.

13. For Miller *egoism* is not a pejorative term: "[E]goism is no problem when the local is the same as the enactment of order in function, in the functioning object, whether yardstick, grammar, logic, or dialectic. In each case the actuality requires a medium. *There* is the cure for vagrant egoism, and it is the only cure" (TO 402). *Egoism* is a disciplined and responsible sense of identity.

14. Tyman clarifies this matter by noting that there are two levels of local-control. First is the type of local-control that is pragmatically oriented toward immediate purposes (i.e., purpose-control). The concern here is with means–ends relations—that is, the technical application of existing distinctions and values. The second type of local-control is directed toward the more encompassing, universal controls of action embodied in symbols (i.e., will-control or, as it will be referred to in §3.3, control-in-principle). At this level, action addresses the prevailing distinctions themselves and develops their form. Local-control, taken as a whole, implies action on both registers. See *Descrying the Ideal* (p. 29), as well as the distinction between ontological and psychological action presented in section 3.1.

15. Part of the general conditions of specific acts is the possibility of criticism. Thus Robert Corrington describes the categories as "structures of criticism" that "derive their validation from practical and local control" (1990, p. 85).

16. Another way of describing this tone of Miller's thinking is terming his

philosophy a form of *voluntarism*. See Corrington's "Finite Idealism: The Midworld and Its History" for a criticism of what he construes as Miller's voluntarism. That charge will be addressed in chapter 4.

17. See Davidson's "Actions, Reasons, and Causes," in *Essays on Actions and Events*, as well as Bishop's development of Davidson's position. Alicia Juarrero, in her *Dynamics in Action*, offers a criticism of the bases of action theory (including Davidson's) on grounds similar to those offered by Miller.

18. See the fifth part of Descartes's *Discourse on Method*.

19. See Emerson's "Experience" (*Essays and Lectures*, p. 487).

CHAPTER 3. SYMBOL

1. See Stephen Tyman's "The Concept of Act in the Naturalistic Idealism of John William Miller" for another account of Miller's treatment of this dilemma.

2. It is Miller's claim that he is establishing the constitutional status of psychology (DP 149).

3. Here one sees what Aristotle found in his *Physics* (198^a14-98^b9)—that is, the convergence of formal and final causes.

4. Miller notes that "will is the form of purpose" (PH 68–69). See sections 3.2 and 3.3, as well as Hannah Arendt's remarks on the will understood as a break in causal relations (1978, vol. 2, p. 213).

5. There are also no *terms*, *universals*, or *orders* apart from psychology, physiology, and the encompassing material world. As always, the relationship is dialectical even if form is given pride of place. We almost always act on both the psychological and the ontological level—for example, the firing of a gun can be described in terms of basic physiology, the psychology of mean-ends thinking, and the formal level of law and criminality. See Hugh McCann's *The Works of Agency*, specifically chapter 1, for a relevant discussion.

6. This is an allusion to G. W. F. Hegel's use of *passion* or *Leidenschaft*, particularly in the Introduction to his *Lectures on the Philosophy of Religion*: "I will speak of passion, and in that sense of the particular uniqueness of a person's character, insofar as the uniqueness of will does not have a merely private content but also drives and motivates actions of a universal scope. Passion is primarily the subjective, and in that sense formal, aspect of energy, will, and activity in which the content or goal remains as yet undetermined" (1827/1988, p. 27).

7. Miller is not guilty of committing the fallacy of *post hoc ergo propter hoc* (because it was, so it is). Because formal and not efficient causality is the model, simple if-then statements do not capture the relationship (cf. Juarrero, 1999).

8. This process, while discontinuous with any chain of efficient causes, is still capable of being understood. The transition is intelligible; it has *reasons* but not

causes. "Whatever is understood, yet is not a case of a lawful change," Miller writes, "is teleological in nature" (MP 9:6). Compare Miller's approach to Donald Davidson's equation of *reasons* and *causes* (Davidson, 1980).

9. This approach cuts through the murkiness of the process of deciding when something counts as an action (e.g., White, 1968, 1–8). Many such discussions end in statements like the following: "A particular happening is an action if it is the exercise of a power to make that happen" (White, 1968, p. 8). The distinguishing features of action are, of course, not apparent and so strictly empirical accounts are difficult. If, however, reflection and history are countenanced then we have characteristics that are diagnostic of action even though we may continue to argue whether intentionality, voluntariness, purposiveness, antecedence, responsibility, and contingency are ingredient.

10. Indeed *psychological* is a term of distinction achieved via teleological controls; this is a development of the conclusion reached in chapter 2—that is, the dialectical primacy, although not independence, of the ontological.

11. This crucial term was not, however, coined by Miller. Rather the debt is to Ralph Waldo Emerson. "We meet only in a 'Mid-world,' as I call it, although the phrase appears in Emerson," Miller writes in 1945 (quoted in personal correspondence, Brockway to Colapietro, November 15, 1990). In the essay "Experience," Emerson wrote of the midworld: "The great gifts are not got by analysis. Everything good is on the highway. The middle region of our being is the temperate zone. We may climb into the thin and cold realm of pure geometry and lifeless science, or sink into that of sensation. Between these extremes is the equator of life, of thought, of spirit, of poetry,—a narrow belt. Moreover, in popular experience everything good is on the highway. . . . The mid-world is best" (1844/1983, pp. 480–81). Emerson's usage emphasizes not just the importance of moral moderation but also suggests an appreciation of the constitutive character of dialectic, of the third element that composes dyads. Life is not in the elements produced via analysis—that is, pure thought, pure sensation—but in the dynamic from which they are derived. Emerson's mid-world also has the tincture of idealism, a concern for structure and form.

12. See Arendt on the "in between" of action (1959, pp. 162–63).

13. In *Language and Reality*, W. M. Urban drew attention to this characteristic of the symbol when he noted that, while not all signs are symbols, *all symbols are signs* (p. 405). This fact will be important to clarifying the interpretation of figure 3.1 in this section, figures 3.2, 3.3, and 3.5 in section 3.3, and for a reinterpretation of figure 3.1 in section 4.5. For while the symbolic sphere is distinct from the sphere of signs, the larger and more accurate story is that all symbols are contained in the sphere of signs. The point of these figures, however, is clarifying the semiotic field under the sway of symbols— that is, the semiotic field interpreted as a region of authoritative control and not mere data.

14. This distinction is not always maintained in Miller's own writing (see PC 119-23 and MS 33). The following works offer differing presentations of this distinction: Suzanne Langer's *Philosophy in a New Key* (pp. 29 ff.); Urban's *Language and Reality* (pp. 402 ff.); and Cassirer's *An Essay on Man* (pp. 31 ff.). Of these three, Miller's writings suggest that he was familiar with only Langer's work.

15. See Josiah Royce's description of what he called a "quasi-mind"—that is, "an object that fulfills the functions of a mind" insofar as it is expressive and determines interpretation (1918/1968, p. 345). When Miller writes of a "portrait" and its "the original," one should be careful to avoid making the symbol into a representation. It is rather an expression of activity, local-control, and energy. It is not a picture of a substantial subject but rather an interpretative vehicle (see DP 159-60).

16. See Colapietro's "Human Symbols as Functioning Objects" for a discussion of Miller's semiotics.

17. Miller warns against proposing a "general theory of signs" (MS 156), and this discussion should be read with this in mind. The problem of addressing the conditions of disclosure was considered in chapter 2. This account of the midworld aims to avoid the errors of objectifying the conditions of disclosure and to remain within a functional vocabulary that highlights symbols as action.

18. In his "Acts and Necessity in the Philosophy of John William Miller," James Diefenbeck highlights some of the interesting distinctions in modes of disclosure (pp. 46-48).

19. Compare to Arthur Danto's concept of *basic actions* as described in *Analytic Philosophy of Action*.

20. See George P. Brockway's essay "Miller on Economics," as well as his *The End of Economic Man* (pp. 41-66), for accounts of money and financial institutions as pure symbols.

21. In a 1973 document (MP 18:7) Miller distinguishes imaginative objects from functioning objects, using the Parthenon as an example of an imaginative object. The distinction is suggestive. Yet this may be the only place that Miller takes this approach to the role of monuments and works of art. Elsewhere in his writings the Parthenon is referred to as a functioning object (PC 128). Yet there is something unique and powerful about the monument or work of art that is not captured in the description of pure symbols offered above. Imaginative objects should be distinguished from functioning objects.

22. This is so even though each artistic work is itself a work of interpretation within a tradition of artistic expression and craft. *Kitsch* is one term applied to reproductions of works of art that clearly distinguishes the artistic expression from the technique of its duplication and commodification. Even high-quality lithographic prints remain reproductions of the painting in question and are never referred to as the painting itself.

23. Diefenbeck's comments (especially pp. 46–47) point in this direction.

24. A caveat is in order. Philosophical practice—and artistic practice more generally—is as productive as it is reflective. The reflective mode of philosophy must be paired with its role in the production of concepts and, more generally, language. Philosophy would then span the class of pure symbols—as a type of language and thus a pure symbol proper, and as an imaginative symbol. On this matter Miller expresses some reservations about connecting philosophy and art when he defines art as a "reminder" of one's commitments and philosophy as "the general theory of all criticism" (PC 167).

25. One of the sections in the "Notes on Language" portion of *The Definition of the Thing* is a response to Morris's positivist semiotics (see DT 180–85). Other essay drafts and notes (MP 4:13; MP 21:1) show how Miller, who took detailed notes on *Foundations of the Theory of Signs*, was responding to what he understood to be the errors of Morris's work.

26. Robert Gahringer writes, "The items of Miller's midworld are indeed in the world; but they are in it as *bearers* of interpretation" (1990, p. 39).

CHAPTER 4. HISTORY

1. Miller is unique in an American tradition that does not say much about history. (See Robert Corrington's essay "John William Miller and the Ontology of the Midworld.") While Charles J. Peirce, William James, and John Dewey show a respect for historicity, none of them made *history* constitutional in the same way as Miller. Regarding the status of history in American philosophy see Morris Cohen's *American Thought: A Critical Sketch*.

2. Stephen Tyman suggests another possibility in *Descrying the Ideal* (p. 73). Tyman draws a connection between what Miller calls the "distrust of time" and what Friedrich Nietzsche diagnosed as *ressentiment*. Contrary to appearances, Nietzsche argued, ressentiment is not an inactive state devoid of will. It is the activity of an unhealthy will; the will is always active even if, at its most debased, it is willing nothing at all (1887/1967, p. 97). The ahistoric temper is not a move away from action but a move toward a subterranean and irresponsible mode of action. Just as Nietzsche referred to the world-altering accomplishments of Christianity, Miller gestures toward science as a parallel example of the will and activity invested in the ahistoric temper.

3. While Miller explicitly addresses history as both a *category* and a *region*, he only suggests the significance of the distinction. One clear mention of it develops in correspondence (MP 22:14). There Miller responds favorably to a proposal that one refer to nature as a region rather than as a category. "You close with an interesting idea," Miller writes, "a difference between 'categories' and 'regions.' This seems to

me to be an excellent distinction. There is something amiss in calling 'Nature,' say, a 'category,' and something suitable in calling it a 'region.'" While no mention of history is made in this context, the extrapolation that the term *region* is as appropriate to history as it is to nature has some basis. *History*, like *nature*, is not just a category in its adjectival form—that is, historic*al* and natur*al*—but a set of relations, a unity of forms of being. History, like nature, is an ongoing process and not just a definition of a type of process. Furthermore if nature is the world seen under one aspect (determinate quantity) and the midworld that same world seen under another (symbolic form), then history can be described as that same world seen under yet another aspect (reflective, revisionary, autonomous, and willful action). Without the midworld, however, there is neither history nor nature (MP 17:15).

    4. Time is a category but the *minute* remains a dependent distinction. For although one cannot do without time, musicians are better served by marking time in terms of *beats*, while farmers prefer articulating time by *sunrises* and *seasons* and are not particularly aided by either *minutes* or *beats*. Each of these distinctions is an instantiation of the pervasive category of time and each has a limited scope of application.

    5. Miller's essay from the 1930s, titled "Idealism," summarizes the sense of *category* by listing ten characteristics: (1) not sensible, (2) neutral to all qualities, (3) applicable to all things, (4) organizational, (5) expressive of an ideal, (6) infinite in direction and application, (7) unverifiable by a particular experience, (8) incomplete, (9) unconditioned, and (10) a source of orientation, judgment, and criticism (PL 274-75).

    6. In terms of the modes of order provided by physics and chemistry, the distillation will have resulted in no change whatsoever—that is, at t_1 and t_3 the same physical state of affairs prevailed and the fact that at the intermediary moment of t_2 (the distilled compound) a different state was in evidence is not in itself important to the prevailing state of affairs. The temporality of any given thing is a dependent mode of organization as compared to its physical relations in space (i.e., their basic, and assumed, simultaneity). In this example, time functions primarily as a placeholder, a secondary mode of distinction. If the lab could afford it, distinctions between similar compounds could be made using an electron microscope and the process of definition could thus bypass time altogether.

    7. This presentation of the role of time in science is reductive. It would be completely apt so long as science treats with closed systems. Miller often states that "physics," and in a sense all science, "invokes the ideally complete" where change is always "in the direction of unification" (PH 25; see MP 20:3). However when a science no longer has as one of its axioms that its subject matter is a closed system of relations then time has a certain efficacy. Any theory of evolution that is not mere determinism (i.e., what Peirce called "anancasm"), must take the element of

time seriously; the genetic sport, certainly, is not reversible. Similarly in moving from mechanics to thermodynamics, and thus to a universe that may very well be irreversibly expanding—that is, moving toward increasing *disorder*—physics gives time a fundamental role. Yet, as will be discussed more thoroughly in section 4.4, none of these estimations of the efficacy of time in science can establish a *historical* sense of time.

8. An example of the difference that Miller is highlighting is that chronology simply tells one that the Fourth Republic of France came to an end in 1958 when it was succeeded by Charles De Gaulle's Fifth Republic. Nothing that chronology says about the event prevents the return of the Fourth Republic; chronology only needs an available date for the transition. History, however, ensures that the Fourth Republic could not reappear in 2006. Whereas a quantity of ozone (O_3) could disappear at one moment in the creation of a quantity of water (H_2O), only to reappear on the separation of the hydrogen, the change represented in the transition between the Fourth and the Fifth Republics is not reflected in a different configuration of the same basic material. The Fifth Republic indicates an actual change of mind, a revolution in interpretation that could only be what it is because it came *after* and indeed *through* the revision of antecedent conditions embodied in the Fourth Republic (see PH 112).

9. Hannah Arendt described this situation as a struggle where a person, lodged in the present, grapples with the demands of the past and the future (1978, vol. 1, pp. 205 ff.).

10. If one reads Paul Feyerabend's somewhat ill-titled book *Against Method* as most do—that is, as being against method, against scientific institutions—then, from Miller's standpoint, he would be dead wrong. In the absence of institutions a person loses her instruments, modes of practice, and, even more radically, nature as such. A more interesting reading of Feyerabend, one that shows him fighting not against method as such but against making certain methods and institutions into idols, places him in Miller's orbit. Here Feyerabend's struggle with routinized method becomes akin to Miller's resistance to static definitions.

11. This is why Bruno Latour exaggerates his case in *We Have Never Been Modern*. The claim that we have *never* been modern undercuts Latour's own interest in reassessing modern ontology organized around the poles of subject and object. Claiming that modern ontology was never quite what it appeared to be is one thing. Denying that it has been constitutive of the very position that one presently holds is entirely another matter.

12. See Arendt's chapter "The Concept of History" in *Between Past and Future*.

13. One owes piety toward history in two respects. First one must be appreciative of history in its *categorical form*—that is, as a term of metaphysics. There is an equivalence between history and philosophy in Miller's thinking in

that both are concerned with putting a person in touch with the very conditions of his endeavors. (See the discussion of metaphysics in the chapter 1 as well as in section 4.5 where the equivalence of history and philosophy is addressed.) Second, a person owes piety toward his *specific history* insofar as that history provides the particular conditions of his experience. On the matter of piety, see Colapietro's review, in *The Journal of Speculative Philosophy*, of Miller's work.

14. Because one's metaphysical terms cannot be subject to further analysis and explanation they, too, must have a metaphorical, or original, element. As was the case with action and symbolism, one must avoid having a *theory* of history. For, while theory treats its subject matter as phenomena, the origin of phenomena cannot itself be reduced to a phenomenon (TO 401; see AH 265; MP 7:22). As Miller writes, history has no cause (PH 27).

15. The following discussion of fate addresses Corrington's charge that Miller sees the world as a made world and does not acknowledge "all of the deeper senses in which the world gives itself to the finite self" (1990, p. 90). For Miller neither the world of nature nor that of culture is "made." It is *disclosed.* As the following account emphasizes, the process of disclosure is complex in character and unruly in its consequences. Working in terms of disclosure deprives the events of nature of none of their integrity. As Miller writes, the midworld "robs nobody of nature" (PC 118; cf. Colapietro, 2003, pp. 114–16.). A hurricane smashes the homes of realists and idealists with equal force.

16. Miller's sense of fate has only a passing resemblance to more common conceptions derived from our understanding of Athenian tragedies. Despite his explicit appropriation of Greek terms (e.g., *nemesis*), this sense of fate is more nuanced than that exemplified in the Greek world (see SF 12–13). Fate is not written in the stars—or in the will of the gods—prior to and independent of any action (e.g., Euripides's *Bacchaea*). Nor does fate simply turn on the ignorance of some aspect of one's identity or past experience (e.g., Sophocles' *Oedipus the King*), although this sense of fate has more relevance to Miller's approach due to its link to the notion of being flawed. *Hamartia*, the flaw of the tragic hero, establishes the conditions for tragedy. In this sense, the tragedy comes from within the hero and not from without; it is connected with character and action. See Johnstone's "The Fatality of Thought" for some considerations of how Miller conceived of the role of fate within the history of thought.

17. This personal connection with the forces of constraint and limitation is an essential ingredient in actualism. The rock a person stumbles on, the cupboard against which she strikes her head, the lightning that sets her fields afire—these things, while undoubtedly forces of resistance, are not the stuff of fate. She is implicated with them only to the extent that the symbolic capacity of the body translates their brute resistance into the articulate terms of touch, vision, and

hearing. They are natural experiences. History, however, is not possible without a more significant measure of self-identification (MP 21:6). The sense of fate implies that a person see, however vaguely, her own hand in the besetting forces. Fate, that is to say, requires *guilt* (see PH 66–69), and history is the story of words claimed as one's own (PL 64).

18. Action, as Hannah Arendt noted, is a risk—we do not know what we will disclose or bring about when we act (1959, p. 160; see 1968, p. 85).

19. Miller draws from Tillich's *The Interpretation of History*. In volume 3 of his *Systematic Theology, Life and Spirit, History and Kingdom of God*, Tillich defined the demonic as follows: "The demonic does not resist self-transcendence as does the profane, but it distorts self-transcendence by identifying a particular bearer of holiness with the holy itself" (p. 102).

20. In this respect it would seem that Miller overstates his case when, in "For Idealism," he writes that dogmas do not conflict (FI 262). Rather the conflict between opposing dogmas is so absolute that there is no ground for the *creative* form of conflict that is the ongoing process of mutual revision. The conflict between dogmas, then, is a cold standoff.

21. Miller expresses some reservations: "I would not want to make the historical event too much a function of its present meaning. I want the event in itself to be historical, so that it may be part of my self-definition in the historical community, or implied by known historical events of that community. An event not historical in itself can never become so apropos of history" (PH 167). If a historical event has the ability to constrain present interpreters and be a guide for action, then it cannot simply be concocted. The distinction between history and fiction remains in force (MP 8:3). Yet present concerns do lend particular urgency of the contemporary interpreter. History is addressed, Miller states, not because the past is a problem but because the present is (MP 17:5).

22. For example, the Constitution was a vehicle of repression and a bearer of demonic interpretation insofar as it institutionalized the practice of slavery and was its legal justification. Yet that very same document provided the resources for amending the status of slavery in the Republic—for example, both a conception of human rights carried over from the Declaration of Independence to the Bill of Rights and procedures of legal revision. By the late twentieth century the symbolic vehicle that is the Constitution has become something that it clearly was not in the late eighteenth century—a symbol enforcing the legal equality and personhood of *all* residents of the United States if not all human beings. This is what the Constitution presently means. In this respect, it took time for the Constitution to become itself and it has not ceased developing via revision.

23. It is for this reason that Miller connects history to the larger educational project of "idealizing the actual" (PC 176; see epilogue).

24. Because of the misunderstandings that inevitably accompany the word *egoism* is it useful to quote Miller: "The sense of fate occurs where our own activity, whether of thought or will, encounters systematic restriction. But there is no sense of fate where there is no program of one's own, where no control has been attempted. Lethargy, indifference, and drift conjure up no systematic opposition. Fate is the correlative of egoism and egoism is not in the passing whim, but in the enduring attitude which seeks control and mastery" (SF 1–2; see also §2.3). How different Miller's understanding of egoism is from the standard dictionary definition: "The ethical doctrine that self-interest is the proper motive for all human conduct" (*Webster's II New Riverside Dictionary*, 1994). The position sketched in *Webster's* is what Miller terms "vagrant" egoism (TO 402–03).

25. In a letter to Colapietro (personal correspondence, July 19, 1989), Fell notes that, while Miller does not think persons are simply embedded in the historical moment, the contrasting position is not a transcendence of history. Fell takes Miller to be presenting an alternative "transtemporal" possibility—that is, the capacity of spanning, but not escaping, history. Such transtemporality is historical temporality and its vehicle, as is now clear, is the symbol.

26. This more formal approach is explored in two essays of commentary: Stahl's "Making the Moral World" and my own "John William Miller's Metaphysics of Democracy." Yet concentrating on history as pure process or, more precisely, pure symbolism misses at least one keen insight of Miller's dialectic: The forms of order are in an ongoing and developmental relationship with that which they bring into order. History can no more be pure than form can be without content. One must come to terms with what Miller means when he addresses history as "an attitude of piety" concerned with "our reconciliation with the conditions of our own endeavors" (PH 149), and particularly our commitment to actual institutions and practices.

27. It should be noted that figure 4.1 differs from figure 3.1 not just in having added the distinction of *symbolic-control*. Here the sphere of signs is also shown to encompass the region of symbols. The reason for this revision is twofold. First the semiotic vocabulary of *control* is attached to the sign. Thus in "The Symbol" Miller writes of the *symbol* as also being a *sign*—that is, an expressive sign. Second, while symbols are distinguishable from signs by their function, all symbols remain signs; the symbol is amenable to being understood as an object in a defined world (e.g., the map understood as scrap paper) rather than an object declaring a world. There is no symbol beyond the sphere of signs. The distinction between symbols and signs is a matter of function or, as in section 3.2, emphasis.

28. Miller's appropriation of Hocking's *Types of Philosophy* is important in this regard. It would be too much to say that the career of reflection is simply progressive. While the career of reflection can undergo reversal, ideally the tendency of reflection is toward a deepening of thoughtfulness and self-consciousness.

See Fell's notes (PH 1-2, Notes 1950-51), Johnstone, Jr.'s essay "The Fatality of Thought," as well as Fell's "John William Miller and Nietzsche's Nihilism."

CHAPTER 5. DEMOCRACY

1. Whitman wrote in *Democratic Vistas*: "In the prophetic literature of these States (the reader of my speculations will miss their principal stress unless he allows well for the point that a new Literature, perhaps a new Metaphysics, certainly a new Poetry, are to be, in my opinion, the only sure and worthy of supports and expressions of the American Democracy), Nature, true Nature, and the true idea of Nature, long absent, must, above all, become fully restored, enlarged, and must furnish the pervading atmosphere to poems, and the test of all high literary and esthetic compositions" (1867/1982, p. 984).

2. Miller's response to Whitman was mixed. Certainly the idea of a metaphysics of democracy struck a cord. Yet, in a letter on the topic of American literature, Miller remarks that, "Whitman has the American note of universality but is scanty on the local and actual as a controlling power." In another letter Miller states more strongly, "I feel the need of reading something on individualism in American literature. We have had to take lying down the encomiastic cult of Whitman, a man without a sense of individuality. But he is the poet of Democracy! It is such attitudes which are 'bunk,' not the personal, the individual, and the private" (personal correspondence, George Brockway). While Whitman's interest in the seething crowds of New York (not to mention the freedom of loafing) buttresses Miller's assessment, the equal concern that Whitman evinced for the personal suggests some limitations to these criticisms. Indeed, there is something to be learned from Emmanuel Mounier's (1949/1995) estimation that Whitman is the American herald of *personalism*—a term Miller himself uses (MP 20:4).

3. On the general topic of morality, see Gary Stahl's "Making the Moral World."

4. In this vein Emerson, in a later essay in *The Conduct of Life* titled "Fate," qualified his conception of nature by describing it as "what you may do." For Emerson the sense of limitation, however, remained predominant: "The Circumstance is Nature. Nature is, what you may do. There is much that you may not. We have two things,—the circumstance and the life. Once we thought, positive power was all. Now we learn, the negative power, or circumstance, is half. Nature is the tyrannous circumstance" (1860/1983, p. 949).

5. This represents not only a criticism of realism but also of idealism and, in particular, subjective idealism. If, as Miller claims, idealism is different from

realism because it is a philosophy of structure rather than content (FI 267), then it is clear that if idealism appeals to content the distinction between the two positions is effectively collapsed (see MS 31).

6. Although the insight offered by actualism is that person and society are coeval, there are perspectives in which one takes precedence over the other. In this section, for instance, it is stressed that the person must be given precedence as a necessary experiential starting place. As Miller points out, if one's interest is in studying ethics it is a mistake to begin from the standpoint of society (OES 1–3). From the standpoint of the temporal order, however, it would be correct to state that the person is primarily a member of a community and only subsequently a person (MP 12:14). The relative veracity of these two points of view confirms the more basic dialectical relationship between person and society: "Society vanishes without personality, just as personality vanishes without society" (MP 9:9).

7. Hocking referred to these external objects, institutions, and practices as *will circuits*. The term suggests a similarity with other circuits of one's vital existence such as processes of digestion, respiration, and sensation. Thus one could say that public institutions are not just an extension of oneself but, rather, an integral part of the individual; for Hocking, the person and her objects form a whole (1926, pp. 363–79). The concept of *will circuits* also serves as Hocking's response to the question as to whether the state itself constitutes an individual mind or will (pp. 351–79). The tradition of thinking of the state as an individual has at least two major exponents—that is, Rousseau in his *Social Contract* and Hegel in his *Philosophy of Right*. Hocking, in contrast to both Rousseau and Hegel, rejected thinking of the state as an individual and agreed that it is only possible to attribute responsibility to individual persons. Miller follows Hocking in this regard, stating that "every will is an individual will" (MP 9:9).

8. On that same page of *The Paradox of Cause*, Miller is careful to distinguish the *moral* universe from a *benevolent* universe. The moral universe establishes the meaning of *good* and *justice* but does not assure any actual outcome. The concern is with structure not content. Similarly the necessity that one be a *moral* person is different from the imperative to be a *good* person. Miller is not making the stronger, and more dubious, claim that insofar as one is a person then one must act according to the moral law. That is a more strictly Kantian point. The actualist position more modestly asserts that personhood is synonymous with *having the moral question before oneself*: "[T]here is reason to suppose that moral problems are pressing. . . . They seem, somehow, problems peculiarly proper to human nature, and definitive of it. One may say that man aspires to do wrong, to know not only the good, but also the difference between good and evil. To know this difference is more important than to be good. This is a distinction without meaning where

no action has occurred. We wish to be wrong in order that we may lay claim to having acted" (MM 9). The fundamental question of morality and ethics is not, then, the good act but the very possibility of acting (PH 19–20, 1952–53, 25–38).

9. Borrowing Hocking's language, Miller refers to legislation as *term-making*. Hocking considered judicial activity to also be term-making and separated the executive function as part of what he called the "commotive process" (1926, pp. 3–21). Miller differs from Hocking in allying the legislative with the historical process whereas Hocking asserted that the executive makes history while the legislative only makes terms (p. 18). The thrust of actualism, of course, is to unite term- and history-making activities.

10. Interpreted in terms of the midworld, nature and the natural object become partners in the process of definition. Nature speaks to one as much as one speaks to, orders, and controls it; natural objects are part of a reciprocal relationship. See *The Definition of the Thing*, particularly pages 38–59, on definition and inductive definition in particular; see also section 2.2.

11. See Jefferson's "First Inaugural Address" (in *Writings*) and Dewey's *Experience and Nature*. See also Miller's remarks about the community of learning in *The Philosophy of History* (pp. 123–26), and "The Scholar as Man of the World" in *The Paradox of Cause*. In this regard comparisons can also be made with Dewey's pragmatism, Peirce's version of critical realism, and Popper's reappropriation of critical realism in *The Open Society and Its Enemies*.

12. Despite Miller's stress on privacy (see §5.2), persons cannot stand aloof from the process of inquiry. Privacy is important in that it establishes social and moral means by which a person can exercise agency. The right to privacy is thus less a claim to the inviolable character of certain relations or practices than it is a statement about nonnegotiable status of agency (see OES 5–7).

13. This statement holds unless one construes *end* so broadly as to encompass freedom, an end that itself appears to be more a process than a conclusion. The distinction between ordinary and constitutional law underlines this matter: Ordinary law is manifestly concerned with ends in their more obvious sense (e.g., limiting highway fatalities) while constitutional law is more concerned with ends in a more attenuated sense (e.g., "form a more perfect union, establish justice, insure domestically tranquility, provide for the common defense, promote the general welfare, and secure the blessings of liberty for ourselves and our posterity"). The true end of constitutional law is to establish the terms or process according to which one can seek ends.

14. See Hocking's *Man and the State* (pp. 308–36) by way of comparison. Although the term is Nietzsche's, Miller uses *will to power* in light of Hocking's interpretation. With respect to power, Hocking thought along the same lines as Nietzsche and refused to define *power* as a property or possession of a being. Yet for

Hocking will to power was more human, or personal, in the sense that "to be in control of forces and to know himself in control is a right status for him, a status in which he feels himself in the line of his destiny" (1926, p. 309). To be powerless is "to fail to be human." It is a person's fundamental will "to be in conscious knowing control of such energies as the universe has, and to work with them in reshaping that universe" (p. 309). For Nietzsche, however, will to power was a metaphysical principle articulating an empirical reality composed of matter and forces. In *Beyond Good and Evil*, Nietzsche wrote: "Suppose, finally, we succeeded in explaining our entire instinctive life as the development and ramification of one basic form of the will—namely, the will to power, as my proposition has it; suppose all organic functions could be traced back to this will to power and one could also find in it the solution of the problem of procreation and nourishment—it is one problem—then one would have gained the right to determine all efficient force univocally as—will to power" (1886/1989, p. 48). For Miller's estimation of Nietzsche see *The Paradox of Cause* (pp. 26–31; cf. Fell, 1997).

15. The question of the priority of the moral or the political is pervasive in the idealist tradition. (See A. J. M. Milne's *The Social Philosophy of English Idealism* on the general topic.) Bosanquet, in specific, articulated the matter in a fashion that has an influence on Miller. In his work, *The Philosophical Theory of the State*, Bosanquet described the state as "the operative criticism of all institutions—the modification and adjustment by which they are capable of playing a rational part in the object of human will" (p. 140). Criticism proceeds via the institutions and practices developed in a political association and compares the present state of one's will not to another or greater will but, rather, to the larger implications of *one's own* will (p. 111). Thus Bosanquet was wary of international federations and considered the state to be "the supreme community," "the guardian of a whole moral world" (p. 302). That moral world is premised on universal commitments grounded in the state itself. Echoes of Bosanquet's position can he heard in Miller when, apropos of discussions about the possibility of trying Mussolini for his role in the Second World War, he wrote: "The state is not, I believe, under another law, a moral law known to all and accepted by all. A state is the expression of a view of morality but is not itself an attempt to express a non-political type of right" (PL 582–83).

16. The comparison of the state to an organism is a staple of idealist thought. Important examples that were influential in Miller's thinking include Hegel's *Philosophy of Right* and Bosanquet's *The Value and Destiny of the Individual*. (See Milne's *The Social Philosophy of English Idealism* for a general consideration of the place of the organic model in idealist thought.) Actualism, however, distinguishes political association from natural forms of order. Yet Miller's own terminology is ambiguous. At certain points he refers to the state as natural (PL 150; PH 5, 1931, 69–70), while at others he designates it as artificial (PH 5, 1931, 107).

This ambiguity is clarified if one considers that Miller picks up the organic model (but not the mechanical model) to show how the state is a perpetual process of change, occurring on a plurality of fronts, and within persons who are born and will die (see MP 29:17; DP 118). The adjective *natural* is also appropriate to the state when interpreted as meaning a *necessary* condition for reflective, historical minds in association with one another. As M. Holmes Hartshorne's notes read: "The state is artificial in a way, yet the expression of a profound characteristic of human mind" (PH 5, 1931, 107). Miller's considered opinion on the status of the state is in keeping with Hocking's estimation that the state has connections with the natural and artificial (1926, pp. 137–50).

17. Political association is not a grouping into which one naturally falls. The free state must be established by force (NS 10–12). The force involved may be martial, economic, or philosophical—whatever is requisite for reconceiving the terms of association and moving beyond similarity and simple calculations of interest. What is finally required is a *change of mind* and, thus, a philosophical conversion of some sort. Indeed Miller notes that political association cannot be *maintained* by force: "Politically, the future will be oriented on the problem of winning power for each man. This is not power over nature, but power for each man over another, and every other. But power of that sort can never be physically enforced. It must proceed from respect" (PC 74).

18. This is an important reversal of Colapietro's statement: "What [Miller] calls functioning objects are not foci of attention but loci of control" (1990, p. 79). In the activity of reflection, the media of disclosure become the objects of critical, although not perceptual, attention.

19. Miller refers to economics, and market relations more generally, as a "school of human relations" (PL 116) and art as a "school of feeling" (PL 641).

20. Politics, unlike nature and history, is not precisely a region; it is a distinguishable *approach* to and *mode* of being within the region of history. Engaging in democratic politics is the paramount way of being a historical being (see §4.1).

21. Interpretation concerns the continuum of action embodied in symbols. It is action that maintains and revises the symbolic conditions of disclosure. Another person, particular event, or concrete experience always provokes such activity. Galileo Galilei's *Starry Messenger*, for example, was provoked by the data revealed through the use of the instrument later to be called the *telescope*. Thus matters of fact were in question. Galileo's theory also challenged structures of authority—ecclesiastical as well as secular—involving issues of practical power and control. Yet, properly speaking, Galileo's struggle was not about the data in question. His true dispute was not with Cardinal Roberto Bellarmino and the authorities of the Roman Catholic Church either. Galileo was engaged in the criticism of the fundamental and common controls of experience—in particular, the Ptolemaic

maps of the cosmos, the standing rules of evidence, and the status of his optical device. What was most in question was which symbols were authoritative.

22. While Miller states that we above all "desire to be immortal in our ideas" (MP 9:9; cf. Hocking, 1926, p. 316), it is important to remember that *ideas* are always symbolically embodied and manifested in practice. These ideas are not fancies but are the articulate symbolic conditions of disclosure that organize experience. Furthermore the *immortality* that Miller claims this effort confers on persons should not be misconstrued as a desire to escape history. *Immortality* in this case is simply a "human form of transcendence" (personal communication, Fell to Colapietro, July 19, 1989). Such transcendence is itself illuminated by the Greek concept of heroism (remembered deeds) as well as by what Miller refers to as the overindividual or transtemporal (symbolically objectified acts).

EPILOGUE

1. See Arendt's *The Human Condition*, as well as the introduction to this book.

2. This point addresses Robert Gahringer's concern that Miller's philosophy not be treated as a speculative theory in the form of process metaphysics (1990, p. 35). Actualism mediates the contemplative and active lives both in terms of its description of the world but also in the very form of the philosophy itself.

3. In the face of "the end of metaphysics," Rorty champions solidarity (1989, 189-98). Miller tends to emphasize the individual and the heroic as an appropriate response to a full estimation of the significance of history. Yet *solidarity* is not inimical to Miller's approach; community, common understandings, and shared actions are all ingredient to his sense of history and politics. Solidarity, however, must also be a form of plurality and individuality—a unified plurality or a plural unity (see PC 174-75).

References

This listing of references contains those works that are cited in the book and is divided into three major sections—Miller's writings, writings on Miller, and additional works cited in the book. For a complete bibliography of Miller's writings, as well as scholarly writings about Miller, see the Web site of the John William Miller Fellowship Fund: http://www.williams.edu/resources/miller.

MILLER'S WRITINGS

Published Books

In Defense of the Psychological. New York: Norton, 1983.
The Definition of the Thing with Some Notes on Language. New York: Norton, 1980.
The Midworld of Symbols and Functioning Objects. New York: Norton, 1982.
The Paradox of Cause and Other Essays. New York: Norton, 1978.
The Philosophy of History with Reflections and Aphorisms. New York: Norton, 1981.

Published Essays

"Afterword: The Ahistoric and the Historic." In José Ortega y Gasset's *History as a System and Other Essays Toward a Philosophy of History.* Trans. Helene Weyl. New York: Norton, 1961.
"For Idealism." *Journal of Speculative Philosophy* 1 (1987): 260–69.
"On Choosing Right and Wrong." *Idealistic Studies* 21 (1992): 74–78.
"The Owl." *Transactions of the Charles S. Peirce Society* 24 (1988): 399–407.

Unpublished Essays

"Communication in Beauty" (1933). Miller Papers, Box 9: Folder 10.
"Economics, Politics, and Ethics" (1949). Miller Papers, Box 3: Folder 6.
"Ethics and Cosmology" (1955). Miller Papers, Box 52: Folder 12.

"History and the Sense of Fate" (1955). Miller Papers, Box 4: Folder 15.
"How to Render Passion Responsible?" (1942). Miller Papers, Box 12: Folder 3.
"The Individual" (1972). Miller Papers, Box 24: Folder 21.
"Moral Man" (undated). Miller Papers, Box 6: Folder 13.
"The National State" (1945). Miller Papers, Box 3: Folder 3.
"The Natural Law" (1956). Miller Papers, Box 4: Folder 21.
"Obstacles to Ethical Study" (undated). Miller Papers, Box 6: Folder 13.
"Rejection as a Moral Factor" (1957). Miller Papers, Box 4: Folder 24.
"Solitude and Community: A Meditation" (1973). Miller Papers, Box 26: Folder 17.
"Sources of Interest in the Idea of History" (undated). Miller Papers, Box 7: Folder 11.
"The Symbol" (1950–52). Miller Papers, Box 4: Folder 13.
"Translation" (1956). Miller Papers, Box 4: Folder 19.

Student Notes

"American Philosophy." Philosophy 8, Williams College, Spring 1951. Transcript compiled and edited by Joseph P. Fell, 1997. Miller Papers, Box 51: Folder 2.
"Maintaining Criticism: The Metaphysics of Ethics and Epistemology." Philosophy 19–20, Williams College, 1952–53. Transcript compiled and edited by Joseph P. Fell, 1998. Miller Papers, Box 51: Folder 2.
"Philosophy of History." Philosophy 7, Williams College, 1951–52. Transcript compiled and edited by Joseph P. Fell, 1993. Miller Papers, Box 51: Folder 2.
"Philosophy of the State." Philosophy 5, Williams College, 1931. Transcript compiled by M. Holmes Hartshorne. Miller Papers, Box 22: Folder 7.
"Types of Philosophy." Philosophy 1–2, Williams College, 1950–51. Transcript compiled and edited by Joseph P. Fell, 1991. Miller Papers, Box 51: Folder 2.

Other Materials

John William Miller Papers, Williamsiana Collection, Williams College.
"Papers and Letters. 1929–1978." Compiled and edited by Eugene R. Miller. 1993. Miller Papers, Box 55.

WRITINGS ON MILLER

Anderson, Douglas R. "Miller's American Scholar: Acting in the Midworld." Paper presented to the American Philosophical Society, Central Division, Kansas City, MO, May 1994.
———. "In the Face of Technology: Toward a Recovery of the Human." Technology in Society 20 (1998): 297–306.

Bradford, Judith. "Telling the Difference: Feminist Philosophy and Miller's Actualist Semiotics." *Journal of Speculative Philosophy* 11 (1997): 297–314.

Brockway, George. "John William Miller." *The American Scholar* 49 (1980): 236–40.

———. "Miller on Economics." In *The Philosophy of John William Miller*, edited by Joseph P. Fell, 125–35. Lewisburg, PA: Bucknell University Press, 1990.

Colapietro, Vincent. "Review of Miller's Five Books." *Journal of Speculative Philosophy* 1 (1987): 239–56.

———. "Reason, Conflict, and Violence." *Transactions of the Charles S. Peirce Society* 25 (1989): 175–90.

———. "Human Symbols as Functioning Objects: A First Look at John William Miller's Contribution to Semiotics." In *The Philosophy of John William Miller*, edited by Joseph P. Fell, 70–84. Lewisburg, PA: Bucknell University Press, 1990.

———. *Fateful Shapes of Human Freedom: John William Miller and the Crises of Modernity*. Nashville, TN: Vanderbilt University Press, 2003.

Corrington, Robert. "John William Miller and the Ontology of the Midworld." *Transactions of the Charles S. Peirce Society* 22 (1986): 165–88.

———. "Finite Idealism: The Midworld and its History." In *The Philosophy of John William Miller*, edited by Joseph P. Fell, 85–95. Lewisburg, PA: Bucknell University Press, 1990.

Diefenbeck, James A. "Acts and Necessity in the Philosophy of John William Miller." In *The Philosophy of John William Miller*, edited by Joseph P. Fell, 43–58. Lewisburg, PA: Bucknell University Press, 1990.

Elias, Robert H. "Literature, History, and What Men Learn." In *The Philosophy of John William Miller*, edited by Joseph P. Fell, 136–52. Lewisburg, PA: Bucknell University Press, 1990.

Fell, Joseph P. "Miller: The Man and His Philosophy." In *The Philosophy of John William Miller*, edited by Joseph P. Fell, 21–31. Lewisburg, PA: Bucknell University Press, 1990.

———. "John William Miller and Nietzsche's Nihilism." *Eidos: The Bucknell Academic Journal* 10 (1997): 5–21.

Fell, Joseph P., ed. *The Philosophy of John William Miller*. Lewisburg, PA: Bucknell University Press, 1990.

Gahringer, Robert E. "On Interpreting J. W. Miller." In *The Philosophy of John William Miller*, edited by Joseph P. Fell, 32–42. Lewisburg, PA: Bucknell University Press, 1990.

Johnstone, Henry W., Jr. "The Fatality of Thought." In *The Philosophy of John William Miller*, edited by Joseph P. Fell, 59–69. Lewisburg, PA: Bucknell University Press, 1990.

McGandy, Michael J. "John William Miller's Metaphysics of Democracy." *Transactions of the Charles S. Peirce Society* 31 (1995): 598–630.

——. "The Midworld: Clarifications and Developments." *Transactions of the Charles S. Peirce Society* 34 (1998): 225–64.

Stahl, Gary. "Making the Moral World." In *The Philosophy of John William Miller*, edited by Joseph P. Fell, 111–24. Lewisburg, PA: Bucknell University Press, 1990.

Strout, Cushing. "When the Truth Is in the Telling." In *The Philosophy of John William Miller*, edited by Joseph P. Fell, 153–66. Lewisburg, PA: Bucknell University Press, 1990.

Tyman, Stephen. "The Problem of Evil in Proto-Ethical Idealism: John William Miller's Ethics in Historical Context." In *The Philosophy of John William Miller*, edited by Joseph P. Fell, 96–110. Lewisburg, PA: Bucknell University Press, 1990.

——. *Descrying the Ideal: The Philosophy of John William Miller*. Carbondale: Southern Illinois University Press, 1993.

——. "The Concept of the Act in the Naturalistic Idealism of John William Miller." *The Journal of Speculative Philosophy* 10 (1996): 161–71.

ADDITIONAL WORKS CITED

Arendt, Hannah. *The Human Condition.* New York: Doubleday, 1959.

——. *Between Past and Future: Eight Exercises in Political Thought.* New York: Viking 1968.

——. *The Life of the Mind.* New York: Harcourt, 1978.

Beardsley, Monroe. "The Metaphorical Twist." In *Philosophical Perspectives on Metaphor*, edited by Mark Johnson. Minneapolis: University of Minnesota Press, 1981.

Bishop, John. *Natural Agency: An Essay on the Causal Theory of Action.* Cambridge, UK: Cambridge University Press, 1989.

Black, Max. "Metaphor." In *Philosophical Perspectives on Metaphor*, edited by Mark Johnson. Minneapolis: University of Minnesota Press, 1981.

Bosanquet, Bernard. *The Value and Destiny of the Individual.* London: Macmillan, 1913.

——. *The Philosophical Theory of the State.* London: Macmillan, 1920.

Brockway, George P. *The End of Economic Man* (3rd ed.). New York: Norton, 1995.

Cassirer, Ernest. *An Essay on Man: An Introduction to a Philosophy of Human Culture.* New Haven, CT: Yale University Press, 1944.

Cohen, Morris R. *American Thought: A Critical Sketch.* La Salle, IL: Open Court, 1962.

Collingwood, Robin George. *The Idea of History.* Oxford, UK: Oxford University Press, 1946.

Conrad, Joseph. *Lord Jim.* New York: Norton, 1981. (Originally published 1900.)

Croce, Benedetto. *History: Its Theory and Practice*. Trans. Douglas Ainslie. New York: Russell & Russell, 1960. (Originally published 1920.)

Danto, Arthur C. *Analytic Philosophy of Action*. Cambridge, UK: Cambridge University Press, 1973.

Davidson, Donald. *Essays on Actions and Events*. Oxford, UK: Claredon Press, 1980.

Derrida, Jacques. *Speech and Phenomena and Other Essays on Husserl's Theory of Signs*. Trans. David B. Allison. Evanston, IL: Northwestern University Press, 1973. (Originally published 1967.)

Descartes, René. *Discourse on Method*. Trans. Donald A. Cress. Indianapolis, IN: Hackett, 1993. (Originally published 1637.)

Dewey, John. *Experience and Nature*. La Salle, IL: Open Court, 1929.

Emerson, Ralph Waldo. *Essays and Lectures*. New York: Library of America, 1983.

Feyerabend, Paul. *Against Method*. London: Verso, 1993.

Fichte, Johann Gottlieb. *The Science of Knowledge*. Trans. Peter Heath and John Lachs. New York: Cambridge University Press, 1982. (Originally published 1802.)

———. *The Vocation of Man*. Trans. Peter Preuss. Indianapolis, IN: Hackett, 1987. (Originally published 1800.)

Galileo. *Discoveries and Opinions of Galileo*. Trans. Stillman Drake. Garden City, NY: Anchor Press, 1956.

Ginet, Carl. *On Action*. Cambridge, UK: Cambridge University Press, 1990.

Hall, David L. *Richard Rorty: Prophet and Poet of the New Pragmatism*. Albany: State University of New York Press, 1995.

Hegel, Georg Wilhelm Friedrich. *The Philosophy of Right*. Trans. T. M. Knox. Oxford, UK: Oxford University Press, 1965. (Originally published 1821.)

———. *The Phenomenology of Spirit*. Trans. A. V. Miller. New York: Oxford University Press, 1977. (Originally published 1807.)

———. *Lectures on the Philosophy of Religion*. Trans. Robert F. Brown and Peter Crafts Hodgson. Berkeley: University of California Press, 1984–1987. (Originally published 1827.)

———. *Introduction to the Philosophy of History*. Trans. Leo Rauch. Indianapolis, IN: Hackett, 1988. (Originally published 1840.)

Heidegger, Martin. *Being and Time*. Trans. John Macquarrie and Edward Robinson. New York: Harper Collins, 1962. (Originally published 1927.)

———. "On the Essence of Truth." In *Basic Writings*, edited by David Farrell Krell, 117–39. San Francisco: Harper Collins, 1977. (Originally published 1949.)

———. *The Question Concerning Technology and Other Essays*. Trans. William Lovitt. New York: Harper & Row, 1977.

Hocking, William Ernest. *Man and the State*. New Haven, CT: Yale University Press, 1926.

——. *The Self, Its Body, and Freedom*. New Haven, CT: Yale University Press, 1928.

——. *Types of Philosophy*, rev. ed. New York: Scribners, 1939.

Hobbes, Thomas. *Leviathan*. London: Penguin, 1985. (Originally published 1651.)

Horkheimer, Max, and Adorno, Theodor. *Dialectic of Enlightenment*. Trans. John Cumming. New York: Continuum, 1989. (Originally published 1944.)

Huntington, E. V. *The Continuum as a Type of Order*. Cambridge, MA: Harvard University, 1905.

Husserl, Edmund. *Ideas: General Introduction to Pure Phenomenology*. Trans. W. R. Boyce Gibson. New York: Collier, 1962. (Originally published 1913.)

James, William. *The Principles of Psychology*. New York: Holt, 1890.

——. *Radical Empiricism and a Pluralistic Universe*. New York: Longmans, Green, & Company, 1943.

Jefferson, Thomas. *Writings*. Ed. Merrill D. Peterson. New York: Library of America, 1984.

Juarrero, Alicia. *Dynamics in Action: Intentional Behavior as a Complex System*. Cambridge, MA: MIT Press, 1999.

Kant, Immanuel. *Critique of Pure Reason*. Trans. Norman Kemp Smith. New York: St. Martin's, 1965. (Originally published 1787.)

——. *Groundwork for the Metaphysics of Morals*. Trans. Lewis White Beck. Indianapolis, IN: Bobbs-Merrill, 1976. (Originally published 1785.)

——. *The Metaphysics of Morals*. Trans. Mary Gregor. Cambridge, UK: Cambridge University Press, 1996. (Originally published 1797.)

Langer, Suzanne K. *Philosophy in a New Key*. Cambridge, MA: Harvard University Press, 1957.

Latour, Bruno. *We Have Never Been Modern*. Trans. Katherine Porter. Cambridge, MA: Harvard University Press, 1993.

Lincoln, Abraham. *Speeches and Writings, 1859–1865*. Ed. Don E. Fehrenbacher. New York: Library of America, 1989.

Locke, John. *Two Treatises of Government*. Ed. Peter Laslett. Cambridge, UK: Cambridge University Press, 1960. (Originally published 1690.)

Lyotard, Jean-François. *Le Postmoderne expliqué aux enfants: Correspondance 1982–1985*. Paris: Editions Galilée, 1988.

Macpherson, C. B. *The Political Theory of Possessive Individualism*. Oxford, UK: Oxford University Press, 1962.

McCann, Hugh J. *The Works of Agency: On Human Action, Will, and Freedom*. Ithaca, NY: Cornell University Press, 1998.

Mead, George Herbert. *The Philosophy of the Act. Works of George Herbert Meade* (Vol. 3). Chicago: University of Chicago Press, 1938.

——. *The Real World of Democracy*. Oxford, UK: Oxford University Press, 1966.

——. *The Life and Times of Democracy*. Oxford, UK: Oxford University Press, 1977.

Menzel, Christopher. "Actualism." In *The Stanford Encyclopedia of Philosophy* (spring 2003 ed.), Edward N. Zalta (ed.). http://plato.stanford.edu/archives/spr2003/entries/actualism/.

Milne, A. J. M. *The Social Philosophy of English Idealism.* London: Allen & Unwin, 1962.

Morris, Charles W. *Foundations of the Theory of Signs.* Chicago: University of Chicago Press, 1938.

Mounier, Emmanuel. *Le Personnalisme.* Paris: Presses Universitaires de France, 1995. (Originally published 1949.)

Nietzsche, Friedrich. *On Genealogy of Morals and Ecce Homo.* Trans. Walter Kaufmann. New York: Vintage, 1967. (*On the Genealogy of Morals* originally published 1887.)

———. *Beyond Good and Evil.* Trans. Walter Kaufmann. New York: Vintage, 1989. (Originally published 1886.)

Ortega y Gasset, José. *History as a System and Other Essays Toward a Philosophy of History.* Trans. Helene Weyl. New York: Norton, 1961.

Paine, Thomas. *Collected Writings.* New York: Library of America, 1995.

Peirce, Charles Sanders. *The Essential Peirce: Selected Philosophical Writings* (Vol. 2, 1893–1913). Ed. Peirce Edition Project. Bloomington: Indiana University Press, 1998.

Popper, Karl. *The Open Society and Its Enemies.* Princeton, NJ: Princeton University Press, 1950.

———. *Conjectures and Refutations.* New York: Routledge, 1992.

Rawls, John. "Justice as Fairness: Political not Metaphysical." *Philosophy and Public Affairs* 14 (1985): 223–51.

———. *Political Liberalism.* New York: Columbia University Press, 1993.

Richards, I. A. *The Philosophy of Rhetoric.* Oxford, UK: Oxford University Press, 1936.

Rorty, Richard. *Philosophy and the Mirror of Nature.* Princeton: Princeton University Press, 1979.

———. *Consequences of Pragmatism.* Minneapolis: University of Minnesota Press, 1982.

———. *Contingency, Irony, Solidarity.* New York: Cambridge University Press, 1990.

———. *Objectivity, Relativism, and Truth.* New York: Cambridge University Press, 1991.

———. *Philosophy and Social Hope.* London: Penguin, 1999.

Rousseau, Jean-Jacques. *The Basic Political Writings.* Trans Donald A. Cress. Indianapolis, IN: Hackett, 1987.

Royce, Josiah. *Problem of Christianity.* Chicago: University of Chicago Press, 1968. (Originally published 1918.)

———. *World and the Individual* (series 1–2). Gloucester, MA: Peter Smith, 1967. (Originally published 1899.)

Schumpeter, Joseph. *Capitalism, Socialism, and Democracy.* New York, Harper & Row, 1976. (Originally published 1947.)

Tillich, Paul. *Systematic Theology 3. Life and the Spirit, History and the Kingdom of God.* Chicago: University of Chicago Press, 1963.

Urban, W. M. *Language and Reality: The Philosophy of Language and the Principles of Symbolism.* London: G. Allen & Unwin, 1939.

White, Alan R. "Introduction." In *The Philosophy of the Act,* edited by Alan R. White, 1–18. Oxford, UK: Oxford University Press, 1968.

Whitman, Walt. *Poetry and Prose.* New York: Library of America, 1982.

Index